INSTANT COOKING

INSTANT COOKING

fabulous food in no time at all

Editor: Jenni Fleetwood

HERMES
HOUSE

First published in 1999 by Hermes House

HERMES HOUSE books are available for bulk purchase
for sales promotion and for premium use. For details, write or
call the sales director, Hermes House, 27 West 20th Street,
New York, NY 10011; (800) 354–9657

Hermes House is an imprint of
Anness Publishing Inc.

ISBN 1 84038 278 3

Publisher: Joanna Lorenz
Editor: Jenni Fleetwood
Project Editor: Felicity Forster
Recipes: Alex Barker, Carla Capalbo, Maxine Clark, Matthew Drennan,
Christine France, Sarah Gates, Shirley Gill, Carole Handslip, Patricia Lousada,
Norma McMillan, Sue Maggs, Sarah Maxwell, Janice Murfitt, Annie Nichols,
Angela Nilsen, Jenny Stacey, Liz Trigg, Hilaire Walden, Laura Washburn,
Steven Wheeler and Elizabeth Wolf-Cohen
Designers: Siân Keogh and Margaret Sadler
Jacket Designer: Simon Balley
Photographers: Karl Adamson, Edward Allwright, Steve Baxter, James Duncan,
Michelle Garrett, Amanda Heywood, Tim Hill and Don Last
Stylists: Madeleine Brehaut, Michelle Garrett, Hilary Guy and Fiona Tillett
Editorial Reader: Kate Henderson
Production Controller: Mark Fennell

Printed and bound in Indonesia

10 9 8 7 6 5 4 3 2 1

CONTENTS

INTRODUCTION

INTRODUCTION

The one ingredient none of us ever seems to have enough of is time. We live life in the fast lane, packing in a million activities between breakfast and bedtime. Even leisure—which should be a laid-back proposition—has become a frenzied pursuit, as we struggle to find time for the exercise sessions we're told are essential for good health and vitality.

Faced with such demanding schedules, most of us—quite literally—put food on the back burner. We snatch sandwiches at delis, fill our freezers with prepared meals and can recite the telephone numbers of all our local take-out places. Good, home-cooked meals are reserved for Saturdays or Sundays, and even then, there's no guarantee that every member of the family will be around to enjoy them.

So what's the answer? Accept the supermarket solution, or fight back by finding a foolproof collection of quick and easy dishes that can be prepared in next to no time? We'd advocate the latter, and to prove how easy it can be to cook delicious meals in under half an hour, we've put together dozens of simple and satisfying recipes.

Easy, effortless cooking takes a bit of planning, of course, but even there, we've done the hard work for you. Included in this book are menu plans, a step-by-step guide to time-saving techniques and suggestions for stocking the pantry, fridge and freezer with items that will make quick cooking a piece of cake—with instant frosting, naturally!

Countdown to Cooking the Easy Way

Quick cooks are made, not born. Those people who walk in from work, fix a quick drink, disappear for 30 minutes and produce an amazing meal weren't born with this knowledge. It takes practice, organization and a certain amount of expertise with a knife, can opener and whisk to whip up great grub in next to no time.

Pen and paper
A lot of unnecessary running around can be prevented by sitting down with pen and paper

and drawing up a plan of action. Too often, ideas get the green light before realizing how much time and effort are needed to produce them. The first question to ask yourself is "How much time and energy do I have?" Be realistic—a lot of

cooks come unstuck when they take on more than they can handle. Be kind to yourself and choose something you can cope with. You'll not only enjoy preparing the meal, you might even be composed enough to sit down and enjoy it.

Choosing your ingredients
Cooking becomes a pleasure when we can recognize and choose the finest ingredients to work with. Being able to see clearly what is good at a glance is one of the secrets of trouble-free cooking. Every item we shop

for has value associated with price, flavor and convenience. If price exceeds flavor, reconsider. If flavor is lost for the sake of convenience – powdered mashed potato, for instance—you should think again. The cook's ultimatum should be flavor and convenience at the right price.

Fresh herbs make a huge difference to quickly cooked meals. Fresh cilantro has a wonderful flavor when stirred into a spicy dish at the end of cooking, basil is wonderful in sauces and salads, and snipped chives make all the difference to an omelet. Growing your own herbs isn't difficult and not only provides you with an instant supply, but is also very rewarding.

Shopping

Shopping with a nose for flavor and freshness is the best way to fight through the consumer jungle and arrive home with quality produce. Choose well and give your cooking the head start that it deserves.

Fresh herbs or herb butter (prepared beforehand) add interest to simple dishes. Look for ready-washed vegetables to save time at home. Buy fish fillets that are already boned and skinned, and meat that is prepared for cooking. To enliven pasta and rice dishes, buy pesto and other flavored sauces.

Do your shopping in one stop and try to write your list in accordance with the layout of the store. Back-tracking for the last few items on your list is no one's idea of fun. When even the simplest of meals is properly thought out, three-quarters of

the work is done. From your list you know exactly what you are cooking, what shopping you need and what you are going to do with the ingredients when you start to get to work in the kitchen.

Kitchen layout

Next, consider your kitchen. No matter how small or ill-equipped it may appear to an outsider, it's where you cook. You're probably stuck with the layout, but consider whether there are any simple changes that will make preparing food a lot easier. The stove and oven, main preparation area and sink should ideally be close together, and to help in this the pots, pans and utensils you use most often within easy reach.

Pots and pans can hang from butcher's hooks or be placed on shelves. Put the ones you rarely

use in cupboards by all means, but keep your wok, favorite frying pan and saucepans where you can easily put your hands on them. The same goes for utensils—drawers are alright for cake decorating sets and those lace napkins your Aunt Clara sent you, but spoons, spatulas and whisks will be much more useful in a jar next to the stove.

It's always worth taking a few minutes to read a recipe through before you start. This should enable you to have all the necessary equipment to hand from the outset. For efficiency, keep knives sharp—this saves time and makes them safer than blunt ones.

It has to be said that some cooks are more organized in their kitchens than others. Some cooks clean and tidy up with near-surgical precision, while

others thrive in varying degrees of chaos. Cooking quickly depends on: a) knowing what you are doing, and b) being able to put your hands on what you need as you go. Most cooks work best of all in a relatively creative mess where somehow everything comes together in the end. Whatever conditions you are comfortable with, make sure they are 'just so' before you begin cooking.

Storage of foods

When storing foods, separate sweet and savory ingredients, except those that are used for both such as flour, eggs and sugar. Ingredients that are used often, including onions, garlic, olive oil and fruit make an attractive display in the kitchen if there is space.

Herbs and spices look great on a rack, but make sure they are not in direct sunlight, and check them frequently, discarding any you've had for

Right: A colorful selection of fresh produce, including root vegetables, green vegetables and salad ingredients.

Below: Simple ingredients such as pasta, vegetables and cheese make a quick and simple lunch or supper dish.

more than a few months. Herbs and spices rapidly lose flavor after being opened and are best bought in small quantities. Like

perfume, they should be used, not saved for special occasions. Many cooks prefer to store spice jars on their sides in a shallow

drawer. This works well, as long as the drawer stays neat and the contents are easily accessible.

Aromatics like onions can be kept in a basket on the work surface or suspended from a string. The same goes for garlic, although you may prefer to buy one bulb at a time and keep it close to your cutting board.

Maintaining your supplies

An essential item for any cook who aspires to being organized is a blackboard or pad of paper, on which any member of the household who notices supplies are running low can make a note. There's nothing more irritating than going to your well-stocked pantry and finding that someone has eaten the noodles you'd had in mind for supper.

Really organized quick cooks also keep a list of supplies on the pantry door. This enables them to see at a glance what's inside, and acts as a reminder of those dried cranberries bought on impulse a month ago that still haven't been used.

Above: A wok is perfect for quick-cooking stir-fries and can also double as a steamer. Choose a heavy, non-stick wok for ease of cooking, and save time washing up, too.

saving tips—you may not be able to declare, "Here's one I made earlier," but, with practice, you'll soon get the hang of keeping a watchful eye on several sauccpans simultaneously. An electric timer—one of those simple battery-operated devices that sticks magnetically to the fridge—can be a huge help.

By using techniques like these you'll soon be whipping up speedy and appealing meals, ...

Above: A bowl of strawberries, crème fraîche and a ready-made flan case are all you need for an impromptu dessert.

Below: A delicious selection of fresh fruit is perfect for a quick snack.

Tl... ......g......

Time management is a skill, like any other. If you are only cooking one dish, just follow the recipe. It will take you through the method step by step. However, if you want to serve accompaniments and dessert, you'll need to plan your time out carefully. Taking a few seconds to figure out the sequence really does pay, as does the time-honored advice of setting out all the ingredients in order. Watch TV cooks for time-

Above: A good *batterie de cuisine* makes for efficiency in a kitchen where fast cooking is a priority.

Right: A heavy, non-stick frying pan allows food to spread over a large area and cook quickly and evenly.

Pantry Ingredients

A well-stocked pantry is the secret of a quick cook's success, and when planning a kitchen it is worth thinking seriously about storage space. Ingredients you use frequently should be close at hand. Open shelves are often better than closed cupboards, and glass jars not only give you the opportunity to create a colorful display, they enable you to see at a glance when stock is running low. The following ingredients are a good way to start your pantry collection.

Arrowroot
Mixed with water, arrowroot is used to thicken sauces and glazes without destroying their clarity.

Baking powder
To make self-rising flour, add baking powder to plain flour in the proportion of 1 tsp to 1 cup.

Bouillon cubes
Buy good-quality beef, chicken, fish and vegetable cubes, plus a can or two of quality broth for those occasions when flavor is paramount.

Bulghur
A whole-wheat grain that is steam-dried and cracked, this is a boon to the busy cook. Soak it in water, drain thoroughly, then squeeze tightly in a clean cloth to remove excess moisture. Mix with chopped vegetables, lemon juice and oil for a satisfying salad.

Cornstarch
Made from corn, this light flour is mainly used for thickening, but is also sometimes mixed with plain flour for making extra-light sponge cakes.

Couscous
Pearl-like pellets of soaked semolina. Instant couscous is great for busy cooks.

Dried mushrooms
Full of flavor, dried mushrooms such as porcini need only a brief soak in warm water before use.

Flour
White and whole-wheat flour in both plain and self-rising versions are essentials. Keep in storage jars in a cool, dry place.

Nuts
Useful for quick desserts, toppings and decorations—a basic selection should include ground and slivered almonds, cashews, peanuts, pecans, pine nuts, pistachios and walnuts. Also keep dry, shredded coconut, and cans of coconut milk on hand.

Oatmeal
Useful for thickening soups and stews and to make crumble toppings.

Pizza crust mix
A real time-saver—use it for family-size pizzas, calzone or pizzettes.

Polenta
Italian cornmeal—look for instant versions.

Skim milk powder
Quick cooks always keep this handy to make custards and sauces when they're out of fresh milk.

Sugar
Granulated sugar, superfine sugar, light and dark brown sugar, and confectioner's sugar are all essential.

Tortillas
Buy refrigerated corn and flour tortillas. Remove the tortillas from the package, wrap them in microwave-safe plastic wrap, heat them for a few seconds in the microwave, then spread with salsa and fill with ground beef, shredded lettuce, chopped tomatoes, sliced onion, avocado and grated cheese.

Right: Wooden shelves with hooks for hanging garlic, fresh herbs and a nutmeg grater are perfect for displaying favorite ingredients. Baskets of lemons, a bowl of eggs and bottles of wine, oils and vinegars are practical as well as pretty.

Pasta, Rice and Lentils

Pasta and rice are ideal for instant meals, as they take very little time to cook and are extremely versatile. With the exception of lentils, dried pulses are less useful, as they must be soaked before long, slow cooking. Use canned beans and chick-peas instead.

Arborio rice
This rounded short-grain rice is used for risotto, as is carnaroli.

Basmati rice
Generally acknowledged to be one of the world's greatest grains, this has a distinctive, fragrant aroma.

Campanelle
Italian pasta tubes with delicate, frilled edges, these are particularly pretty.

Capellini
Also known as angel-hair pasta, capellini consists of extremely fine strands.

Cellophane noodles
These Asian noodles are made from ground mung beans and are also known as bean thread, transparent or glass noodles. They must always be soaked in warm water before being cooked.

Egg noodles
Widely used throughout China, Japan, Malaysia and Thailand, these can be fresh, but are more often sold dried. Many types need only be soaked in boiling water before use, and are ideal for quick cooking.

Lentils
Red lentils cook quickly without soaking, so are perfect for fast meals. French or European brown lentils take a little longer.

Long-grain rice
For speed, use instant white or brown long-grain rice. This has been treated and partially cooked, so the grains will rapidly become tender and remain separate.

Pasta bows (farfalle)
A popular pasta shape, which takes its Italian name from the butterflies it resembles.

Penne
These short, tubular pasta shapes make great quick comfort food as they are substantial and hold sauce well.

Rice noodles
Also called bahn trang, these are made from ground rice and water. They range in thickness from very thin to wide ribbons (sold in skeins) and sheets. Always rinse rice noodles in warm water and drain before use.

Soba noodles
Made from a mixture of buckwheat and wheat flour, these popular Japanese noodles are cooked in simmering water, then drained.

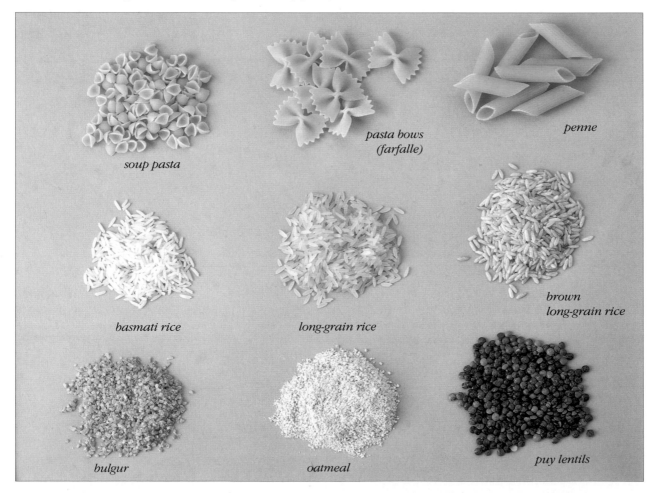

soup pasta

pasta bows (farfalle)

penne

basmati rice

long-grain rice

brown long-grain rice

bulgur

oatmeal

puy lentils

Left: For speedy meals, make the most of pasta, rice, lentils and grains, such as bulgur and oatmeal.

Somen noodles
Delicate, thin, white Japanese noodles made from wheat flour, these are usually sold dried, in bundles held together with a paper band.

Soup pasta
This is the collective term for a wide range of tiny shapes, which cook almost on contact when added to soups.

Spaghetti
The most popular form of pasta, spaghetti is long thin strands of pasta.

Tagliatelle
Italian flat, long ribbon noodles. The green version is flavored with spinach.

Udon noodles
Wheat flour and water are used to make these Japanese noodles. They are usually round, but can be flat. The pre-cooked variety is best for quick cooking.

Vermicelli
Very fine pasta, this cooks rapidly. Italians make it from durum wheat, and there is also an Asian rice version.

Wild rice
Not a true rice, but the seed of an aquatic grass. The brown, long grains open when cooked. Wild rice is expensive, so is often mixed with long-grain rice. It makes a delicious side dish and is also widely used in salads.

Right: Dried noodles cook quickly. The picture shows (clockwise from top left): ribbon noodles, somen noodles, udon noodles, soba noodles, egg ribbon noodles, medium egg noodles, cellophane noodles, rice sheets, rice vermicelli, egg noodles and (center) rice ribbon noodles.

Herbs and Spices

It's a myth that all herbs and spices need long, slow cooking to bring out their flavor: most fresh herbs and many spices are best added to dishes shortly before serving.

Basil
One of the most delicious fresh herbs, basil has an affinity for tomato, and is wonderful in salads and sauces.

Black peppercorns
For the best flavor, use black peppercorns freshly ground; the taste and aroma vanish quickly.

Caraway seeds
The warm, sweet flavor of caraway seeds makes them a popular addition to braised cabbage.

Cardamom
Pods and ground cardamom add a warm, pungent flavor to curries and other spicy dishes, while the black seeds are used in some desserts.

Cayenne
The finely ground powder from a fiery chili. Use sparingly.

Chiles
Canny cooks use fresh chiles when they can get them, but keep a jar of bottled chiles and a packet of dried chiles for emergencies.

Chili powder
Available in various strengths—mild chili powder is a popular spice for quick cooking.

Chives
Snip fresh chives into omelets, rice dishes or salads.

Cilantro/Coriander
Fresh cilantro has a wonderful flavor and is often used as an edible garnish. Ground coriander is deliciously warm and aromatic.

Cinnamon
Sticks add subtle flavor—try using one to stir hot chocolate—while ground cinnamon is a popular addition to cakes.

Cumin
Both seeds and ground cumin are valued for their warm, earthy flavor.

Curry powder and paste
Cooks with time on their hands roast and grind their own spices, but hurried hosts and hostesses find good-quality powders and pastes a real boon.

Five-spice powder
A mixture of Szechuan pepper, cinnamon or cassia, cloves, fennel seeds and star anise, this is a popular Chinese spice.

Garam masala
A warm Indian spice mix which is often sprinkled over a finished dish to enhance the flavors.

Garlic
Some quick cooks use garlic paste or minced garlic, but it takes only seconds to crush your own.

Ginger
Keep fresh ginger in the freezer and grate it as needed. It will thaw as soon as it is added to a hot dish.

Herbes de Provence
A dried herb mixture of thyme, savory, rosemary, marjoram and oregano.

Mint
Fresh mint is great in salads and chilled soups.

Mustard seeds
These pop when added to hot oil to release a wonderful nutty flavor.

Nutmeg
Keep whole nutmegs near the cooker and grate them as needed.

Oregano
This aromatic and highly flavored herb is wonderful in tomato sauces and is traditionally sprinkled over the top of pizzas.

Paprika
A mild, sweet red powder, paprika adds color.

Parsley
The clean, fresh taste of both curly parsley and the flat-leaf variety makes it a favorite herb.

Rosemary
Fresh rosemary is traditionally served with lamb but is also delicious with vegetables.

Saffron
The dried stigmas of a type of crocus, saffron is very expensive, but imparts a wonderful flavor and color to food.

Sage
Wonderful with fried liver, sage has a strong flavor, so don't overdo it.

Salt
For seasoning, use sea-salt flakes or refined table salt.

Thyme
Fresh or dried, thyme is a popular herb. Whole sprigs can be used as a garnish.

Turmeric
This bright yellow powder is largely used for coloring. It has a pungent, bitter flavor and should be used sparingly.

saffron

red chili flakes

cilantro

mild chili powder

fresh red chilies

chives

curly parsley

Italian parsley

ground cumin

herbes de Provence

nutmeg

thyme

sage

rosemary

oregano

basil

black peppercorns

sea salt

Food Stored in Bottles and Jars

Quick cooks keep favorite ingredients close at hand, making a display of beautifully bottled oils and vinegars.

Capers
The pickled flower buds of a bush native to the Mediterranean, capers have a strong, sharp flavor you either love or loathe. If you're a lover, try them with cottage cheese on a sandwich, or add them to our Tomato Sauce.

Gherkins
These are small cucumbers, grown specifically for pickling. Use them in salads and cold sauces.

Green peppercorns
Pickled in brine, these are often used in steak sauces. They have an affinity with mustard.

Lemon and lime juice
Although it is preferable to use freshly squeezed lemon or lime juice in most recipes, bottled juices are very useful for those occasions when the fruit bowl is bare. Keep citrus juices in the fridge after opening and use as soon as possible.

Mayonnaise
It isn't difficult to make your own mayonnaise, but because the recipe uses raw egg yolks, the homemade product is not recommended for very young children or the elderly. Good-quality bought mayonnaise is very useful. Keep it in the fridge after opening.

Mustard
A little mustard will often bring out the flavor of other ingredients. In dressings, mustard is used as an emulsifier, helping to bring oil and vinegar together. As with oils, experiment to find your favorite type. A basic pantry should include both powdered and ready-made mustards, including a whole-grain variety and a mild Dijon type.

Oils
Keep the oils you use most often close to the stove, but not so close that they will be affected by the heat. Exposure to bright sunlight is harmful to oils, especially olive oil, which is why the latter is often sold in green glass bottles. For general cooking, choose corn or sunflower oil, which can be heated to a high temperature without smoking. Sunflower oil is particularly useful for delicate dishes, as the flavor is not overpowering. Safflower oil has a higher concentration of polyunsaturated fatty acids than other oils. Olive oil is prized for its contribution to a healthy diet and is widely used in the recipes in this book. It tends to smoke at high temperatures, so use a light olive oil or a mixture of olive oil and sunflower oil for cooking. For salads, use virgin or extra-virgin oils.

Olives
Sold at different stages of ripeness (black olives are fully ripe), olives are ideal for quick meals. They are very good in salads, sauces and on pizzas.

Peanut butter
Although most often thought of as a spread, peanut butter is an important ingredient in Indonesian cooking. Saté sauce, which is superb with pork and pineapple kebabs, is a case in point.

Vinegars
It is important to use the recommended type of vinegar in a recipe. Flavors and strengths vary widely, depending on the base, which can be wine, beer or fruit juice. Red and white wine vinegars are widely used for dressings and marinades, while sherry vinegar is preferred when a more full-bodied flavor is required. Rice wine vinegar and cider vinegar are often less sour than other types, so are used to give sauces, stir-fries and dressings a tangy taste. One of the quick cook's best allies is good balsamic vinegar. This dark Italian wine vinegar is rich and robust, but not harsh. A few drops, added to a sauce, will really boost the flavor. Malt vinegar is used for pickling, as a table condiment (with fish and chips, for instance), and is the traditional choice for making mint sauce. Raspberry vinegar is mild and sweet. It is used in some dressings and can be served with pancakes.

Wine
A dash or two gives a lift to soups and sauces—and has a similar effect on the cook! The recipes in this collection make judicious use of wine, spirits and liqueurs, but in most instances these can be omitted if preferred.

Italian olive oil

Spanish olive oil

lemon

Italian olive oil

safflower oil

hazelnut oil

walnut oil

peanut oil

French olive oil

Italian olive oil

garlic oil

white-wine vinegar

olives

limes

capers

mustard

Sauces and Pastes

When you want a speedy meal, buy the sauce pre-made. A wide range of sauces and pastes is available in bottles or squeezable tubes. They keep well, so it is worth buying and trying new varieties, and building up a versatile and tasty range of flavors.

Anchovy paste
Sold in tubes, anchovy paste is useful for adding a subtle flavor to a sauce to be served with fish. For a more robust taste, use pounded salted or drained canned anchovies. Look for anchovy extract, too.

Carbonara sauce
Although your own version will be much better, a jar or two of the ready-made sauce will prove useful when you need to make a meal in double-quick time. Add sautéed fresh mushrooms or more bacon if desired.

Garlic paste
Squeeze it from the tube whenever you need it. Alternatively, buy a jar of chopped garlic—a great time-saver.

Horseradish sauce
Creamed horseradish sauce is the classic accompaniment to roast beef, but also tastes wonderful in a shrimp cocktail.

Mushroom paste
Some Italian delicatessens sell this delicious delicacy. Mix a generous spoonful with some crème fraîche to make a quick pasta sauce. Mushroom paste is a very useful item in the quick cook's armory—a small splash will intensify the flavor of any mushroom-based sauce, and will also add interest to a risotto, omelet or gravy.

Olive paste
Olive paste—tapenade—is available in jars and tubes, in both green and black varieties. The black is particularly tasty: toss a small amount with freshly cooked spaghetti for a superb treat. Tapenade is also very good with boiled new potatoes.

Pesto
The best option is to make your own, but fresh basil isn't always available. Look for "fresh" pesto, sold in tubs in the refrigerated section of some supermarkets and health food shops. Third choice—but not necessarily an unacceptable option—is to buy pesto in the jar. Brands vary, so experiment until you find a good one. Red pesto is made from tomatoes and red bell peppers. It makes a delicious addition to soups and sauces, and can also be tossed with freshly cooked pasta.

Soy sauce
Soy sauce is famously used in stir-fries, but also gives cooked sauces and gravies a lift. Recipes in this book use both light and dark soy sauce, and kecap manis (sweet soy sauce). Other invaluable Asian sauces include Hoisin sauce, black bean sauce, oyster sauce, fish sauce and sweet chili sauce.

Sun-dried tomatoes
For quick cooking, use the ones preserved in oil to deepen the flavor of tomato-based dishes.

Tabasco sauce
Hot chili sauces like Tabasco are very useful for pepping up all kinds of savory dishes. Use sparingly and stir in well.

Tomato paste
Concentrated tomato paste comes in tubes and cans and is absolutely invaluable for enriching the flavor of soups and sauces. Look for sun-dried tomato paste, which has an excellent flavor and less dominant color.

Tomato sauce
Making your own pasta sauce only takes minutes, but when you are really pressed for time, it can be very handy to have a jar or two of ready-made sauce. Spice it up by stirring in chopped anchovies or olives and a sprinkling of chopped fresh herbs. A splash of red wine, vermouth or balsamic vinegar can improve a bought sauce considerably.

Tomatoes, canned
No self-respecting pantry should be without these. The range is extensive, so choose chopped or whole tomatoes, as you prefer. Passata, sold in jars and cans, is pulped tomato that has been strained to remove the seeds.

Worcestershire sauce
An old friend that is easily overlooked in the host of newer sauces that crowd supermarket shelves. Add a few drops of Worcestershire to sauces, gravies and meat dishes for instant flavor, but avoid using it in strict vegetarian cooking, as it contains anchovies.

passata

mushroom paste

salted anchovies

olive paste

tomato paste

carbonara sauce

chopped tomatoes

canned plum tomatoes

capers

tomato sauce

fresh pesto

red pesto

pesto

sun-dried tomatoes in oil

chopped garlic

Dessert Ingredients

Instant desserts can be much more than
a package of powder whipped with water or
milk. Add these extras to your pantry and
you'll have the makings of delicious
quick desserts.

Cakes
Foil-wrapped cakes can be
easily transformed into simple
desserts. Chocolate cake with
liqueur, cherries, ice cream and
whipped cream makes a great
sundae, while gingerbread and
bananas with a brûlée topping
is delicious.

Chocolate
Buy good-quality dark chocolate
for quick desserts. Melted with
cream, it makes an instant sauce
for ice cream and cream puffs.

Cocoa powder
Use cocoa powder in drinks
and desserts for a rich
chocolate taste.

Dessert cookies
Many kinds of cookies can be
served with creamy desserts, and
are also useful as the basis of
instant desserts. As a filling for
nectarines, macaroons have no
equal, while ladyfingers dipped
in black coffee and brandy, then
layered with whipped cream,
make a quick tiramisù.

Eggs
Always buy eggs from a
reputable supplier. Store in
the fridge, but bring to room
temperature before using.

Extracts
Vanilla extract is the most
popular of these. Buy pure
vanilla extract rather than a
mere flavoring; the taste will
be much better. Almond extract
will also prove useful.

Fruit
Fresh fruit is the best and
simplest sweet treat, but canned
and dried fruit have an
important part to play in the
creation of quick desserts.
Include canned peaches,
apricots, pineapple rings and
black cherries in your pantry,
and make sure you have
packages of ready-to-use dried
apricots, raisins, currants,
prunes and dates, as well as
more exotic fruits like mango.

Instant coffee
Great for making mocha sauces.
Use strong coffee for dipping
ladyfingers when making
tiramisù and similar desserts.

Jams and preserves
Keep a selection of good-quality
jams in small jars for filling cakes
and making quick fruit sauces
and glazes. Croissants spread
with ricotta and strawberry jam
taste heavenly when toasted.

Marshmallows
Marshmallows melted with
cream make a quick fondue
for dipping fruit kebabs.
Alternatively, stir some crème de
menthe into the mixture, pour it
into a cookie crust and leave it
in the fridge until set. Decorate
the pie with shaved chocolate
before serving.

Marzipan
Use to fill apples for baking,
or mix with cookie crumbs as a
filling for peaches.

Meringues
Shop around for good-quality
meringues and store them in an
airtight jar for impromptu
desserts. Meringues can be
sandwiched with whipped cream
and served with chocolate sauce,
broken and stirred into ice
cream, and made into mini
pavlovas with berries and
whipped cream.

Muesli
Much more than a breakfast
food, muesli makes a good,
quick crumble topping. For
the easiest-ever dessert, layer
raspberries with muesli and
plain yogurt.

Sponge cake shells
Just fill with fruit and whipped
cream for instant sweet success.

The Vegetable Basket

Speedy cooks love vegetables. What other savory ingredients look so beautiful, taste so good and cook so quickly? With only minutes to spare you can toss a salad or steam a medley of snow peas, baby carrots and miniature ears of corn. Simply add dressing or make a dipping sauce and you have a great quick meal. The sheer variety and range of vegetables now available at our supermarkets and farm stands is dazzling, but for flavor, it is still best to seek out seasonal produce. Summer's sun-ripened vine tomatoes will be much tastier than those that have come from a cold store, and freshly dug new potatoes are not only full of flavor, but can be cleaned with very little effort, as the skins simply rub off under running water. Carrot batons, cauliflower and broccoli florets, sliced leeks, trimmed beans and ready-to-cook snap peas are all there for the taking, along with shiny bell peppers of every hue, cook-in-the-bag spinach, wild and cultivated mushrooms and every member of the onion family.

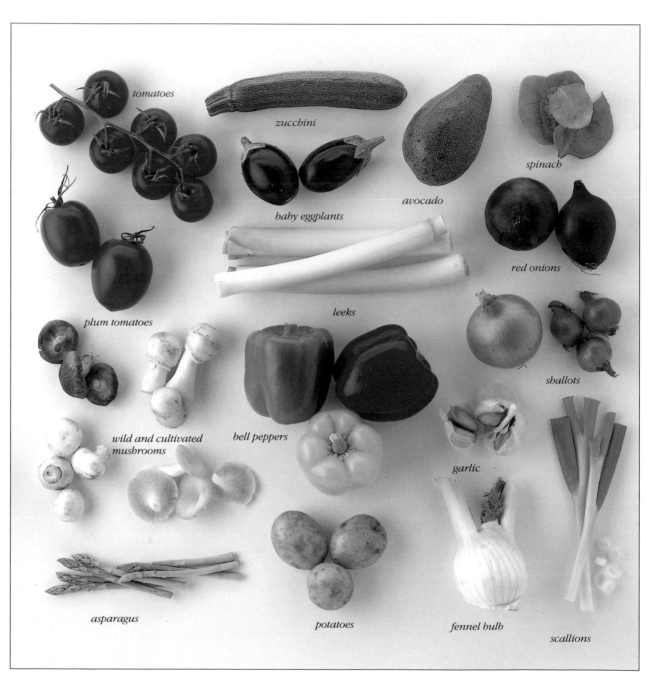

tomatoes

zucchini

spinach

avocado

baby eggplants

red onions

plum tomatoes

leeks

shallots

wild and cultivated mushrooms

bell peppers

garlic

asparagus

potatoes

fennel bulb

scallions

The Fruit Bowl

It is no coincidence that most of the desserts featured in this book are based on fresh fruit. When nature has provided such a wide range of delicious sweet treats for our consumption, why look elsewhere? Fruit needs little or no preparation, looks luscious and actually promotes good health.

Fast cooks know that with a well-stocked fruit bowl, dessert will often take care of itself. A perfect pear, a bunch of grapes, a simple salad of kiwi and orange segments—these are the sweetest solutions to the problem of what to serve when you don't have much time to make dessert.

The next step is a simple combination of two or more complementary types of fruit. Try chilled melon with wild strawberries, peaches with raspberries, or pineapple with lychees and oranges.

If you like hot fruit desserts, the good news for contemporary cooks is that you can produce delicious results in very little time. Grilling, frying and poaching are popular methods, and desserts like Caramelized Apples, Fruit Kebabs, and Pineapple Wedges with Rum Butter Glaze can be made while the dinner dishes are being cleared, giving your guests a brief respite before the meal's final flourish.

When shopping, choose fruit that is fresh, unblemished and ready to eat. Contrary to all those household hints that involve paper bags and chunks of apple, hard, unyielding fruit will seldom ripen satisfactorily at home.

Knowing just when a fruit is at its peak can be tricky, however. Most of us are familiar with apples and pears, but feel less confident when faced with exotic or unfamiliar fruit like papayas or cantaloupes. Some stores label some packs with the slogan "ready to eat," but in the absence of this advice, here are a few tips:

Bananas should have no hint of green. A light mottling of brown indicates that the fruit is ready to eat, and will be easy to digest, but you should avoid any fruits that are bruised.

Citrus fruits are at their best in winter, when individual fruits feel heavy for their size. To persuade an orange or lemon to yield its juice, roll it on the work surface or work it firmly between the palms of your hands.

Mangoes are ready to eat when the skin has a red blush and sweet, perfumed aroma.

When it comes to choosing pineapples or melons, your nose is often your best judge. Ripe pineapples have a wonderful, sweet smell. Cantaloupes and similar melons, with a "netted" rather than a hard, smooth skin, will have a lovely scent when ripe, and the skin will yield to the touch around the blossom end. Papayas become yellow-green when ripe, and yield gently to pressure in the hand.

Strawberries, raspberries and other berries are often sold in cartons. The fruit on top may look perfect, but it isn't easy to know what lies beneath. Check the bottom of the carton—if it is at all soggy, leave it well alone.

For convenience, quick cooks keep cans of apricot halves, peach slices, pineapple chunks, red cherries and mandarin segments, plus dried fruits including apricots, mangoes and peaches, which can be poached, then puréed for instant mousses.

Right: Fresh fruits can be used in both sweet and savory salads. Ensure they are ripe and in peak condition.

lollo rosso

Salad Leaves

When time is short, nothing is swifter than a salad. Supermarkets speed the process still further by providing bags of crisp, washed leaves, so all the cook has to do is dress for dinner.

Arugula
The leaves have a peppery, slightly lemony taste and are often used to add zest and flavor to mixed salads.

Batavian endive
Similar to escarole, but with a slightly sweeter, softer taste, Batavian endive is suited to most salads. With an underlying hint of bitterness, it stands up to a well-flavored dressing.

Escarole
More robust than regular lettuce, escarole has a bitter flavor. It is best during the winter months. The bitterness is usually offset with a sweet dressing.

Frisée
Frisée is a member of the chicory family. It has a clean, bitter taste and combines well with milder-flavored salad leaves.

Iceberg lettuce
Compact and firm, this is a popular ingredient for salads, despite having little intrinsic flavor. Tops for texture, it can be torn or shredded, and is very versatile.

Lamb's lettuce
Also known as maché, this has small, spoon-shaped leaves with a sweet, slightly nutty flavor.

Little gem
Little gem or sucrine is a small, sweet, compact lettuce that keeps well. The flavor resembles that of romaine.

Lollo biondo (Green leaf lettuce)
A loose-leafed lettuce with a curly edge, lollo biondo or green lollo has a mild flavor and goes well with stronger-tasting leaves.

Lollo rosso (Red leaf lettuce)
Although this pretty, loose-leafed lettuce has lost a little of its star status, it is still very popular for its attractive red-tinged leaves and mild flavor.

Oakleaf lettuce
The dark color and mild taste of these broad wavy leaves combine well with escarole and curly endive.

Romaine lettuce
With its faintly nutty taste, this is considered by many to have the finest flavor of all the salad leaves. It is the classic choice for Caesar salad.

Spinach
Young spinach leaves have a rich, sweet flavor and taste particularly good in a salad that includes crumbled bacon.

Watercress
Peppery and slightly pungent, watercress is extremely rich in vitamins. Scatter sprigs in salads or use to make sauces or soups.

Batavian endive

frisée

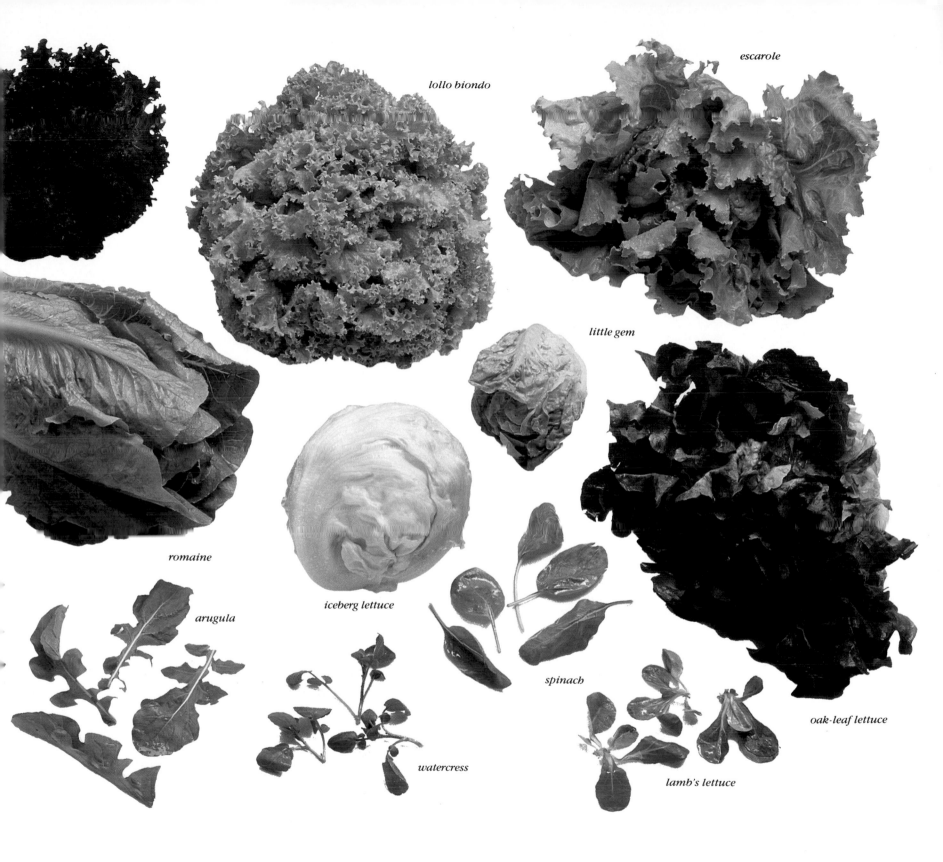

lollo biondo

escarole

little gem

romaine

iceberg lettuce

spinach

oak-leaf lettuce

arugula

watercress

lamb's lettuce

Meat and Fish

When the focus is on fast food, choose meats and fish that come ready-cooked or can be sautéed or stir-fried swiftly and with as little fuss as possible. Choose lean, ready-trimmed portions and cut them into small, even-sized pieces for sautéeing or stir-frying.

Beef
Ground beef is the number one choice for quick cooking, with strips of steak coming a close second. Ground beef is the basis for burgers, pasta sauces, meatballs and chili, while strips star in sizzling beef dishes, sukiyaki and stir-fries.

Chicken
Skinless, boneless chicken breasts are the best choice for the quick cook. Allow one per person unless you are cooking a stir-fry with plenty of vegetables, in which case one breast will stretch surprisingly and will certainly serve two. Smoked chicken is a good buy at most delis. Use it for sandwiches and in salads—it combines very well with fruit, especially melon.

Chorizo
This cured pork sausage comes from Spain and is flavored with garlic and paprika. It goes well with canned chick-peas or black beans and is particularly popular as a pizza topping.

Crab
Canned crab is ready to use. Use it as the basis of a sophisticated salad.

Ham
Cooked ham is ideal for quick snacks and salads. Don't automatically assume the most expensive choice at the deli counter is the best: shoulder often has a finer flavor than more costly cuts. Smoked ham is delicious wrapped around asparagus.

Italian salami
Serve with ricotta salata or feta and black olives for a tasty tapa or snack.

Lamb
Buy lean, boneless lamb from the leg for stir-frying. It tastes particularly good with a fruity glaze.

Mixed seafood
It is the preparation that takes time when it comes to seafood. Packages of mixed, prepared squid, mussels and shrimp are great for fish soups and delicious, quick casseroles.

Pancetta
This is pork belly, cured with salt and spices, and comes from Italy. Like bacon, which it resembles, it is available in both unsmoked and smoked forms and is generally sold thinly sliced. It used to be difficult to locate pancetta, but increased demand is making it more widely available. If you can't find it, use bacon instead.

Parma ham
Also known as prosciutto crudo, this salted and air-dried ham is a delicacy. It is usually thinly sliced and served with figs or melon.

Pepperoni
A salami-type sausage, this is made from pork and beef, flavored with fennel and red pepper. Thin slices of pepperoni are a favorite pizza topping.

Pork
For speed, choose fillet or pork steaks to make kebabs, stir-fries or seared specialities.

Sausages
Sausages are not just an ingredient—they're an industry. Every possible flavor is now available, so keep a few favorites in the freezer. Always thaw sausages thoroughly and make sure they are cooked through before serving. Chipolatas cook more quickly than regular sausages.

Shrimp
Cooked shrimp are perfect for quick meals. Just add mayonnaise or a seafood dressing. If using shrimp in a composite dish, such as a risotto, take care not to let them overcook or they will toughen.

Smoked salmon
One of the swift cook's favorite ingredients, smoked salmon can be formed into cones and filled with mousse or cream cheese, served simply in a salad, snipped into scrambled eggs, used to top pizzettes or star in a tasty sandwich.

pancetta

smoked chicken

smoked ham

sausages

chorizo

canned crab

Parma ham

shrimp

pepperoni

Italian salami

mixed seafood

ground beef

chicken

smoked salmon

Cheeses

Cheese is an excellent choice for the quick cook. Remove any rind and it is ready to use. There's a flavor for every occasion and every palate. Serve it solo, use it in salads or sandwiches, or team it with other ingredients. Whether hard or soft, cheese is equally at home in appetizers, main courses, desserts and even some soups.

Bavarian smoked cheese
With its distinctive, smoky flavor, this is a good choice for grilling. Try mixing it with Cheddar for a distinctive pizza topping.

Cheddar
Great for grating and grilling, this is arguably the world's most popular cheese. Flavors can vary from mild to extra mature. Cheddar is ideal for cooking, as it melts without forming threads.

Dolcelatte
An Italian blue-veined cheese with a piquant flavor, Dolcelatte is semi-soft. Try crumbling it into a white sauce or serve it with apples or pears.

Edam
This ball-shaped Dutch cheese has a mild, nutty flavor which is particularly popular with children. Cubes of Edam alternating with pineapple chunks, red bell pepper squares and cucumber slices make delicious kebabs.

Feta
Preserved in brine, this crumbly cheese comes from Greece. It is wonderful in salads and has an affinity for tomatoes and olives. Try it baked, in filo pastry.

Goat cheeses
These can be hard or soft, the latter being the most popular type. Sold in logs, rounds, pyramids or ovals, the soft cheeses range in flavor from fresh and creamy to strong and tangy, depending on the diet enjoyed by the goats. Goat cheese is delicious with roasted vegetables.

Gorgonzola piccante
This cheese has a pleasantly sharp flavor, with a soft texture and blue-green veins. It makes a marvellous gratin with cauliflower and walnuts, and is good with all types of pasta, especially tagliatelle.

Gruyère
A hard cheese with a distinctive sweet and nutty taste, Gruyère is popular for cooking as it melts well.

Mozzarella
Good mozzarella should be very white, fairly elastic and moist when cut. It is often served in salads, but is also an excellent melting cheese—the prime choice for pizzas.

Oak-smoked Cheddar
This is just one of many Cheddar variants worth investigating. It can be used in any recipe specifying a hard grating cheese.

Parmesan
Parmesan and pasta are an obvious pairing, but this wonderful cheese is also excellent in salads and on risottos. Buy fresh Parmesan in a chunk if possible, and grate or shave it as needed.

Pecorino
An Italian sheep's milk cheese, this is used in much the same way as Parmesan. It has a distinctive, fairly strong flavor.

Red Leicester
This cheese has a mild flavor. The bright color makes it a good choice for sauces. Mix it with mature Cheddar if you want to deepen the flavor.

Ricotta
The delicate flavor of this smooth, soft, Italian whey cheese makes it first choice for desserts and baked dishes.

Smoked mozzarella
This cheese has a creamy, smoky taste. Whether you prefer it to plain mozzarella is a matter of choice. Try it and see—it has the same excellent melting properties as the plain variety.

red Leicester

Gruyère

smoked mozzarella

Cheddar

oak-smoked Cheddar

goat cheese

Gorgonzola

Parmesan

Edam

ricotta

mozzarella

Bavarian smoked cheese

Dolcelatte

Pecorino

feta

Quick Cookware

It isn't so much what cookware you have, but how you store it that is the main consideration for quick cooking. Have favorite pans and utensils close at hand—searching in drawers wastes time and sparks stress.

Colanders and sieves
You need at least one metal colander and a good-sized sieve. A small sieve or tea strainer is useful for dusting confectioner's sugar.

Cutting boards
The jury is still out on whether plastic or wooden cutting boards are best. The important thing is to have separate boards for raw and cooked ingredients, and to scrub them thoroughly after use.

Saucepans
A few good-sized saucepans with well-fitting lids are a must. Buy the best quality you can afford, but don't necessarily buy a boxed set. You may well end up with sizes you never use. Start with two or three reasonably sized pans, then double up on the size you use most. Choose heavy-based or non-stick pans that will be easy to clean—there isn't much point saving time cooking if you have to spend hours washing up afterward. For quick cooking, you'll need several frying pans. A good wok is essential, as is a deep skillet with a lid and a pancake or crepe pan.

Knives
It pays to buy good-quality knives. A really sharp knife can halve your preparation time.

Knives are very personal possessions—every cook will have his or her favorites—but for most purposes a short, sharp vegetable knife, a flat-bladed cook's knife, a medium serrated knife and a bread knife will work. Store knives in a block, if possible, or on a rack. In a drawer they are liable to get knocked around and damaged.

Utensils
Store whisks, spoons and spatulas on a rack or in a jar on the work surface. It is useful to have both long and short-handled wooden spoons, and at least two whisks. Miniature whisks are handy for small quantities in cups. A reamer—a wooden utensil with a shaped end—is ideal for juicing lemons and limes. Tongs are another essential item, but comparison shop before buying: you need a pair that is sturdy and easy to manipulate. You'll also need a draining spoon, potato masher and one or two spatulas. Good-quality rubber spatulas are ideal for getting the last of a mixture out of a bowl, or scraping the sides of a food processor. For speed, it pays to buy a sturdy peeler. The type with a U-shaped handle and a blade across the top works fast and well.

wooden spatula

ladle

scissors

knives and peelers

vegetable knife

bread knife

whisks

draining
spoon

serving
spoon

chopping
board

grater

colander

saucepans

wok

frying pan

TECHNIQUES AND BASIC RECIPES

Mastering a few simple techniques for food preparation will really speed
up your cooking; making basic recipes in bulk is another great time-saver.

Peeling and Seeding Tomatoes

A simple and efficient way of preparing tomatoes.

1 Holding each tomato in turn, firmly (and keeping your fingers out of the way), cut a small cross on the bottom with a sharp knife.

2 Turn the tomato over and carefully cut out the core with the tip of the knife.

3 Immerse the tomato in boiling water for 10–15 seconds, then transfer to a bowl of cold water using a slotted spoon.

4 As soon as the tomato is cool enough to handle, lift it out and use the side of the knife blade to peel off the skin, which should be easy to remove.

5 Cut the tomato in half horizontally and squeeze out the seeds into a bowl. Discard the seeds.

6 Use a large knife to cut the peeled tomato into strips, then chop across the strips to make dice.

Chopping Onions

Uniform-sized dice make cooking easy. This method can't be beaten.

1 Peel the onion. Cut it in half with a large knife and set it cut-side down on a cutting board. Make lengthwise vertical cuts along the onion, cutting almost, but not quite, through to the root.

2 Using a cook's knife, make 2 horizontal cuts from the stalk end toward the root, cutting almost, but not completely through it, so that the onion remains sufficiently intact to be manageable.

3 With the knife blade down, cut the onion neatly, first in one direction, then the other, so that it forms small, even dice. The size of the dice will be dictated by the recipe; small dice cook more quickly.

Slicing Onions

Use thin slices for sautéeing or to flavor oils for stir-frying, or use sweet onion slices in salads.

1 Peel the onion. Cut it in half with a large knife and set it cut-side down on a cutting board.

2 Using the tip of a sharp knife, cut out a triangular piece of the core from each half.

3 Holding the onion firmly (and keeping your fingers out of the way) cut across each half in vertical slices.

Shredding Cabbage

This method is useful for coleslaws, pickled cabbage or any cooked dish.

1 Put the cabbage on a board and hold it securely. Use a large cook's knife to cut the cabbage into quarters. If the knife is sharp, it should slide through the cabbage easily; if not, you may need to use a sawing action.

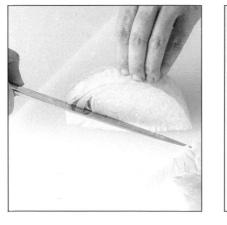

2 Place each quarter in turn on a cutting board. Rest it on one of the flat sides for safety, then use a sharp knife to cut out the core.

3 Holding the cabbage securely, slice across each quarter to form fine, even shreds. If the recipe requires the cabbage to be blanched, add the shreds to boiling water, cook for 1–2 minutes, then drain thoroughly.

Cutting Carrot Julienne

Julienne strips of any vegetable make decorative accompaniments, or can be used in stir-fries.

1 Peel the carrot and use a large knife to cut it into 2 in lengths. Cut a thin sliver from one side of each piece so that it sits flat on the board.

2 Using a sharp cook's knife (or your favorite vegetable knife) cut the piece of carrot into thin lengthwise slices.

3 Stack the slices and cut through them to make fine strips.

Chopping Fresh Ginger

Fresh ginger imparts a clean, refreshing taste. Follow the instructions to chop finely.

1 Break off small knobs of ginger from the main root. Using a small, sharp knife, or a swivel-bladed peeler, remove the outer skin.

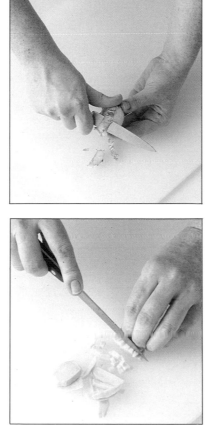

2 Slice the ginger flesh lengthwise and cut into strips.

3 Cut across the strips to form small, even dice.

COOK'S TIP

Fresh ginger can be frozen. Wrap the knobs well and remove them from the freezer as and when you need them. Frozen ginger is very easy to grate and does not need to be peeled. Just add the frozen grated ginger to hot food; it will thaw on contact.

Chopping Chiles

Handle chiles with care. Always work in a well-ventilated area and keep away from your eyes.

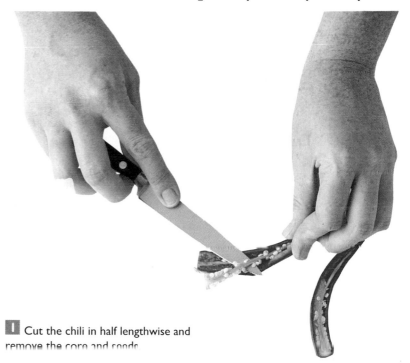

1 Cut the chili in half lengthwise and remove the core and seeds.

2 Cut it into lengthwise strips.

3 Cut across the strips to form small, even dice.

Pitting Olives

Using a pitter is the easiest way to remove the pit from an olive, but you can also use a sharp knife.

1 Put the olive in the pitter, with the pointed end on top.

2 Squeeze the handles together to extract the pit.

COOK'S TIP
For speed, buy olives pre-pitted. It is also possible to obtain jars of sliced olives in brine, which are very handy for the quick cook.

Chopping Herbs

Use this method to chop herbs until they are as coarse or fine as you wish.

1 Strip the leaves from the stalk and pile them on a cutting board.

2 Using a sharp knife, cut the herbs into small pieces, holding the tip of the blade against the board and rocking the blade back and forth. A mezzaluna (a crescent-shaped blade with a handle at either end) does the job even more easily and efficiently.

Seasoning a Wok

If you are using a new wok or frying pan you will need to prepare it as follows to ensure the best results.

1 Heat the wok or frying pan with 2–3 tbsp salt for about 15 minutes. Wipe out the salt. The wok is now ready for use.

2 To clean your wok, wipe out the inside with paper towels, keeping washing with detergent to a minimum. Seasoning a pan by the method described here will create a good non-stick surface.

Preparing Scallions

Scallions can be used in stir-fries to flavor oil, as vegetables in their own right, or as decoration.

1 This technique can also be used for the larger scallions. Trim off the root of each scallion with a sharp knife.

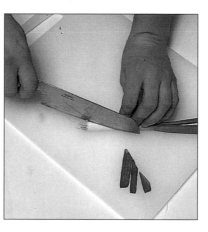

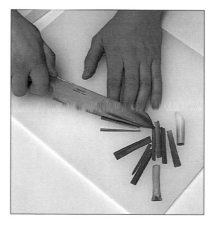

2 For an intense flavor, cut into matchsticks and stir-fry with vegetables of the same size.

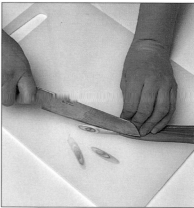

3 Slice thinly to stir-fry with crushed garlic to flavor the cooking oil.

COOK'S TIP

Scallion greens can be used as decoration. If they are young and tender, snip as you would chives. Long pieces can be blanched in boiling water, dried, and used to tic carrots in bundles for garnishing.

Speedy Stir-frying

Stir-frying takes very little actual cooking time, often no more than a matter of minutes. For this reason it is important that all the ingredients are prepared ahead of time—washed, peeled or grated as required, and cut to approximately the same shape and size, to ensure even cooking.

1 Always heat the wok (or frying pan, if using) for a few minutes before adding the oil or any other ingredients.

2 If adding oil, swirl the oil into the wok and allow it to heat up before adding the next ingredients.

3 When adding the first ingredients, reduce the heat a little. This will ensure they are not overcooked or burnt by the time the remaining ingredients have been added to the wok.

4 Once all the ingredients have been added, quickly increase the heat, as this will allow the dish to cook in the least possible time. This ensures that the ingredients retain a crisp, fresh texture, and prevents them from becoming soggy or laden with oil.

5 Use a long-handled scoop or spatula to turn the ingredients as you stir-fry. This will allow the ingredients to cook evenly and quickly.

6 It may be easier to slice meat for stir-frying if it has been frozen slightly for an hour or so. By the time you have sliced it, the meat will have thawed.

Cooking Pasta

1 Throw the pasta into a large pan of boiling salted water. Stir once to prevent sticking. The addition of 1 tbsp vegetable or olive oil will help stop the water from boiling over and prevent the pasta from sticking. Do not cover or the water will boil over.

2 Quickly bring the pasta back to a rolling boil and boil until al dente (literally "to the tooth") – the pasta should be just firm to the bite. It should not have a hard center or be very floppy.

Cooking Times for Fresh and Dried Pasta

Calculate the cooking time from the moment the water returns to the boil after the pasta has been added.

Unfilled pasta
Fresh: 2–3 minutes, though some very thin pasta is ready as soon as the water returns to the boil.
Dried: 8–12 minutes, but keep checking, as this is only a guide.

Filled pasta
Fresh: 8–10 minutes.
Dried: 15–20 minutes.

Above: Cook unfilled pasta until al dente, or firm to the bite.

3 Quickly drain the pasta well, using a large colander or strainer.

4 Immediately rinse the pasta with boiling water to wash off any starch and to prevent it from sticking together. Toss the pasta in a little olive oil or butter, or dress with sauce. Serve hot pasta immediately.

5 It is up to you whether you toss the pasta with the sauce before serving or serve it with the sauce on top.

Below: Filled pasta takes a little longer to cook than unfilled.

Scone Pizza Dough

The joy of using a scone mixture is that it is quick to make and uses pantry ingredients.

MAKES
1 x 10 in round pizza crust
1 x 12 x 7 in oblong pizza crust

INGREDIENTS
1 cup self-raising flour
1 cup self-rising whole-wheat
    flour
pinch of salt
$1/4$ cup butter, diced
$2/3$ cup milk

1 Combine the flours and salt in a mixing bowl. Rub in the butter until the mixture resembles fine bread crumbs.

2 Add the milk and mix with a wooden spoon to a soft dough.

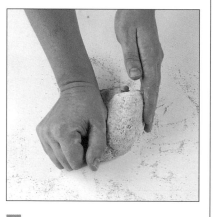

3 Knead gently on a lightly floured surface until smooth. The dough is now ready to use.

Superquick Pizza Dough

If you're really pressed for time, try a packaged pizza dough mix. For best results roll out the dough to a 10–12 in circle; this is slightly larger than stated on the package, but it does produce a perfect thin, crispy crust. For a deep-pan version, use two packages.

MAKES
1 x 10–12 in circle
4 x 5 in round pizza crusts
1 x 12 x 7 in oblong pizza crust

INGREDIENTS
1 x 5 oz package pizza crust mix
$1/2$ cup lukewarm water

1 Empty the contents of the package into a mixing bowl.

2 Pour in the water and mix with a wooden spoon into a soft dough.

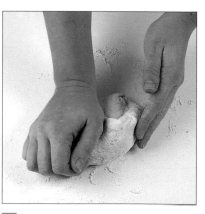

3 Transfer the dough to a lightly floured surface and knead for 5 minutes, until smooth and elastic. The dough is now ready to use.

Using a Food Processor

For speed, make superquick pizza dough in a food processor; let the machine do the mixing and kneading.

Ready-made Pizza Crusts

Fortunately for the busy cook it is now possible to buy fresh or frozen pizza crusts from most supermarkets. Many are enriched with additional ingredients like cheese, herbs and onions. All you have to do is add your chosen topping and bake in the oven in the usual way. For a different pizza crust, without having to make your own dough, try using French bread, pita bread or English muffins.

1 Put the pizza crust mix in a food processor. Process briefly.

2 Measure the water into a jug. With the machine running, add it and process until the dough forms a soft ball. Let rest for 2 minutes, then process for 1 more minute to knead the dough.

3 Put the dough on a lightly floured surface and roll it out into a large circle, or cut small rounds for pizzettes.

Tomato Sauce

Homemade tomato sauce can be used in a wide range of recipes and is an invaluable asset to the quick cook.

MAKES
about 1 cup

INGREDIENTS
1 tbsp olive oil
1 onion, finely chopped
1 garlic clove, crushed
1 x 14 oz can chopped tomatoes
1 tbsp tomato paste
1 tbsp chopped fresh mixed
    herbs, such as parsley,
    thyme, basil and oregano
pinch of sugar
salt and black pepper

1 Heat the oil in a pan, add the onion and garlic, and gently fry for about 5 minutes until softened.

2 Add the tomatoes, tomato paste, herbs, sugar and seasoning.

3 Simmer, uncovered, stirring occasionally for 10–15 minutes or until the tomatoes have reduced to a thick pulp. Let cool.

Flavored Oils

Brush these over pizza crusts before adding the topping. They can also be used in salad dressings, or tossed with pasta.

CHILI OIL
INGREDIENTS
²⁄₃ cup olive oil
2 tsp tomato paste
1 tbsp dried red chili flakes

1 Heat the oil in a pan until very hot but not smoking. Stir in the tomato paste and chili flakes. Let cool.

2 Pour the chili oil into a small jar or bottle. Cover and store in the fridge for up to 2 months (the longer you keep it, the hotter it gets).

GARLIC OIL
INGREDIENTS
3–4 whole garlic cloves
¹⁄₂ cup olive oil

1 Peel the garlic cloves and put them into a small jar or bottle.

2 Pour in the oil, cover and keep in the fridge for up to 1 month.

Salad Dressing/Baste

A good salad dressing can double up as an effective baste for the grill. This dressing is delicious with white meats or fish.

MAKES
7 tbsp

INGREDIENTS
6 tbsp olive oil
1 tbsp white wine vinegar
1 tsp French mustard
½ garlic clove, crushed
¼ tsp sugar

1 Pour the oil and vinegar into a screw-topped jar.

2 Add the mustard, garlic and sugar.

3 Shake well, and use as a dressing or marinade for salad, meat and fish.

Mayonnaise

Although bought mayonnaise is fine for fast meals, it takes very little time to make your own. Make sure the egg yolks are at room temperature, and add the oil very gradually at the start. Home-made mayonnaise is made with raw egg yolks and may therefore be considered unsuitable for young children, pregnant mothers and the elderly.

MAKES
about 1¼ cups

INGREDIENTS
2 egg yolks
1 tsp French mustard
⅔ cup extra-virgin olive oil
⅔ cup sunflower oil
2 tsp white wine vinegar
salt and pepper

2 Add the olive oil a little at a time while the processor is running. When the mixture is thick, add the remainder of the oil in a slow, steady stream.

1 Place the egg yolks and mustard in a food processor and blend smoothly.

COOK'S TIP
Should mayonnaise separate during blending, add 2 tbsp boiling water and beat until smooth. Store mayonnaise in the refrigerator for up to 1 week, sealed in a screw-topped jar.

3 Add the vinegar and season to taste with salt and pepper.

MENU PLANS

All of the recipes in this book can be prepared individually in 30 minutes or less, but they can also be combined with other dishes to provide a three-course meal. Below are some suggested menus, using different combinations of quick recipes from the book.

MENU 1

Butterfly Shrimp, p. 74

Stir-fried Sweet and Sour Chicken, p. 149

Peach Melba, p. 406

MENU 2

French Onion Soup, p. 59

Zucchini Puffs with Salad and Balsamic Dressing, p. 236

Char-grilled Apples on Cinnamon Toasts, p. 374

MENU 3

Chilled Fresh Tomato Soup, p. 67

Veal Escalopes with Artichokes, p. 127

Red Berry Sponge Tart, p. 392

MENU 4

Creamy Parmesan and Cauliflower
Soup with Pasta Bows, p. 60

Grilled Snapper with Hot Mango
Salsa, p. 170

Chocolate Mousse on the Loose,
p. 408

MENU 5

Mini Spring Rolls, p. 78

Stir-fried Pork with Mustard, p. 134

Mango and Coconut Stir-fry, p. 380

MENU 6

Buckwheat Couscous with Goat
Cheese and Celery, p. 112

Warm Stir-fried Salad, p. 266

Fruit Kebabs with Chocolate and
Marshmallow Fondue, p. 376

MENU 7

Sesame Seed Chicken Bites, p. 80

Indonesian Pork and Peanut Saté,
p. 142

Broiled Pineapple with Rum-custard
Sauce, p. 387

MENU 8

Asparagus Rolls with Herb Butter
Sauce, p. 224

Beet and Celeriac Gratin, p. 231

Black Forest Sundae, p. 410

QUICK
APPE

You've arrived home **late** and your guests are due in under an hour. Surely you don't have time to make an appetizer? Oh **yes**, you do. The recipes in this chapter have been especially selected for the **ease** and **speed** with which they can be

TIZERS

prepared. Crab and Egg Noodle Broth looks as

sophisticated as its name suggests, yet takes only

minutes to make. Butterfly Shrimp takes even less time

to prepare and is always popular, while crisp and

tender Deep-fried Florets with Tangy Thyme Mayonnaise is

the perfect choice for vegetarians.

Crab and Egg Noodle Broth

This delicious broth is an ideal solution when you are hungry and time is short, and you need something fast, nutritious and filling.

Serves 4

INGREDIENTS

3 oz fine egg noodles
2 tbsp unsalted butter
1 small bunch scallions, chopped
1 celery stick, sliced
1 medium carrot, peeled and cut
   into sticks
5 cups chicken stock
4 tbsp dry sherry
4 oz white crab meat, fresh
   or frozen
pinch of celery salt
pinch of cayenne pepper
2 tsp lemon juice
1 small bunch cilantro or flat-leaf
   parsley, to garnish

celery

egg noodles

crab meat

scallions *cilantro*

1 Bring a large saucepan of salted water to a boil. Toss in the egg noodles and cook according to the instructions on the package. Cool under cold running water and leave immersed in water until required.

2 Heat the butter in another large pan, add the scallions, celery and carrot, cover and soften the vegetables over a gentle heat for 3–4 minutes.

3 Add the chicken stock and sherry, bring to a boil and simmer for a further 5 minutes.

4 Flake the crab meat between your fingers onto a plate and remove any stray pieces of shell.

5 Drain the noodles and add to the broth together with the crab meat. Season to taste with celery salt and cayenne pepper, and sharpen with the lemon juice. Return to a simmer.

6 Ladle the broth into shallow soup plates, scatter with roughly chopped cilantro or parsley and serve.

Chicken Vermicelli Soup with Egg Shreds

This soup is very quick and easy – you can add all sorts of extra ingredients to vary the taste, using up lurking leftovers such as scallions, mushrooms, a few shrimp, chopped salami and so on.

Serves 4–6

INGREDIENTS
3 large eggs
2 tbsp chopped fresh cilantro or parsley
6¼ cups good chicken stock or canned consommé
1 cup dried vermicelli or angel hair pasta
¼ lb cooked chicken breast, sliced
salt and pepper

vermicelli

chicken breast

eggs

cilantro

THAI CHICKEN SOUP

To make a Thai variation, use Chinese rice noodles instead of pasta. Stir ½ tsp dried lemon grass, 2 small whole fresh chilies and 4 tbsp coconut milk into the stock. Add 4 sliced scallions and plenty of chopped fresh cilantro.

1 First make the egg shreds. Whisk the eggs together in a small bowl and stir in the cilantro or parsley.

2 Heat a small nonstick skillet and pour in 2–3 tbsp egg, swirling to cover the base evenly. Cook until set. Repeat until all the mixture is used up.

3 Roll each pancake up and slice thinly into shreds. Set aside.

4 Bring the stock to a boil and add the pasta, breaking it up into short lengths. Cook for 3–5 minutes until the pasta is almost tender, then add the chicken, salt, and pepper. Heat through for 2–3 minutes, then stir in the egg shreds. Serve immediately.

Fresh Pea and Ham Soup

Frozen peas provide flavor, freshness and color in this delicious winter soup, which is filling enough to make a light main course or a starter.

Serves 4

INGREDIENTS
4 oz small pasta shapes
2 tbsp vegetable oil
1 small bunch scallions, chopped
3 cups frozen peas
5 cups chicken stock
8 oz raw unsmoked ham
    or bacon
4 tbsp heavy cream
salt and freshly ground black pepper
warm crusty bread, to serve

ham

pasta

cream

peas

scallions

1 Bring a large saucepan of salted water to a boil. Toss in the pasta and cook according to the instructions on the package. Drain, cover with cold water and set aside until required.

2 Heat the vegetable oil in a large heavy saucepan and cook the scallions until soft. Add the peas and stock, then simmer for 10 minutes.

3 Liquidize the soup in a blender and return to the saucepan. Cut the ham or bacon into short fingers and add it together with the pasta to the saucepan. Simmer for 2–3 minutes and season to taste. Stir in the cream and serve with the warm crusty bread.

VARIATION

Any pasta shapes can be used for this soup, although hoops or shells seem to work best of all.

Broccoli and Almond Soup

The creaminess of the toasted almonds combines perfectly with the slight bitterness of the taste of broccoli.

Serves 4–6

INGREDIENTS
⅔ cup ground almonds
1½ lb broccoli
3¾ cups fresh vegetable stock or
  water
1¼ cups skim or low-fat milk
salt and freshly ground black pepper

ground almonds

skim milk

broccoli

1 Preheat the oven to 350°F. Spread the ground almonds evenly on a cookie sheet and toast in the oven for about 10 minutes, or until just golden. Reserve ¼ of the almonds and set aside for the garnish.

2 Cut the broccoli into small florets and steam for 6–7 minutes or until tender.

3 Place the remaining toasted almonds, broccoli, stock or water and milk in a blender and blend until smooth. Season to taste.

4 Reheat the soup and serve sprinkled with the reserved toasted almonds.

French Onion Soup

In the time it takes to soften a few onions and brown some cheese on toast, this delicious soup appears on the table steaming hot and ready to eat. It makes a substantial starter or lunch dish.

Serves 4

INGREDIENTS
2 tbsp vegetable oil
3 medium onions, sliced
3¾ cups beef stock
4 slices French bread
butter, for spreading
1 cup grated Gruyère, Beaufort or
  Emmenthal cheese

onions

cheese

French bread

1 Heat the vegetable oil in a large frying pan and brown the onions over a steady heat, taking care they do not burn.

2 Transfer the browned onions to a large saucepan, cover with beef stock and simmer for 10 minutes.

3 Preheat the broiler to a moderate temperature and toast the French bread on both sides. Spread one side with butter and top with grated cheese. Ladle the soup into four flameproof dishes, float the cheesy crusts on top and grill until crispy and brown.

Creamy Parmesan and Cauliflower Soup with Pasta Bows

A silky smooth, mildly cheesy soup that isn't overpowered by the cauliflower. It is an elegant dinner party soup served with the crisp melba toast.

Serves 6

INGREDIENTS
1 large cauliflower
5 cups chicken or vegetable stock
1½ cups pasta bows (farfalle)
⅔ cup light cream or milk
freshly grated nutmeg
pinch of cayenne pepper
4 tbsp freshly grated Parmesan cheese
salt and pepper

MELBA TOAST
3–4 slices day-old white bread
freshly grated Parmesan cheese, for
    sprinkling
¼ tsp paprika

cauliflower

pasta bows

Parmesan cheese

nutmeg

1 Cut the leaves and central stalk away from the cauliflower and discard. Divide the cauliflower into florets.

2 Bring the stock to a boil and add the cauliflower. Simmer for about 10 minutes or until very soft. Remove the cauliflower with a perforated spoon and place in a food processor.

3 Add the pasta to the stock and simmer for 10 minutes until tender. Drain, reserve the pasta, and pour the liquid over the cauliflower in the food processor. Add the cream or milk, nutmeg, and cayenne to the cauliflower. Blend until smooth, then press through a strainer. Stir in the cooked pasta. Reheat the soup and stir in the Parmesan. Taste and adjust the seasoning.

4 Meanwhile make the melba toast. Preheat the oven to 350°F. Toast the bread lightly on both sides. Quickly cut off the crusts and split each slice in half horizontally. Scrape off any doughy bits and sprinkle with Parmesan and paprika. Place on a baking sheet and bake in the oven for 10–15 minutes or until uniformly golden. Serve with the soup.

Red Onion and Beet Soup

This beautiful vivid ruby-red soup will look stunning at any dinner party.

Serves 4–6

INGREDIENTS
1 tbsp olive oil
12 oz red onions, sliced
2 garlic cloves, crushed
10 oz cooked beets, cut into
 thin sticks
5 cups fresh vegetable stock or water
1 cup cooked soup pasta
2 tbsp raspberry vinegar
salt and freshly ground black pepper
low-fat yogurt or ricotta cheese, to
 garnish
snipped chives, to garnish

garlic

red onion

beets

pasta

chives

1 Heat the olive oil and add the onions and garlic.

2 Cook gently for about 20 minutes or until soft and tender.

COOK'S TIP
Try substituting cooked barley for the pasta to give extra nuttiness.

3 Add the beets, stock or water, cooked pasta shapes and vinegar and heat through. Season to taste.

4 Ladle into bowls. Top each one with a spoonful of yogurt or ricotta cheese and sprinkle with chives.

Cauliflower, Flageolet and Fennel Seed Soup

The sweet, anise-liquorice flavor of the fennel seeds gives a delicious edge to this hearty soup.

Serves 4–6

INGREDIENTS
1 tbsp olive oil
1 garlic clove, crushed
1 onion, chopped
2 tsp fennel seeds
1 cauliflower, cut into small florets
2 × 14 oz cans flageolet beans, drained and rinsed
5 cups fresh vegetable stock or water
salt and freshly ground black pepper
chopped fresh parsley, to garnish
toasted slices of French bread, to serve

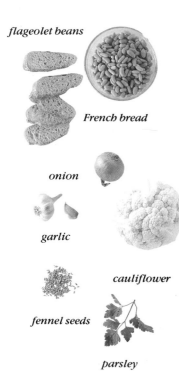

flageolet beans

French bread

onion

garlic

cauliflower

fennel seeds

parsley

1 Heat the olive oil. Add the garlic, onion and fennel seeds and cook gently for 5 minutes or until softened.

2 Add the cauliflower, half of the beans and the stock or water.

3 Bring to a boil. Reduce the heat and simmer for 10 minutes or until the cauliflower is tender.

4 Pour the soup into a blender and blend until smooth. Stir in the remaining beans and season to taste. Reheat and pour into bowls. Sprinkle with chopped parsley and serve with toasted slices of French bread.

Speedy Beet and Lima Bean Soup

This soup is a simplified version of borscht, and is prepared in a fraction of the time. Serve with a spoonful of sour cream and a scattering of chopped fresh parsley.

Serves 4

INGREDIENTS
2 tbsp vegetable oil
1 medium onion, halved and sliced
1 tsp caraway seeds
finely grated zest of ½ orange
9 oz cooked beets, grated
5 cups fresh or canned beef stock
   or rassol
1 × 14 oz can lima beans, drained
1 tbsp wine vinegar
4 tbsp sour cream
4 tbsp chopped fresh parsley,
   to garnish

caraway seeds

beets

sour cream

onion

orange

beans

1 Heat the oil in a large saucepan and cook the onion, caraway seeds and orange zest until soft but not colored.

2 Add the beets, stock, lima beans and vinegar and simmer for a further 10 minutes.

3 Divide the soup between four bowls, add a spoonful of sour cream to each and scatter with chopped fresh parsley.

COOK'S TIP
Rassol is a beet broth used for its strong color and flavor. You are most likely to find it in Kosher food stores.

Baby Carrot and Fennel Soup

Sweet tender carrots find their moment of glory in this delicately spiced soup. Fennel provides an anise flavor without overpowering the carrots.

Serves 4

INGREDIENTS
4 tbsp butter
1 small bunch scallions, chopped
5 oz fennel bulb, chopped
1 celery stalk, chopped
1 lb baby carrots, grated
½ tsp ground cumin
5 oz new potatoes, peeled and diced
5 cups fresh or canned chicken or
    vegetable stock
4 tbsp heavy cream
salt and freshly ground black pepper
4 tbsp chopped fresh parsley,
    to garnish

carrots

fennel bulb

celery

cream

scallions

1 Melt the butter in a large saucepan and add the scallions, fennel, celery, carrots and cumin. Cover and cook for 5 minutes until soft.

2 Add the potatoes and stock, and simmer for a further 10 minutes.

3 Liquidize the mixture in the pan with a hand-held mixer. Stir in the cream and season to taste. Serve in individual bowls and garnish with chopped fresh parsley.

COOK'S TIP
For convenience, you can freeze the soup in portions before adding the cream, seasoning and parsley.

Succotash Soup Plate

Succotash is a North American Indian dish of corn and lima beans. Originally the dish was enriched with bear fat, although modern day succotash is finished with milk or cream. This version makes an appetizing and filling main course soup.

Serves 4

INGREDIENTS
4 tbsp butter
1 large onion, chopped
2 large carrots, peeled and cut into
    short sticks
3¾ cups milk
1 vegetable bouillon cube
2 medium-sized waxy potatoes,
    peeled and diced
1 thyme sprig
2 cups frozen corn
3 cups frozen lima beans or broad
    beans
2 tbsp chopped fresh parsley,
    to garnish

carrots

corn

thyme

lima beans

potatoes

parsley

1 Heat the butter in a large saucepan. Add the onion and carrots and cook over a gentle heat for 3–4 minutes, to soften without coloring.

2 Add the milk, bouillon cube, potatoes, thyme, corn and lima beans or broad beans. Simmer for 10 minutes until the potatoes are cooked through.

3 Season to taste, ladle into soup plates and garnish with chopped fresh parsley.

COOK'S TIP

Frozen corn and lima beans are best for flavor and convenience in this soup, although the canned variety may also be used.

Melon and Basil Soup

A deliciously refreshing, chilled fruit soup, just right for a hot summer's day.

Serves 4–6

INGREDIENTS
2 canteloupe or honeydew melons
⅓ cup superfine sugar
¾ cup water
finely grated zest and juice of 1 lime
3 tbsp shredded fresh basil
fresh basil leaves, to garnish

basil

sugar

lime

melon

I Cut the melons in half across the middle. Scrape out the seeds and discard. Using a melon baller, scoop out 20–24 balls and set aside for the garnish. Scoop out the remaining flesh and place in a blender or food processor.

2 Place the sugar, water and lime zest in a small pan over a low heat. Stir until dissolved, bring to the boil and simmer for 2–3 minutes. Remove from the heat and leave to cool slightly. Pour half the mixture into the blender or food processor with the melon flesh. Blend until smooth, adding the remaining syrup and lime juice to taste.

3 Pour the mixture into a bowl, stir in the basil and chill. Serve garnished with basil leaves and melon balls.

COOK'S TIP

Add the syrup in two stages, as the amount of sugar needed will depend on the sweetness of the melon.

Chilled Fresh Tomato Soup

This effortless uncooked soup can be made in minutes.

Serves 4–6

INGREDIENTS
3–3½ lb ripe tomatoes, peeled and
   roughly chopped
4 garlic cloves, crushed
2 tbsp extra-virgin olive oil (optional)
2 tbsp balsamic vinegar
freshly ground black pepper
4 slices wholewheat bread
low-fat ricotta cheese, to garnish

*wholewheat
bread*

garlic

ricotta cheese

peppercorns

tomato

COOK'S TIP

For the best flavor, it is important to
use only fully ripened, succulent
tomatoes in this soup.

1 Place the tomatoes in a blender with
the garlic and olive oil if using. Blend until
smooth

2 Pass the mixture through a sieve to
remove the seeds. Stir in the balsamic
vinegar and season to taste with pepper.
Chill quickly by adding several ice cubes
or some crushed ice to the mixture, but
be careful not to dilute it too much.

3 Toast the bread lightly on both sides.
While still hot, cut off the crusts and slice
in half horizontally. Place the toast on a
board with the uncooked sides facing
down and, using a circular motion, rub to
remove any doughy pieces of bread.

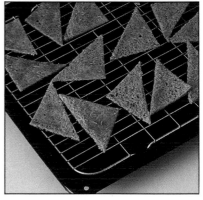

4 Cut each slice into 4 triangles. Place
on a griddle and toast the uncooked sides
until lightly golden. Garnish each bowl of
soup with a spoonful of ricotta cheese and
serve with the melba toast.

Deep-fried Florets with Tangy Thyme Mayonnaise

Cauliflower and broccoli make a sensational snack when coated in a beer batter and deep-fried. Serve with a tangy mayonnaise.

Serves 2–3

INGREDIENTS
6 oz cauliflower
6 oz broccoli
2 eggs, separated
2 tbsp olive oil
1 cup beer
1¼ cups all-purpose flour
pinch of salt
2 tbsp shredded fresh basil
vegetable oil for deep-frying
⅔ cup good quality mayonnaise
2 tsp chopped fresh thyme
2 tsp grated lemon rind
2 tsp lemon juice
sea salt, for sprinkling

eggs
basil
all-purpose flour
mayonnaise
broccoli
beer
cauliflower
thyme
lemon

1 Break the cauliflower and broccoli into small florets, cutting large florets into smaller pieces. Set aside.

2 Beat the egg yolks, olive oil, beer, flour and salt in a bowl. Strain the batter, if necessary, to remove any lumps.

3 Whisk the egg whites until stiff. Fold into the batter with the basil.

4 Heat the oil for deep-frying to 350°F or until a cube of bread, when added to the oil, browns in about 30–45 seconds. Dip the florets in the batter, and deep-fry in batches for 2–3 minutes until the coating is golden and crisp. Drain on paper towels.

5 Mix the mayonnaise, thyme, lemon rind and juice in a small bowl.

6 Sprinkle the florets with sea salt and then serve with the thyme mayonnaise.

Caponata

Caponata is a quintessential part of Sicilian antipasti and is a rich, spicy mixture of eggplants, tomatoes, capers and celery.

Serves 4

INGREDIENTS
4 tbsp olive oil
1 large onion, sliced
2 celery stalks, sliced
1 lb eggplant, diced
5 ripe tomatoes, chopped
1 garlic clove, crushed
3 tbsp red wine vinegar
1 tbsp sugar
2 tbsp capers
12 olives
pinch of salt
4 tbsp chopped fresh parsley,
   to garnish
warm crusty bread, to serve
olives, to serve

celery

eggplants

onion   *tomatoes*

   olives

capers

1 Heat half the oil in a large heavy saucepan. Add the onion and celery and cook over a gentle heat for about 3–4 minutes to soften.

2 Add the remainder of the oil with the eggplants and stir to absorb the oil. Cook until the eggplants begin to color, then add the chopped tomatoes, garlic, vinegar and sugar.

3 Cover the surface of the vegetables with a circle of waxed paper and simmer for 8–10 minutes.

4 Add the capers and olives, then season to taste with salt. Turn the caponata out into a bowl, garnish with parsley and serve at room temperature with warm crusty bread and olives.

Broiled New Zealand Mussels with Cumin

Large New Zealand mussels have a more distinctive flavor than the more common small black variety. If you can't find these the black mussels are also delicious prepared this way.

Serves 4

INGREDIENTS
3 tbsp fresh parsley
3 tbsp fresh cilantro
1 garlic clove, crushed
pinch of ground cumin
2 tbsp unsalted butter,
  softened
3 tbsp brown bread crumbs
freshly ground black pepper
12 New Zealand mussels or
  24 small mussels on the half-shell
chopped fresh parsley, to garnish

butter

parsley

garlic

bread

coriander

mussels

1 Chop the herbs finely.

2 Beat the garlic, herbs, cumin and butter together with a wooden spoon.

3 Stir in the bread crumbs and freshly ground black pepper.

4 Spoon a little of the mixture onto each mussel and broil for 2 minutes. Serve with chopped fresh parsley.

Crispy "Seaweed" with Flaked Almonds

This popular appetizer in Chinese restaurants is in fact usually made not with seaweed but spring greens such as collard or chard! It is easy to make at home.

Serves 4-6

INGREDIENTS
1 lb spring greens
peanut oil, for deep-frying
¼ tsp sea salt flakes
1 tsp caster sugar
½ cup flaked almonds,
   toasted

spring greens

almonds

peanut oil

sea salt

sugar

COOK'S TIP
It is important to dry the spring greens thoroughly before deep-frying them, otherwise it will be difficult to achieve the desired crispness without destroying their vivid color.

1 Wash the spring greens under cold running water and then pat well with paper towels to dry thoroughly. Remove and discard the thick white stalks from the greens.

2 Lay several leaves on top of one another, roll up tightly and, using a sharp knife, slice as finely as possible into thread-like strips.

3 Half-fill a wok with oil and heat to 350°F. Deep-fry the greens in batches for about 1 minute until they darken and crisp. Remove each batch from the wok as soon as it is ready and drain on paper towels.

4 Transfer the "seaweed" to a serving dish, sprinkle with the salt and sugar, then mix well. Garnish with the toasted flaked almonds sprinkled over.

Hot Spicy Crab Claws

Crab claws are used to delicious effect in this quick appetizer based on an Indonesian dish called *Kepiting Pedas*.

Serves 4

INGREDIENTS
12 fresh or frozen and thawed
  cooked crab claws
4 shallots, coarsely chopped
2-4 fresh red chilies, seeded and
  coarsely chopped
3 garlic cloves, coarsely chopped
1 tsp grated fresh ginger
½ tsp ground coriander
3 tbsp peanut oil
4 tbsp water
2 tsp sweet soy sauce
  (kecap manis)
2-3 tsp lime juice
salt, to taste
fresh cilantro, to garnish

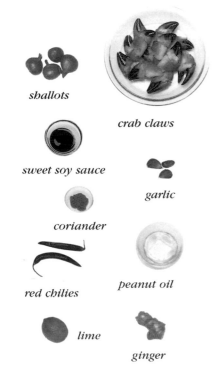

shallots

crab claws

sweet soy sauce

garlic

coriander

red chilies

peanut oil

lime

ginger

1 Crack the crab claws with the back of a heavy knife to make eating easier. Set aside. In a mortar, pound the chopped shallots with the pestle until pulpy. Add the chilies, garlic, ginger and ground coriander and pound until the mixture forms a coarse paste.

2 Heat the wok over medium heat. Add the oil and swirl it around. When it is hot, stir in the chili paste. Stir-fry for about 30 seconds. Increase the heat to high. Add the crab claws and stir-fry for another 3–4 minutes.

3 Stir in the water, sweet soy sauce, lime juice and salt to taste. Continue to stir-fry for 1–2 minutes. Serve at once, garnished with fresh cilantro. The crab claws are eaten with the fingers, so provide finger bowls.

COOK'S TIP
If whole crab claws are unavailable, look out for frozen prepared crab claws. These are shelled with just the tip of the claw attached to the white meat. Stir-fry for about two minutes until heated through.

Butterfly Shrimp

Use raw shrimp if you can because the flavor will be better, but if you substitute cooked shrimp, cut down the stir-fry cooking time by one third.

Serves 4

INGREDIENTS
1 in piece ginger root
12 oz raw shrimp, thawed
 if frozen
½ cup raw peanuts, roughly
 chopped
3 tbsp vegetable oil
1 clove garlic, crushed
1 red chili, finely chopped
3 tbsp smooth peanut butter
1 tbsp fresh cilantro, chopped
fresh cilantro sprigs, to garnish

FOR THE DRESSING
⅔ cup natural low-fat yogurt
2 in piece cucumber, diced
salt and freshly ground black pepper

1 To make the dressing, mix together the yogurt, cucumber and seasoning in a bowl, then leave to chill while preparing and cooking the shrimp.

2 Peel the ginger, and chop it finely.

3 Prepare the shrimp by peeling off the shells, leaving the tails intact. Make a slit down the back of each shrimp and remove the black vein, then slit the shrimp completely down the back and open it out to make a "butterfly."

diced cucumber

peanuts

shrimp

coriander

chili

4 Heat the wok and dry-fry the peanuts, stirring constantly until golden brown. Leave to cool. Wipe out the wok with paper towels.

5 Heat the wok, add the oil and when hot add the ginger, garlic and chili. Stir-fry for 2–3 minutes until the garlic is softened but not brown.

6 Add the shrimp, then increase the heat and stir-fry for 1–2 minutes until the shrimp turn pink. Stir in the peanut butter and stir-fry for 2 minutes. Add the chopped cilantro, then scatter in the peanuts. Garnish with cilantro sprigs and serve with the cucumber dressing.

Chicken Goujons

Serve as a first course for eight people or as a filling main course for four. Delicious served with new potatoes and salad.

Serves 8

INGREDIENTS
4 boned and skinned chicken breasts
3 cups fresh bread crumbs
1 tsp ground coriander
½ tsp ground paprika
½ tsp ground cumin
3 tbsp all-purpose flour
2 eggs, beaten
oil, for deep-frying
salt and freshly ground black pepper
lemon slices, to garnish
sprigs of fresh cilantro, to garnish

FOR THE DIP
1¼ cups plain yogurt
2 tbsp lemon juice
4 tbsp chopped fresh cilantro
4 tbsp chopped fresh parsley

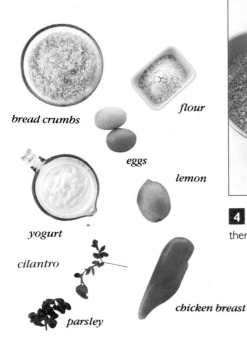

bread crumbs

flour

eggs

lemon

yogurt

cilantro

parsley

chicken breast

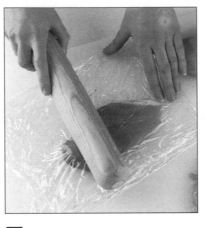

1 Divide the chicken breasts into two natural fillets. Place them between two sheets of plastic wrap and, using a rolling pin, flatten each one to a thickness of about ¼ in.

2 Cut into 1 in strips diagonally across the fillets.

3 Mix the bread crumbs with the spices and seasoning. Toss the chicken fillet pieces (goujons) into the flour, keeping them separate.

4 Dip the fillets into the beaten egg and then coat in the bread crumb mixture.

5 Thoroughly mix all the ingredients for the dip together, and season to taste. Chill until required.

6 Heat the oil in a heavy-based pan. It is ready for deep-frying when a cube of bread tossed into the oil sizzles on the surface. Fry the goujons in batches until golden and crisp. Drain on paper towels and keep warm in the oven until all the chicken has been fried. Garnish with lemon slices and sprigs of fresh cilantro.

Mini Spring Rolls

Eat these light crispy parcels with your fingers. If you like slightly spicier food, sprinkle them with a little cayenne pepper before serving.

Makes 20

INGREDIENTS
1 green chili
½ cup vegetable oil
1 small onion, finely chopped
1 clove garlic, crushed
3 oz cooked chicken breast
1 small carrot, cut into fine
    matchsticks
1 scallion, finely sliced
1 small red pepper, seeded and cut
    into fine matchsticks
1 oz bean sprouts
1 tsp sesame oil
4 large sheets filo pastry
1 medium egg white, lightly beaten
long chives, to garnish (optional)
3 tbsp light soy sauce, to serve

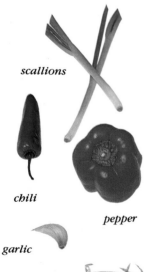

scallions

chili

pepper

garlic

bean sprouts

1 Carefully remove the seeds from the chili and chop finely, wearing rubber gloves to protect your hands, if necessary.

2 Heat the wok, then add 2 tbsp of the vegetable oil. When hot, add the onion, garlic and chili. Stir-fry for 1 minute.

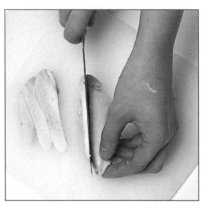

3 Slice the chicken thinly, then add to the wok and fry over a high heat, stirring constantly until browned.

4 Add the carrot, scallion and red pepper and stir-fry for 2 minutes. Add the bean sprouts, stir in the sesame oil and leave to cool.

COOK'S TIP

Always keep filo pastry sheets covered with a dry, clean cloth until needed, to prevent them drying out.

5 Cut each sheet of filo into 5 short strips. Place a small amount of filling at one end of each strip, then fold in the long sides and roll up the pastry. Seal and glaze the parcels with the egg white, then chill uncovered for 15 minutes before frying.

6 Wipe out the wok with paper towels, heat it, and add the remaining vegetable oil. When the oil is hot, fry the rolls in batches until crisp and golden brown. Drain on paper towels and serve dipped in light soy sauce.

COOK'S TIP

Be careful to avoid touching your face or eyes when deseeding and chopping chilies because they are very potent and may cause burning and irritation to the skin. Try preparing chilies under running water.

Sesame Seed Chicken Bites

Best served warm, these crunchy bites are delicious accompanied by a glass of chilled dry white wine.

Makes 20

INGREDIENTS
6 oz raw chicken breast
2 cloves garlic, crushed
1 in piece ginger root, peeled
    and grated
1 medium egg white
1 tsp cornstarch
¼ cup shelled pistachios, roughly
    chopped
4 tbsp sesame seeds
2 tbsp grapeseed oil
salt and freshly ground black pepper

FOR THE SAUCE
¼ cup hoisin sauce
1 tbsp sweet chili sauce

TO GARNISH
ginger root, finely shredded
pistachios, roughly chopped
fresh dill sprigs

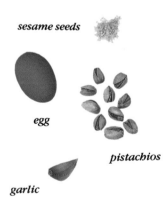

sesame seeds

egg

pistachios

garlic

ginger

1 Place the chicken, garlic, grated ginger, egg white and cornstarch into the food processor and process them to a smooth paste.

2 Stir in the pistachios and season well with salt and pepper.

3 Roll into 20 balls and coat with sesame seeds. Heat the wok and add the oil. When the oil is hot, stir-fry the chicken bites in batches, turning regularly until golden. Drain on paper towels.

4 Make the sauce by mixing together the hoisin and chili sauces in a bowl. Garnish the bites with shredded ginger, pistachios and dill, then serve hot, with a dish of sauce for dipping.

Welsh Rarebit Toasts

Welsh Rarebit is the gourmet's answer to cheese on toast. Serve as a tasty starter with drinks.

Serves 4

INGREDIENTS
scant 1 cup beer
4 tbsp flour
2 tsp mustard (powdered or ready-made)
½ tsp celery salt
pinch of cayenne pepper
1½ cups grated Cheddar cheese
6 thick slices white or whole wheat bread
3 celery stalks, to serve

bread

Cheddar cheese

flour

mustard

beer

1 Measure ¼ cup of the beer into a mixing bowl and combine with the flour, mustard, celery salt and cayenne pepper. Mix well.

2 Bring the remaining beer to a boil in a heavy saucepan together with the cheese. Pour over the mixed ingredients and stir to blend evenly. Return to the saucepan and simmer gently, stirring continuously, to thicken.

COOK'S TIP

Welsh Rarebit mixture will keep in the refrigerator for up to a week and is perfect for a fast snack at any time of the day.

3 Preheat a moderate broiler and toast the bread on both sides. Spread thickly with the mixture, then broil until golden brown and bubbly. Cut into fingers and serve with celery stalks.

 The whole point about snacks is that they must be **quick** and **easy** to make. When you get an attack of the munchies, the last thing you want to do is wait, so these recipes are really **rapid**. Protein-packed omelets are ideal, but can be a little dull. Try our **exciting** variations: Tomato Omelet Envelopes, Spanish Omelet or Soufflé Omelet. Nobody said you couldn't cheat a little, so make the **most** of tacos, tortillas and baked goods such as croissants. With a lot of imagination and a little time, they can be transformed into astonishingly **tasty** treats.

SPEEDY SNACKS

Tomato Omelet Envelopes

Delicious chive omelet, folded and filled with a tasty tomato mixture and lots of melting Camembert cheese.

Serves 2

INGREDIENTS
1 small onion
4 tomatoes
2 tbsp vegetable oil
4 eggs
2 tbsp chopped fresh chives
4 oz Camembert cheese, rind removed and diced
salt and freshly ground black pepper

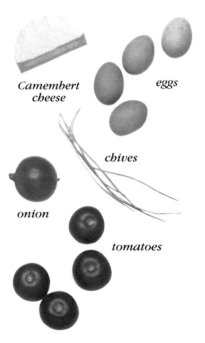

Camembert cheese

eggs

chives

onion

tomatoes

1 Cut the onion in half. Cut each half into thin wedges. Cut the tomatoes into wedges of similar size.

2 Heat 1 tbsp of the oil in a frying pan. Cook the onion for 2 minutes over a moderate heat. Then raise the heat, and add the tomato wedges. Cook for 2 minutes more. Then remove the pan from the heat.

3 Beat the eggs with the chives in a bowl. Add salt and pepper to taste. Heat the remaining oil in an omelet pan. Add half the egg mixture, and tilt the pan to spread thinly. Cook for 1 minute.

4 Flip the omelet over, and cook for 1 minute more. Remove from the pan, and keep hot. Make a second omelet with the remaining egg mixture.

5 Return the tomato mixture to a high heat. Add the cheese, and toss the mixture over the heat for 1 minute.

6 Divide the mixture between the omelets, and fold them over. Serve at once. Add crisp lettuce leaves and chunks of whole wheat bread, if desired.

COOK'S TIP
You may need to wipe the pan clean between the omelets, and reheat a little more oil.

Spanish Omelet

Spanish omelet belongs in every cook's repertoire and can vary according to what you have in store. This version includes white beans and is finished with a layer of toasted sesame seeds.

VARIATION
You can also use sliced cooked potatoes, any seasonal vegetables, baby artichoke hearts and chick-peas in a Spanish omelet.

Serves 4

INGREDIENTS
2 tbsp olive oil
1 tsp sesame oil
1 Spanish onion, chopped
1 small red bell pepper, deseeded and diced
2 celery stalks, chopped
1 × 14 oz can soft white beans, drained
8 eggs
3 tbsp sesame seeds
salt and freshly ground black pepper
4 oz green salad, to serve

celery

red bell pepper

white beans

sesame oil

sesame seeds

eggs

1 Heat the olive and sesame oils in a 12 in paella or frying pan. Add the onion, pepper and celery and cook to soften without coloring.

2 Add the beans and continue to cook for several minutes to heat through.

3 In a small bowl beat the eggs with a fork, season well and pour over the ingredients in the pan.

4 Stir the egg mixture with a flat wooden spoon until it begins to stiffen, then allow to firm over a low heat for about 6–8 minutes.

5 Preheat a moderate broiler. Sprinkle the omelette with sesame seeds and brown evenly under the broiler.

6 Cut the omelet into thick wedges and serve warm with a green salad.

Soufflé Omelet

This delectable soufflé omelet is light and delicate enough to melt in your mouth.

Serves 1

INGREDIENTS
2 eggs, separated
2 tbsp cold water
1 tbsp chopped fresh cilantro
salt and freshly ground black pepper
½ tbsp olive oil
2 tbsp mango chutney
¼ cup Jarlsberg or Swiss cheese, grated

Jarlsberg

mango chutney

eggs

cilantro

COOK'S TIP

A light hand is essential to the success of this dish. Do not overmix the egg whites into the yolks or the mixture will be heavy.

1 Beat the egg yolks together with the cold water, cilantro and seasoning.

2 Whisk the egg whites until stiff but not dry and gently fold into the egg yolk mixture.

3 Heat the oil in a frying pan, pour in the egg mixture and reduce the heat. Do not stir. Cook until the omelet becomes puffy and golden brown on the underside (carefully lift one edge with a spatula to check).

4 Spoon on the chutney and sprinkle on the Jarlsberg. Fold over and slide onto a warm plate. Eat immediately. (If preferred, before adding the chutney and cheese, place the pan under a hot broiler to set the top.)

Omelette aux Fines Herbes

Eggs respond well to fast cooking and combine beautifully with a handful of fresh herbs. Serve with French fries and a green salad.

Serves 1

INGREDIENTS
3 eggs
2 tbsp chopped fresh parsley
2 tbsp chopped fresh chervil
2 tbsp chopped fresh tarragon
1 tbsp chopped fresh chives
1 tbsp butter
salt and freshly ground black pepper
12 oz frozen French fries,
    to serve
4 oz green salad, to serve
1 tomato, to serve

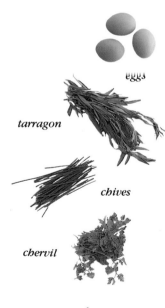

eggs

tarragon

chives

chervil

butter

parsley

1 Break the eggs into a bowl, season to taste and beat with a fork, then add the chopped herbs.

2 Heat an omelet or frying pan over a high heat, add the butter and cook until it foams and browns. Quickly pour in the beaten egg and stir briskly with the back of the fork. When the egg is two-thirds scrambled, let the omelet finish cooking for 10–15 seconds more.

3 Tap the handle of the omelet or frying pan sharply with your fist to make the omelet jump up the sides of the pan, fold and turn onto a plate. Serve with French fries, green salad and a halved tomato.

COOK'S TIP

From start to finish, an omelet should be cooked and on the table in less than a minute. For best results use free-range eggs at room temperature.

Filled Croissants

Croissants are very versatile and can be used with sweet or savory fillings.

Makes 2

INGREDIENTS
2 croissants
knob of butter
2 eggs
salt and pepper
1 tablespoon heavy cream
2 oz smoked salmon, chopped
1 sprig fresh dill, to garnish

croissants

smoked salmon

eggs

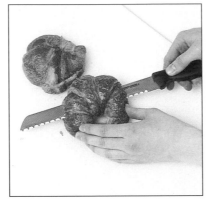

1 Preheat the oven to 350°F. Slice the croissants in half horizontally and warm in the oven for 5–6 minutes.

2 Melt a knob of butter in a small pan. Beat the eggs in a bowl with seasoning to taste.

3 Add the eggs to the pan and cook for 2 minutes, stirring constantly.

4 Remove from the heat and stir in the cream and smoked salmon.

5 Spoon the smoked salmon mixture into the warmed croissants and garnish.

PEAR AND STILTON FILLING

Soften 4 oz Stilton cheese with a fork and mix in 1 peeled, cored, and chopped ripe pear and 1 tbsp chopped chives with a little black pepper. Spoon into a split croissant and bake in a preheated oven for 5 minutes.

Croque Monsieur

Probably the most popular snack food in France, this hot cheese and ham sandwich can be either pan-fried or broiled.

Makes 2

INGREDIENTS
4 slices white bread
2 tbsp softened butter
2 thin slices lean ham
2 oz Swiss cheese, thinly sliced
1 sprig flat-leaf parsley, to garnish

white bread

Swiss cheese

ham

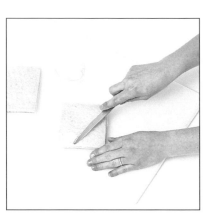

1 Spread the bread with butter.

2 Lay the ham on 2 of the buttered sides of bread.

3 Lay the Swiss cheese slices on top of the ham and sandwich with the buttered bread slices. Press firmly together and cut off the crusts.

4 Spread the top with butter, place on a rack, and cook for 2½ minutes under the broiler preheated to a low to moderate temperature.

5 Turn the sandwiches over, spread the remaining butter over the top, and return to the broiler for 2½ minutes more, until the bread is golden brown and the cheese is beginning to melt. Garnish with a sprig of flat-leaf parsley.

COOK'S TIP

A flavored butter can be used to complement a sandwich filling – for example, horseradish butter with beef, mustard butter with ham, lemon and dill butter with fish. To make these just beat the chosen flavoring into the softened butter with some seasoning. Other useful flavorings for butter are: anchovy or curry paste, garlic, herbs, Tabasco, or chili. These butters can also be used in open-face sandwiches.

Spiced Chicken Livers

Chicken livers can be bought frozen, but make sure that you defrost them thoroughly before using. Serve as a first course or light meal along with a mixed salad and garlic bread.

Serves 4

INGREDIENTS
12 oz chicken livers
1 cup all-purpose flour
½ tsp ground coriander
½ tsp ground cumin
½ tsp ground cardamom seeds
¼ tsp ground paprika
¼ tsp ground nutmeg
6 tbsp olive oil
salt and freshly ground black pepper
garlic bread, to serve

chicken livers

olive oil

flour

coriander

cardamom seeds

cumin

paprika

nutmeg

1 Dry the chicken livers on paper towels, removing any unwanted pieces. Cut the large livers in half and leave the smaller ones whole.

2 Mix the flour with all the spices and the seasoning.

3 Coat the first batch of livers with spiced flour, separating each piece. Heat the oil in a large frying pan and fry the livers in small batches. (This helps to keep the oil temperature high and prevents the flour from becoming soggy.)

4 Fry quickly, stirring frequently, until crispy. Keep warm and repeat with the remaining livers. Serve immediately with warm garlic bread.

Chili Beef Tacos

These easy-to-prepare sandwiches are now equally at home on both sides of the border. But don't limit yourself to the taco shell, soft flour tortillas are also authentically Mexican.

Makes 4

INGREDIENTS
1 tbsp oil
1 small onion, chopped
2 garlic cloves, chopped
6 oz ground beef
½ tbsp flour
7 oz can tomatoes
½ tbsp finely chopped Jalapeño
   peppers
salt
4 wheat or corn tortillas
3 tbsp sour cream
½ avocado, peeled, pitted and sliced
1 tomato, sliced
Tomato Salsa, to serve (optional)

*ground
beef*

avocado

tortillas

onion

garlic

Jalapeño peppers

1 Heat the oil in a skillet, add the onion, and fry until softened. Add the garlic and beef and cook, stirring so that the meat is broken up as it sears.

2 Stir in the flour, then add the canned tomatoes, peppers, and salt to taste.

3 Heat the tortillas one at a time in a medium-hot lightly oiled pan.

4 Spread a spoonful of the meat mixture over each tortilla.

5 Top each tortilla with some sour cream and avocado and tomato slices. Roll up and eat immediately with Tomato Salsa if liked.

Stilton Burger

Slightly more up-market than the traditional burger, this tasty recipe contains a delicious surprise. The lightly melted Stilton cheese encased in a crunchy burger is absolutely delicious.

Serves 4

INGREDIENTS
1 lb/4 cups ground beef
1 onion, finely chopped
1 celery stalk, chopped
1 tsp dried mixed herbs
1 tsp prepared mustard
½ cup crumbled Stilton cheese
4 burger buns
salt and freshly ground black pepper

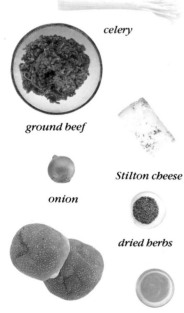

celery

ground beef

Stilton cheese

onion

dried herbs

hamburger buns

mustard

1 Place the ground beef in a bowl together with the onion and celery. Season well.

2 Stir in the herbs and mustard, bringing them together to form a firm mixture.

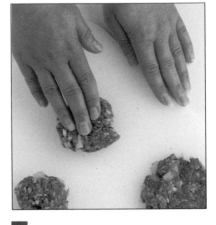

3 Divide the mixture into eight equal portions. Place four on a chopping board and flatten each one slightly.

4 Place the crumbled cheese in the center of each.

5 Flatten the remaining mixture and place on top. Mold the mixture together encasing the crumbled cheese and shape into four burgers.

6 Grill under a medium heat for 10 minutes, turning once or until cooked through. Split the hamburger buns and place a burger inside each. Serve with salad, ketchup, and mustard pickle.

Fritters

A variation on beef patties, coated in batter and lightly fried, this tasty alternative need only be served with a light salad to provide a substantial snack.

Serves 4

INGREDIENTS
FOR THE PATTIES
8 oz/2 cups ground beef
1 onion, grated
2 tsp chopped fresh oregano
½ cup canned corn, drained
1 tsp mustard
2 cups fresh white bread crumbs
oil for deep-frying
salt and freshly ground black pepper

FOR THE BATTER
1 cup flour
¼ cup warm water
3 tbsp melted butter
¼ cup cold water
1 egg white

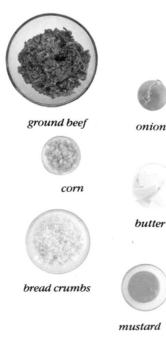

ground beef

onion

corn

butter

bread crumbs

oregano

mustard

1 For the patties, place the ground beef in a bowl and mash with a fork. Add the onion, oregano, corn, mustard and bread crumbs. Season well.

2 Form into eight round patties with lightly floured hands.

3 For the batter, sift the flour into a bowl and stir in the warm water and melted butter. Mix to a smooth batter with the cold water. Whisk the egg white until peaking and fold into the mixture.

4 Heat the oil for deep-frying to 325°F. Dip the patties into the batter to coat and fry two at a time in the oil. Drain on paper towels and serve with tomato pickle and green salad.

Nachos

The addition of beef to this Mexican appetizer makes a hearty meal. Guacamole on the side makes the dish even more delicious.

Serves 4

INGREDIENTS
8 oz/2 cups ground beef
2 red chilies, chopped
3 scallions, chopped
6 oz nachos
1¼ cups sour cream
½ cup freshly grated medium-sharp
  Cheddar cheese
salt and freshly ground black pepper

chili

cheese

ground beef

nachos

cream

scallions

1 Dry-fry the ground beef and chilies in a large pan for 10 minutes, stirring all the time.

2 Add the scallions, season and cook for a further 5 minutes.

3 Arrange the nachos in four individual flameproof dishes.

4 Spoon on the ground beef mixture, top with sour cream and grated cheese. Broil under a medium heat for 5 minutes.

Sardines with Warm Herb Salsa

Plain grilling is the very best way to cook fresh sardines; served with this luscious herb salsa the only other essential item is fresh, crusty bread, to mop up the tasty juices.

Serves 4

12–16 fresh sardines
oil for brushing
juice of 1 lemon

FOR THE SALSA
1 tbsp butter
4 scallions, chopped
1 garlic clove, finely chopped
2 tbsp finely chopped fresh
    parsley
2 tbsp finely snipped fresh
    chives
2 tbsp finely chopped fresh
    basil
2 tbsp green olive paste
2 tsp balsamic vinegar
zest of 1 lemon
salt and freshly ground black
    pepper

sardines

butter

green olive paste

balsamic vinegar

lemon

scallions

parsley

basil

chives

1 To clean the sardines, use small scissors to slit them along the belly and pull out the innards. Wipe the fish with paper towels and then arrange on a grill rack.

2 Melt the butter and gently sauté the scallions and garlic for about 2 minutes, shaking the pan occasionally, until softened but not browned.

3 Add the lemon rind and remaining ingredients and keep warm on the edge of the barbecue. Do not allow to boil.

4 Brush the sardines lightly with oil and sprinkle with lemon juice, salt and pepper. Cook for about 2 minutes on each side, over a moderate heat. Serve with the warm salsa and crusty bread.

Deep fried Whitebait

A spicy coating on these fish gives this favorite dish a crunchy bite.

Serves 6

INGREDIENTS
1 cup flour
½ tsp curry powder
½ tsp ground ginger
½ tsp ground cayenne pepper
pinch of salt
2½ lb fresh or frozen whitebait, thawed
vegetable oil for deep-frying
lemon wedges, to garnish

cayenne pepper

ground ginger

curry powder

lemon

1 Mix together all the dry ingredients in a large bowl.

2 Coat the fish in the flour.

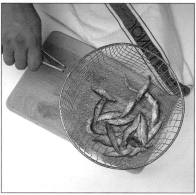
whitebait

3 Heat the oil in a large, heavy-based saucepan until it reaches a temperature of 375°F. Fry the whitebait in batches for 2–3 minutes until the fish is golden and crispy.

4 Drain well on absorbent paper towels. Serve hot garnished with lemon wedges.

English Muffins with Sole, Spinach and Mushrooms

English muffins, frozen spinach and a few mushrooms form the beginning of this nourishing fish course. Any flatfish will do, although sole works best of all.

Serves 2

INGREDIENTS

½ cup butter, plus extra for
    buttering muffins
1 medium onion, chopped
4 oz cremini mushrooms,
    sliced
2 fresh thyme sprigs, chopped
10 oz frozen leaf spinach, thawed
3 lb sole or flounder to yield
    1½ lb skinned fillet
2 white English muffins, split
4 tbsp crème fraîche or heavy cream
salt and freshly ground black pepper

1 Heat 4 tbsp of the butter in a saucepan and add the onion. Cook over a gentle heat until soft but not colored.

2 Add the mushrooms and thyme, cover and cook for a further 2–3 minutes. Remove the lid and increase the heat to drive off excess moisture.

English muffins

spinach

crème fraîche

thyme

sole

onion

3 Using the back of a large spoon, press the thawed frozen spinach in a sieve to extract the moisture.

4 Heat a further 2 tbsp butter in a saucepan, add the spinach, heat through and season to taste.

5 Melt the remaining butter in a large frying pan, season the fillets and, with skin side uppermost, cook for 4 minutes, turning once.

COOK'S TIP

Approximately half of the weight of flatfish is bone, so if buying your fish whole, ask the fishmonger to give you the correct weight of boned fish.

6 Toast and butter the muffins. Divide the fillets between them, top with spinach and a layer of mushrooms, then finish with a spoonful of crème fraîche or heavy cream.

Tostadas with Refried Beans

A tostada is a crisp, fried tortilla used as a base on which to pile the topping of your choice – a variation on a sandwich and a very tasty snack popular on both sides of the border.

Makes 6

INGREDIENTS
2 tbsp oil
1 onion, chopped
2 garlic cloves, chopped
½ tsp chili powder
15 oz can borlotti or pinto beans, drained
⅔ cup chicken stock
1 tbsp tomato paste
2 tbsp chopped fresh cilantro
salt and pepper
6 corn tortillas
3 tbsp Tomato Salsa
2 tbsp sour cream
½ cup grated Cheddar cheese
fresh cilantro leaves, to garnish

beans

onion

tortillas

garlic

chili powder

tomato paste

Cheddar cheese

cilantro

1 Heat the oil in a pan and fry the onion until softened.

2 Add the garlic and chili powder and fry for 1 minute, stirring.

3 Mix in the beans and mash very roughly with a potato masher.

4 Add the stock, tomato paste, chopped cilantro, and seasoning to taste. Mix thoroughly and cook for a few minutes.

5 Fry the tortillas in hot oil for 1 minute, turning once, until crisp, then drain on paper towels.

TOMATO SALSA

Makes about 1¼ cups

1 small onion, chopped
1 garlic clove, crushed
2 fresh green chilies, seeded and
  finely chopped, or 1 tsp bottled
  chopped chilies
1 lb tomatoes, skinned and chopped
salt
2 tbsp chopped fresh cilantro

Stir all the ingredients together until
well mixed.

6 Put a spoonful of refried beans on
each tostada, spoon over some Tomato
Salsa, then some sour cream, sprinkle
with grated Cheddar cheese, and garnish
with cilantro.

Cucumber and Alfalfa Tortillas

Wheat tortillas are extremely simple to prepare at home. Served with a crisp, fresh salsa, they make a marvelous light lunch or supper dish.

COOK'S TIP
When peeling the avocado be sure to scrape off the bright green flesh from immediately under the skin as this gives the sauce its vivid green color.

Serves 4

INGREDIENTS
2 cups flour, sifted
pinch of salt
3 tbsp olive oil
½-⅔ cup warm water
lime wedges, to garnish

FOR THE SALSA
1 red onion, finely chopped
1 fresh red chili, seeded and finely
  chopped
2 tbsp chopped fresh dill or cilantro
½ cucumber, peeled and chopped
6 oz alfalfa sprouts

FOR THE SAUCE
1 large ripe avocado, peeled and
  pitted
juice of 1 lime
2 tbsp soft goat cheese
pinch of paprika

avocado

goat cheese

red chilli

cucumber

dill

alfalfa sprouts

1 Mix all the salsa ingredients together in a bowl and set aside.

2 To make the sauce, place the avocado, lime juice and goat cheese in a food processor or blender and blend until smooth. Place in a bowl and cover with plastic wrap. Dust with paprika just before serving.

3 To make the tortillas, place the flour and salt in a food processor, add the oil and blend. Gradually add the water (the amount will vary depending on the type of flour). Stop adding water when a stiff dough has formed. Turn out onto a floured board and knead until smooth. Cover with a damp cloth.

4 Divide the mixture into 8 pieces. Knead each piece for a couple of minutes and form into a ball. Flatten and roll out each ball to a 9 in circle.

5 Heat an ungreased cast-iron pan. Cook 1 tortilla at a time for about 30 seconds on each side. Place the cooked tortillas in a clean dish-towel and repeat until you have 8 tortillas.

6 To serve, spread each tortilla with a spoonful of avocado sauce, top with salsa and roll up. Garnish with lime wedges.

Pasta with Spinach and Anchovy Sauce

Deliciously earthy, this would make a good entree or light supper dish. Add golden raisins for something really special.

Serves 4

INGREDIENTS

2 lb fresh spinach or 1¼ lb frozen leaf
    spinach, thawed
1 lb angel hair pasta
salt
4 tbsp olive oil
3 tbsp pine nuts
2 garlic cloves, crushed
6 canned anchovy fillets or whole
    salted anchovies, drained and
    chopped
butter, for tossing the pasta

olive oil

pine nuts

spinach

anchovy fillets

garlic   *angel hair pasta*

1 Wash the spinach well and remove the tough stalks. Drain thoroughly. Place in a large saucepan with only the water that still clings to the leaves. Cover with a lid and cook over a high heat, shaking the pan occasionally, until the spinach is just wilted and still bright green. Drain.

2 Cook the pasta in plenty of boiling salted water according to the manufacturer's instructions.

3 Heat the oil in a saucepan and fry the pine nuts until golden. Remove with a perforated spoon. Add the garlic to the oil in the pan and fry until golden. Add the anchovies.

4 Stir in the spinach, and cook for 2–3 minutes or until heated through. Stir in the pine nuts. Drain the pasta, toss in a little butter, and transfer to a warmed serving bowl. Top with the sauce and fork through roughly.

Cheese-stuffed Pears

These pears, with their scrumptious creamy topping, make a sublime dish when served with a simple salad.

Serves 4

INGREDIENTS
¼ cup ricotta cheese
¼ cup Saga blue cheese
1 tbsp honey
½ celery stalk, finely sliced
8 green olives, pitted and roughly chopped
4 dates, pitted and cut into thin strips
pinch of paprika
4 ripe pears
⅔ cup apple juice

honey

pear

apple juice

dates

Saga blue

celery

olives

COOK'S TIP

Choose ripe pears in season such as Bartlett or Comice.

1 Preheat the oven to 400°F. Place the ricotta in a bowl and crumble in the Saga blue cheese. Add the rest of the ingredients except for the pears and apple juice and mix well.

2 Halve the pears lengthwise and use a melon baller to remove the cores. Place in a ovenproof dish and divide the filling equally between them.

3 Pour in the apple juice and cover the dish with foil. Bake for 20 minutes or until the pears are tender.

4 Remove the foil and place the dish under a hot broiler for 3 minutes. Serve immediately.

Sweet Potato Roulade

Sweet potato works particularly well as the base for this roulade. Serve in thin slices for a truly impressive dinner party dish.

Serves 6

INGREDIENTS
1 cup low-fat ricotta cheese
5 tbsp low-fat yogurt
6–8 scallions, finely sliced
2 tbsp chopped brazil nuts, roasted
1 lb sweet potatoes, peeled and
    coarsely cubed
12 allspice berries, crushed
4 eggs, separated
¼ cup Edam or Gouda cheese, finely
    grated
salt and freshly ground black pepper
1 tbsp sesame seeds

yogurt

sesame seeds

sweet potato

ricotta cheese

Edam

brazil nuts

scallions

peppercorns

egg

1 Preheat the oven to 400°F. Grease and line a 13 × 10 in jelly roll pan with parchment paper, snipping the corners with scissors to fit neatly into the pan.

2 In a small bowl, mix together the ricotta, yogurt, scallions and brazil nuts. Set aside.

3 Boil or steam the sweet potato until tender. Drain well. Place in a food processor with the allspice and blend until smooth. Spoon into a bowl and stir in the egg yolks and Edam. Season to taste.

4 Whisk the egg whites until stiff but not dry. Fold ⅓ of the egg whites into the sweet potatoes to lighten the mixture before gently folding in the rest.

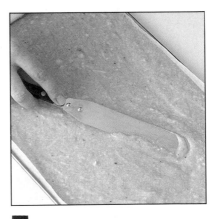

5 Pour into the prepared pan, tipping it to get the mixture right into the corners. Smooth gently with a spatula and cook in the oven for 10–15 minutes.

COOK'S TIP

Choose the orange-fleshed variety of sweet potato for the most striking color.

6 Meanwhile, lay a large sheet of waxed paper on a clean dish-towel and sprinkle with the sesame seeds. When the roulade is cooked, tip it onto the paper, trim the edges and roll it up. Leave to cool. When cool carefully unroll, spread with the filling and roll up again. Cut into slices to serve.

Buckwheat Couscous with Goat Cheese and Celery

Couscous is made from cracked, partially cooked wheat, which is dried and then reconstituted in water or stock. It tastes of very little by itself, but carries the flavor of other ingredients very well.

Serves 4

INGREDIENTS
1 egg
2 tbsp olive oil
1 small bunch scallions, chopped
2 celery stalks, sliced
1 cup couscous
½ cup buckwheat
3 tbsp chopped fresh parsley
finely grated zest of ½ lemon
¼ cup chopped walnuts, toasted
5 oz strongly flavored goat
    cheese
salt and freshly ground black pepper
Romaine lettuce leaves, to serve

1 Boil the egg for 10 minutes, cool, peel and set aside. Heat the oil in a saucepan and add the scallions and celery. Cook for 2–3 minutes until soft.

buckwheat

celery

egg

goat cheese

parsley

walnuts

2 Add the couscous and buckwheat and cover with 2½ cups of boiling salted water. Cover and return to a simmer. Remove from the heat and allow the couscous to soften and absorb the water for about 3 minutes. Transfer the mixture to a large bowl.

3 Grate the hard-boiled egg finely into a small bowl and add the chopped parsley, lemon zest and walnuts. Fold into the couscous, season, and crumble in the goat cheese. Mix well and then turn out into a shallow dish. Serve warm with a salad of Romaine lettuce.

VARIATION
Couscous is ideal as a filling for pita breads when accompanied with crisp salad leaves.

Stuffed Garlic Mushrooms with a Parsley Crust

These garlic mushrooms are perfect for dinner parties, or you could serve them in larger portions as a light supper dish with a green salad. Try them stuffed with a healthy dose of freshly chopped parsley.

Serves 4

INGREDIENTS
12 oz large field mushrooms, stems removed
3 garlic cloves, crushed
¾ cup butter, softened
3 cups finely crumbled fresh white breadcrumbs
1 cup fresh parsley, chopped
1 egg, beaten
salt and cayenne pepper
8 cherry tomatoes, to garnish

parsley

butter　　*egg*

garlic

mushrooms

breadcrumbs

1 Preheat the oven to 375°F. Arrange the mushrooms cup side uppermost on a baking tray. Mix together the crushed garlic and butter in a small bowl and divide ½ cup of the butter between the mushrooms.

2 Heat the remaining butter in a frying pan and lightly fry the breadcrumbs until golden brown. Place the chopped parsley in a bowl, add the breadcrumbs, season to taste and mix well.

3 Stir in the egg and use the mixture to fill the mushroom caps. Bake for 10–15 minutes until the topping has browned and the mushrooms have softened. Garnish with quartered tomatoes.

COOK'S TIP

If you are planning ahead, stuffed mushrooms can be prepared up to 12 hours in advance and kept in the fridge before baking.

MEAT

When the family's in a feeding **frenzy**, prove you can put a meal on the table in under half an hour with these **simple** and satisfying meat dishes. Stir-fries are the obvious solution—and you'll find some **wonderful** ways of using your wok to its full potential. Dishes like Sizzling Beef with

IN MINUTES

Celeriac Straw, Glazed Lamb, and Stir-fried Duck with Blueberries are **tasty** and **colorful** as well as being quick, while the broiler offers equally **delicious** options such as Mexican Beef Burgers, Pork and Pineapple Satay, and Chicken Liver Kebabs.

Sizzling Beef with Celeriac Straw

The crisp celeriac matchsticks look like fine pieces of straw when cooked and have a mild celery-like flavor that is quite delicious.

Serves 4

INGREDIENTS
1 lb celeriac
⅔ cup vegetable oil
1 red pepper
6 scallions
1 lb rump steak
4 tbsp beef stock
2 tbsp sherry vinegar
2 tsp Worcestershire sauce
2 tsp tomato paste
salt and freshly ground black pepper

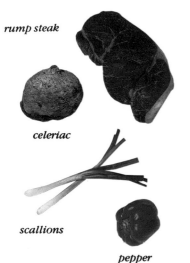

rump steak

celeriac

scallions

pepper

1 Peel the celeriac and then cut it into fine matchsticks, using a cleaver.

4 Chop the beef into strips, across the grain of the meat.

5 Heat the wok, and then add the remaining oil. When the oil is hot, stir-fry the chopped scallions and red pepper for 2–3 minutes.

2 Heat the wok, then add two-thirds of the oil. When the oil is hot, fry the celeriac matchsticks in batches until golden brown and crispy. Drain well on paper towels.

3 Chop the red pepper and the scallions into approximate 1 in lengths, using diagonal cuts.

6 Add the beef strips and stir-fry for a further 3–4 minutes until well browned. Add the stock, vinegar, Worcestershire sauce and tomato paste. Season well and serve with the celeriac straw.

Sukiyaki-style Beef

This Japanese dish is a meal in itself; the recipe incorporates all the traditional elements – meat, vegetables, noodles and bean curd. If you want to do it all properly, eat the meal with chopsticks, and a spoon to collect the stock juices.

Serves 4

INGREDIENTS
1 lb thick rump steak
7 oz Japanese rice noodles
1 tbsp peanut oil
7 oz firm bean curd, cut
    into cubes
8 shiitake mushrooms, trimmed
2 medium leeks, sliced into 1 in
    lengths
3½ oz baby spinach, well washed,
    to serve

FOR THE STOCK
1 tbsp superfine sugar
6 tbsp rice wine
3 tbsp dark soy sauce
½ cup water

rice noodles

leek

baby spinach

shiitake mushrooms

rump steak

1 Cut the beef into thin slices.

2 Blanch the noodles in boiling water for 2 minutes. Strain well.

3 Mix together all the stock ingredients in a bowl.

4 Heat the wok, then add the oil. When the oil is hot, stir-fry the beef for about 2–3 minutes, until it is cooked but still pink in color.

5 Pour the stock over the beef.

6 Add the remaining ingredients and cook for 4 minutes, until the leeks are tender. Serve a selection of the different ingredients, with a few baby spinach leaves, to each person.

Tex-Mex Burgers in Tortillas

If you yearn for a change from ordinary burgers, try this easy Tex-Mex version. Serve with a crisp green salad.

Serves 4

1¼ lb lean ground beef
1 small onion, finely chopped
1 small green bell pepper,
  seeded and finely chopped
1 garlic clove, crushed
oil for brushing
4 fresh tortillas
chopped fresh cilantro, to
  garnish

FOR THE GUACAMOLE SAUCE
2 ripe avocados
1 garlic clove, crushed
2 tomatoes, chopped
juice of 1 lime or lemon
½ small green chili, chopped
2 tbsp chopped fresh cilantro
salt and freshly ground black
  pepper

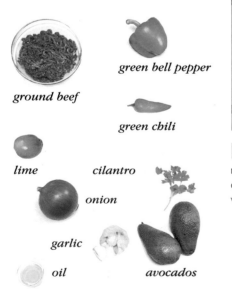

ground beef

green bell pepper

green chili

lime *cilantro*

onion

garlic

oil *avocados*

1 Mix together the ground beef, onion, pepper and garlic, and then season well with salt and pepper.

2 Using your hands, shape the mixture into four large, round burgers and brush them with oil.

3 For the guacamole sauce, cut the avocados in half, remove the pit and scoop out the flesh.

4 Mash the avocado flesh roughly and mix in the garlic, tomatoes, lime juice, chili and cilantro. Adjust the seasoning with salt and pepper.

5 Cook the burgers on a medium hot barbecue for 8–10 minutes, turning once, until golden brown.

6 When the burgers are almost cooked, heat the tortillas quickly on the barbecue for about 15 seconds each side and then place a spoonful of guacamole and a burger on each. Wrap the tortilla around the filling to serve, garnished with cilantro.

COOK'S TIP

The guacamole sauce should be made not more than about an hour before it's needed, or it will start to brown. If it has to be left to stand, sprinkle a little extra lime juice over the top and stir it in just before serving.

Mexican Beef Burgers

Nothing beats the flavor and quality of a home-made burger. This version is from Mexico and is seasoned with cumin and fresh cilantro.

Makes 4

INGREDIENTS
4 ears of corn
1 cup stale white bread crumbs
6 tbsp milk
1 small onion, finely chopped
1 tsp ground cumin
½ tsp cayenne pepper
½ tsp celery salt
3 tbsp chopped fresh cilantro
2 lb lean ground beef
4 sesame buns
4 tbsp mayonnaise
4 tomato slices
½ iceberg lettuce or other leaves
    such as frisée or Romaine
salt and freshly ground black pepper
1 large packet corn chips,
    to serve

iceberg lettuce

ground beef

onion

tomatoes

sesame buns

white bread

1 Bring a large saucepan of water to a boil, add a good pinch of salt and cook the corn for 15 minutes.

2 Combine the bread crumbs, milk, onion, cumin, cayenne, celery salt and fresh cilantro in a large bowl.

3 Add the beef and mix by hand until evenly blended.

4 Divide the beef mixture into four portions and flatten between sheets of plastic wrap.

5 Preheat a moderate broiler and cook for 10 minutes for medium burgers or 15 minutes for well-done burgers, turning once during the cooking time.

6 Split and toast the buns, spread with mayonnaise and sandwich the burgers with the tomato slices, lettuce leaves and seasoning. Serve with corn chips and the ears of corn.

COOK'S TIP
If planning ahead, freeze the burgers between sheets of wax paper or plastic wrap. Covered, they will keep well for up to twelve weeks. Defrost before cooking.

Black Pepper Beef Steaks with Red Wine Sauce

Every cook should know how to rustle up a pan-steak dinner with an impressive sauce to go with it. Black peppercorns follow the French tradition and combine well with the other bold flavors in the sauce.

Serves 4

INGREDIENTS

12 oz frozen fried potatoes or
    4 baking potatoes
1 tbsp black peppercorns
4 × 8 oz sirloin steaks
1 tbsp olive oil
chopped fresh parsley, to garnish
5 oz green salad, to serve

FOR THE RED WINE SAUCE

½ cup red wine
3 oz field mushrooms, sliced
¼ oz dried morel mushrooms, soaked
    (optional)
1¼ cups beef stock
1 tbsp cornstarch
1 tsp Dijon mustard
½ tsp anchovy paste (optional)
2 tsp red wine vinegar
2 tbsp butter
salt and freshly ground black pepper

1 Preheat the oven according to the instructions on the package for frozen fried potatoes and cook. Alternatively, if you require baked potatoes, cook in the microwave on high power (100%) for 8 minutes and then place in a preheated oven at 375°F for a further 10 minutes. Crush the peppercorns using a pestle and mortar, or coarsely grind in a pepper mill. Coat both sides of the steak with the crushed peppercorns and brush lightly with olive oil.

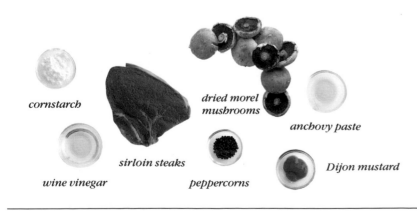

cornstarch

wine vinegar

sirloin steaks

peppercorns

dried morel mushrooms

anchovy paste

Dijon mustard

2 Heat a heavy bare metal frying pan. Fry the steaks for 6–8 minutes for medium-rare or 12–16 minutes for well-done steaks, turning once throughout the cooking time.

3 Transfer the steaks to a plate, cover and keep warm. Pour off the excess fat from the frying pan, return to the heat and brown the sediment. To make the sauce, add the wine and stir with a flat wooden spoon to loosen the sediment.

4 Add the mushrooms to the frying pan with the dried morels, if using. Pour in the stock and cook briefly to soften.

5 Measure the cornstarch, mustard and anchovy paste, if using, into a small bowl. Add 2 tbsp of water and blend together to a smooth paste. Add to the pan, stirring continuously, and simmer to thicken.

COOK'S TIP
Non-stick frying pans are not suitable for making pan sauces. Only bare metal pans allow a rich sediment to form, which is essential to the flavor of a good sauce.

6 Add the vinegar to taste. Toss in the butter and swirl the contents in the pan with a circular motion until the butter has melted. Season to taste, return the steaks and heat through. Arrange the steaks on four plates, pour over the sauce and sprinkle with parsley. Serve with fries or baked potatoes and a green salad.

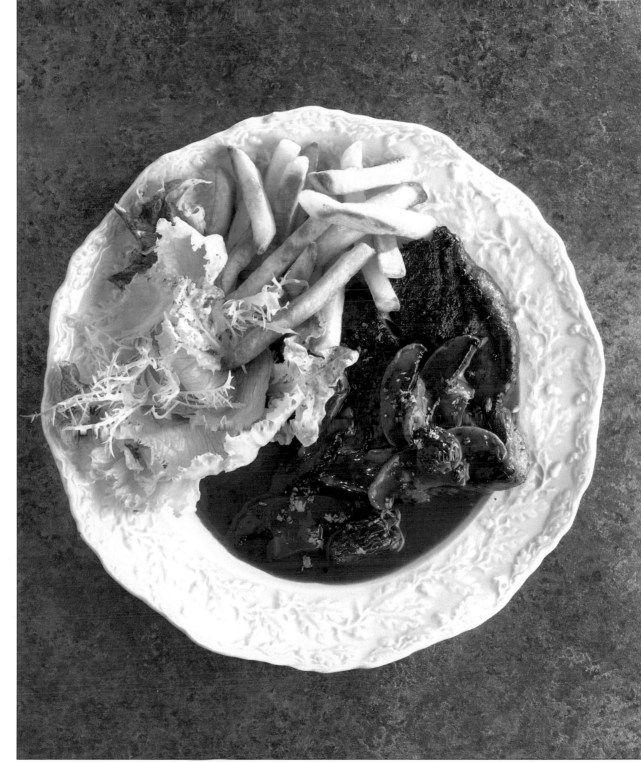

Spicy Beef

Promoting a fast-growing trend in worldwide cuisine, the wok is used in this recipe to produce a colorful and healthy meal.

Serves 4

INGREDIENTS
1 tbsp oil
1 lb/4 cups ground beef
1 in fresh ginger root, sliced
1 tsp Chinese five-spice powder
1 red chili, sliced
2 oz snow peas
1 red bell pepper, chopped
1 carrot, sliced
4 oz beansprouts
1 tbsp sesame oil

pepper

snow peas

sesame oil

five-spice

beansprouts

ground beef

ginger

carrot

chili

1 Heat the oil in a wok until almost smoking. Add the ground beef and cook for 3 minutes, stirring all the time.

2 Add the ginger, Chinese five-spice powder and chili. Cook for 1 minute.

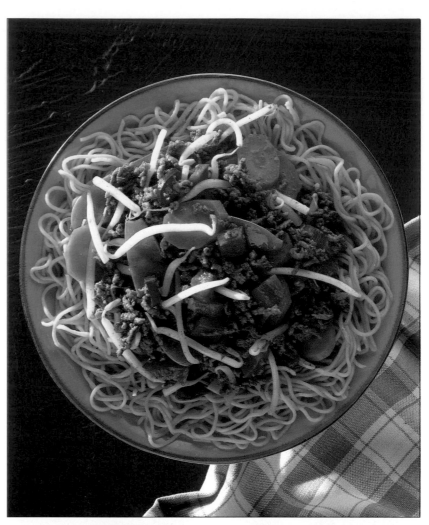

3 Add the snow peas, pepper and carrot and cook for a further 3 minutes, stirring continuously.

4 Add the beansprouts and sesame oil and cook for a final 2 minutes. Serve immediately with noodles.

Veal Escalopes with Artichokes

Artichokes are very hard to prepare fresh, so use canned artichoke hearts, instead — they have an excellent flavor and are simple to use.

Serves 4

INGREDIENTS
1 lb veal escalopes
1 shallot
4 oz lean smoked bacon, finely
  chopped
1 × 14 oz can of artichoke hearts in
  brine, drained and quartered
⅔ cup veal stock
3 fresh rosemary sprigs
4 tbsp heavy cream
salt and freshly ground black pepper
fresh rosemary sprigs, to garnish

veal escalopes

heavy cream

artichoke hearts

1 Cut the veal into thin slices.

2 Using a sharp knife, cut the shallot into thin slices.

3 Heat the wok, then add the bacon. Stir-fry for 2 minutes. When the fat is released, add the veal and shallot and stir-fry for 3–4 minutes.

4 Add the artichokes and stir-fry for 1 minute. Stir in the stock and rosemary and simmer for 2 minutes. Stir in the heavy cream, season with salt and pepper and serve immediately, garnished with sprigs of fresh rosemary.

Glazed Lamb

Lemon and honey make a classically good combination in sweet dishes, and this lamb recipe shows how well they work together in savory dishes, too. Serve with a fresh mixed salad to complete this delicious dish.

Serves 4

INGREDIENTS
1lb boneless lean lamb
1 tbsp grapeseed oil
6 oz snow peas, topped
   and tailed
3 scallions, sliced
2 tbsp honey
juice of half a lemon
2 tbsp fresh cilantro, chopped
1 tbsp sesame seeds
salt and freshly ground pepper

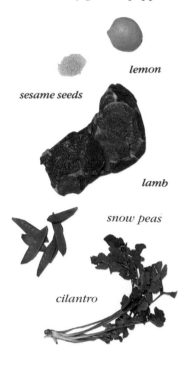

lemon

sesame seeds

lamb

snow peas

cilantro

1 Using a sharp knife, cut the lamb into thin strips.

2 Heat the wok, then add the oil. When the oil is hot, stir-fry the lamb until browned all over. Remove from the wok and keep warm.

3 Add the snow peas and sliced scallions to the hot wok and stir-fry for 30 seconds.

4 Return the lamb to the wok and add the honey, lemon juice, cilantro and sesame seeds, and season well. Bring to a boil and bubble for 1 minute until the lamb is well coated in the honey mixture.

Minted Lamb

Ask your butcher to remove the bone from a leg of lamb – it is sometimes called a butterflied leg of lamb – so that the meat can be sliced easily.

Serves 4

INGREDIENTS

1 lb boneless leg of lamb
2 tbsp fresh mint, chopped
½ lemon
1¼ cups natural low-fat yogurt
1 tbsp sunflower oil
salt and freshly ground black pepper
lemon wedges and fresh mint sprigs,
    to garnish

lemon

sunflower oil

mint

1 Using a sharp knife, cut the lamb into ¼-in thick slices. Place in a bowl.

2 Sprinkle half the mint over the lamb, season well with salt and pepper and leave for 20 minutes.

3 Roughly cut up the lemon and place in the food processor. Process until finely chopped. Empty it into a bowl, then stir in the yogurt and remaining mint.

4 Heat the wok, then add the oil. When the oil is hot, add the lamb and stir-fry for 4–5 minutes until cooked. Serve with the yogurt dressing, garnished with a lemon wedge and fresh mint sprigs.

Mixed Grill Skewers with Horseradish Butter

A hearty, classic selection of meats all cooked together on a skewer, drizzled with a delicious hot horseradish butter. Vary the meats as you like, but keep them all about the same thickness so they cook evenly.

Serves 4

4 small lamb noisettes, about
  1 in thick
4 lamb's kidneys
4 bacon strips
8 cherry tomatoes
8 chipolata sausages
12–16 bay leaves

FOR THE HORSERADISH BUTTER:
2 tbsp horseradish
3 tbsp melted butter
salt and freshly ground black
  pepper

bacon strips

chipolata sausages

lamb's kidneys

lamb noisettes

melted butter

horseradish

bay leaves

cherry tomatoes

COOK'S TIP
Try using your favorite mustard instead of horseradish, for a tangy mustard butter.

1 Trim any excess fat from the lamb noisettes. Halve the kidneys and remove the cores with scissors.

2 Cut each strip of bacon in half across the middle and wrap each piece around a tomato or a half-kidney.

3 Thread the lamb, kidneys, tomatoes, chipolatas and bay leaves onto four long metal skewers.

4 Stir together the horseradish and butter until thoroughly mixed.

5 Brush a little of the horseradish butter over the meat and sprinkle with salt and pepper.

6 Cook on a medium-hot barbecue for 12–15 minutes, turning occasionally, until golden brown and thoroughly cooked. Serve with the remaining horseradish butter poured over.

Pan-fried Pork with Peaches and Green Peppercorns

When peaches are in season, consider this speedy pork dish, brought alive with green peppercorns.

Serves 4

INGREDIENTS
2 cups long-grain rice
4 cups chicken stock
4 × 7 oz pork chops or
    loin pieces
2 tbsp vegetable oil
2 tbsp dark rum or sherry
1 small onion, chopped
3 large ripe peaches
1 tbsp green peppercorns
1 tbsp white wine vinegar
salt and freshly ground black pepper

onion

pork chops

dark rum

oil

green peppercorns

white wine vinegar

peaches

VARIATION

If peaches are not ripe when picked, they can be difficult to peel. Only tree ripened fruit is suitable for peeling. If fresh peaches are out of season, a can of sliced peaches may be used instead.

1 Cover the rice with 3¾ cups chicken stock. Stir, bring to a simmer and cook uncovered for 15 minutes. Switch off the heat and cover for 5 minutes. Meanwhile, season the pork with a twist of black pepper. Heat a large bare metal frying pan and moisten the pork with 1 tbsp oil. Cook the pork for 12 minutes, turning once.

2 Transfer the meat to a warm plate. Pour off the excess fat from the pan and return to the heat. Allow the sediment to sizzle and brown, add the rum or sherry and loosen the sediment with a flat wooden spoon. Pour the pan contents over the meat, cover and keep warm. Wipe the pan clean.

3 Heat the remaining vegetable oil in the pan and soften the onion over a steady heat.

4 Cover the peaches with boiling water to loosen the skins, then peel, slice and discard the pits.

5 Add the peaches and peppercorns to the onion and coat for 3–4 minutes, until they begin to soften.

6 Add the remaining chicken stock and simmer briefly. Return the pork and meat juices to the pan, sharpen with vinegar, and season to taste. Serve with the rice.

Stir-fried Pork with Mustard

Fry the apples for this dish very carefully, because they will disintegrate if they are overcooked.

Serves 4

INGREDIENTS
1¼ lb pork fillet
1 tart apple, such as Granny Smith
3 tbsp unsalted butter
1 tbsp superfine sugar
1 small onion, finely chopped
2 tbsp Calvados, Applejack or
    other brandy
1 tbsp Meaux or coarse-grain
    mustard
⅔ cup heavy cream
2 tbsp fresh parsley, chopped
salt and freshly ground black pepper
flat-leaf parsley sprigs, to garnish

pork fillet

onion

mustard

apple

1 Cut the pork fillet into thin slices.

2 Peel and core the apple. Cut it into thick slices.

3 Heat the wok, then add half the butter. When the butter is hot, add the apple slices, sprinkle over the sugar, and stir-fry for 2–3 minutes. Remove the apple and set aside. Wipe out the wok with paper towels.

4 Heat the wok, then add the remaining butter and stir-fry the pork fillet and onion together for 2–3 minutes, until the pork is golden and the onion has begun to soften.

5 Stir in the Calvados, Applejack or other brandy and boil until it is reduced by half. Stir in the mustard.

6 Add the cream and simmer for 1 minute, then stir in the parsley. Serve garnished with sprigs of flat-leaf parsley.

Pork and Pineapple Satay

This variation on the classic satay has added pineapple, but keeps the traditional coconut and peanut sauce.

If you cannot buy coconut milk, look for creamed coconut in a block. Dissolve a 2 oz-piece in $^2/_3$ cup boiling water and use as below.

Serves 4

1$^1/_4$ lb pork fillet
1 small onion, chopped
1 garlic clove, chopped
4 tbsp soy sauce
finely grated zest of $^1/_2$ lemon
1 tsp ground cumin
1 tsp ground coriander
1 tsp ground turmeric
1 tsp dark raw sugar
8 oz can pineapple chunks, or
    1 small fresh pineapple,
    peeled and diced
salt and freshly ground black
    pepper

FOR THE SATAY SAUCE
$^3/_4$ cup coconut milk
6 tbsp crunchy peanut butter
1 garlic clove, crushed
2 tsp soy sauce
1 tsp dark raw sugar
1 tsp chili powder

1 Trim any fat from the pork fillet and cut it into 1 in cubes. Place the meat in a large bowl.

2 Place the onion, garlic, soy sauce, lemon zest, spices and sugar in a blender or food processor. Add two pieces of pineapple and process until the mixture is almost smooth.

3 Add the paste to the pork, tossing well to coat evenly. Thread the pieces of pork onto bamboo skewers, with the remaining pineapple.

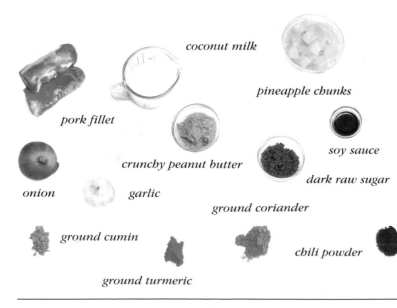

coconut milk

pineapple chunks

pork fillet

crunchy peanut butter

soy sauce

onion

garlic

dark raw sugar

ground coriander

ground cumin

chili powder

ground turmeric

4 For the sauce, pour the coconut milk into a small pan and stir in the peanut butter. Stir in the remaining sauce ingredients and heat gently over the barbecue, stirring until smooth and hot. Cover and keep warm on the edge of the barbecue.

5 Cook the pork and pineapple skewers on a medium-hot barbecue for 10–12 minutes, turning occasionally, until golden brown and thoroughly cooked. Serve with the satay sauce.

Sausage Popovers

This quick dish is always well received. The mashed potatoes and gravy make it a filling and tasty meal.

Serves 4

INGREDIENTS
2 lb baking potatoes
1 lb pork or beef sausages or
   chipolatas
1 × 14 oz can petit pois, to serve
   (optional)

FOR THE BATTER
3 eggs
1¼ cups whole milk
1 cup flour
salt and freshly ground black pepper

FOR THE ONION GRAVY
2 tbsp vegetable oil
1 medium onion, chopped
1 tbsp flour
scant 1 cup fresh or canned chicken
   or beef stock
1 tsp balsamic or red wine
   vinegar

onion

eggs   *flour*

sausages

1 Cut the potatoes into small pieces to reduce the cooking time. Bring them to a boil in salted water and cook for 15 minutes. Preheat the oven to 450°F and partly cook the sausages or chipolatas for 5 minutes.

2 To make the batter, beat the eggs together with a good pinch of salt and a twist of black pepper in a bowl.

3 Add half of the milk and all of the flour and stir into a smooth batter. Pour in the remaining milk and combine evenly.

4 Arrange the partly cooked sausages in a shallow muffin tin.

5 Pour in the batter, transfer to the preheated oven and bake for 10 minutes until well risen and golden.

COOK'S TIP

When making risen batter dishes, it is important to put the mixture into a fiercely hot oven.

6 To make the onion gravy, heat the vegetable oil in a large saucepan and brown the onion for 3–4 minutes, then add the flour. Remove from the heat, gradually stir in the stock and sharpen with vinegar to taste. Mash the potatoes and serve with the popovers, gravy and petit pois if desired.

Wild Mushroom Rösti with Bacon and Eggs

Dried ceps or porcini mushrooms, commonly found in Italian delicatessens, are a good substitute for fresh. Cook them in a potato rösti and serve with bacon and a fried egg for breakfast or a lazy supper.

COOK'S TIP

A large rösti can be made in a non-stick frying pan. Allow 12 minutes to cook. Half-way through the cooking time, invert the rösti on a large plate and slide back into the pan.

Serves 4

INGREDIENTS
1½ lb baking potatoes, peeled
¼ oz dried ceps or porcini
   mushrooms
2 fresh thyme sprigs, chopped
2 tbsp chopped fresh parsley
4 tbsp vegetable oil, for frying
4 × 4 oz unsmoked bacon
pinch of salt
4 eggs, to serve
1 bunch watercress or flat-leaf parsley,
   to serve

bacon

thyme

parsley

potatoes

dried ceps

watercress

eggs

1 Bring the potatoes to a boil in a pan of salted water and cook for 5 minutes.

2 Cover the mushrooms with boiling water to soften, then chop roughly.

3 Drain the potatoes, allow them to cool and grate them coarsely. Add the mushrooms, thyme and parsley and combine together well.

4 Heat 2 tbsp of the oil in a frying pan, spoon in the rösti mixture in heaps and flatten. Fry for 6 minutes, turning once during cooking.

5 Preheat a moderate broiler and cook the bacon slices until sizzling.

6 Heat the remaining oil in a frying pan and fry the eggs as you like them. Serve the rösti together with the eggs and bacon and a watercress salad.

Indonesian Pork and Peanut Saté

These delicious skewers of pork are popular street food in Indonesia. They are quick to make and eat.

Serves 4

INGREDIENTS
2 cups long-grain rice
1 lb lean pork
pinch of salt
2 limes, quartered, to garnish
4 oz green salad, to serve

FOR THE BASTE AND DIP
1 tbsp vegetable oil
1 small onion, chopped
1 garlic clove, crushed
½ tsp hot chili sauce
1 tbsp sugar
2 tbsp soy sauce
2 tbsp lemon or lime juice
½ tsp anchovy paste (optional)
4 tbsp smooth peanut butter

lemon

lime

rice

peanut butter

pork

garlic

chili sauce

1 In a large saucepan, cover the rice with 3¾ cups of boiling salted water, stir and simmer uncovered for 15 minutes until the liquid has been absorbed. Switch off the heat, cover and stand for 5 minutes. Slice the pork into thin strips, then thread zig-zag fashion onto 16 bamboo skewers.

2 Heat the vegetable oil in a pan. Add the onion and cook over a gentle heat to soften without coloring for about 3–4 minutes. Add the next 5 ingredients and the anchovy paste, if using. Simmer briefly, then stir in the peanut butter.

3 Preheat a moderate broiler, spoon a third of the sauce over the pork and cook for 6–8 minutes, turning once. Spread the rice out onto a serving dish, place the pork saté on top and serve with the dipping sauce. Garnish with quartered limes and serve with a green salad.

VARIATION
Indonesian saté can be prepared with lean beef, chicken or shrimp.

Jambalaya

The perfect way to use up left-over cold meat –
Jambalaya is a fast, fortifying meal for a hungry family.

Serves 4

INGREDIENTS
3 tbsp vegetable oil
1 medium onion, chopped
1 celery stalk, chopped
½ red bell pepper, chopped
2 cups long-grain rice
4 cups fresh or canned chicken stock
1 tbsp tomato paste
3–4 shakes of Tabasco sauce
8 oz cold roast chicken or pork,
   thickly sliced
4 oz cooked sausage, such as chorizo
   or kabanos, sliced
¾ cup frozen peas

1 Heat the oil in a heavy saucepan and add the onion, celery and pepper. Cook to soften without coloring.

roast chicken

peas

tomato paste

onion

celery

sausages

red bell pepper

rice

2 Add the rice, chicken stock, tomato paste and Tabasco sauce. Simmer uncovered for 10 minutes.

3 Stir in the cold meat, sausage and peas and simmer for a further 5 minutes. Switch off the heat, cover and leave to stand for 5 minutes more before serving.

VARIATION

You could also add cooked ham, smoked cod or haddock and fresh shellfish to a Jambalaya.

Chinese Duck in Pita

This recipe is based on Chinese crispy duck but uses duck breast instead of whole duck. After 15 minutes cooking, the duck breast will still have a pinkish tinge. If you like it well-done, leave it in the oven for about 5 minutes more.

Makes 2

INGREDIENTS
1 duck breast, weighing about 6 oz
3 scallions
3 in piece hothouse cucumber
2 round pita breads
2 tbsp hoi-sin sauce
radish chrysanthemum and scallion tassel, to garnish

pita breads

cucumber

duck breast

hoi-sin sauce

scallions

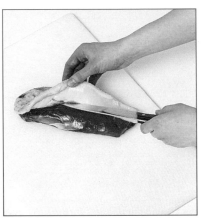

1 Preheat the oven to 425°F. Skin the duck breast, place the skin and breast separately on a rack, and cook in the oven for 10 minutes.

2 Remove the skin from the oven, cut into pieces, and return to the oven for 5 minutes more.

3 Meanwhile, cut the scallions and cucumber into fine shreds about 1 ½ in long.

4 Heat the pita bread in the oven for a few minutes until puffed up, then split in half to make a pocket.

5 Slice the duck breast thinly.

6 Stuff the duck breast into the pita bread with a little scallion, cucumber, crispy duck skin, and some hoi-sin sauce. Serve garnished with a radish chrysanthemum and scallion tassel.

Apricot Duck Breasts with Bean Sprout Salad

Duck is rich in fat, so it stays beautifully moist when cooked on a barbecue but any excess fat drains away.

Serves 4

4 plump duck breasts, with skin
1 small red onion, thinly sliced
³/₄ cup ready-to-eat dried
    apricots
1 tbsp honey
1 tsp sesame oil
2 tsp ground star anise
salt and freshly ground black
    pepper

FOR THE SALAD
¹/₂ head bok choy, finely
    shredded
2 cups bean sprouts
2 scallions, shredded
1 tbsp light soy sauce
1 tbsp peanut oil
1 tsp sesame oil
1 tsp clear honey

I Place the duck breasts, skin-side down, on a board and cut a long slit down one side, cutting not quite through, to form a large pocket.

2 Tuck the slices of onion and the apricots inside the pocket and press the breast firmly back into shape. Secure with metal skewers.

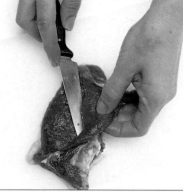

ready-to-eat dried apricots

scallions

duck breasts

red onion

sesame oil   *bok choy*

ground star anise   *bean sprouts*

honey

light soy sauce

3 Mix together the honey and sesame oil and brush over the duck, particularly the skin. Sprinkle over the star anise and season with salt and pepper.

4 To make the salad, mix together the shredded bok choy bean sprouts and scallions.

COOK'S TIP

If you prefer not to eat the bean sprouts raw, they can be blanched first, by plunging them into boiling water for 1 minute. Drain and rinse in cold water.

5 Shake together all the remaining salad ingredients in a screw-topped jar. Season to taste with salt and pepper. Toss into the salad.

6 Cook the duck over a medium-hot barbecue for 12–15 minutes, turning once, until golden brown. The duck should be slightly pink in the center.

Stir-fried Duck with Blueberries

Serve this conveniently quick dinner party dish with sprigs of fresh mint, which will give a wonderful fresh aroma as you bring the meal to the table.

Serves 4

INGREDIENTS
2 duck breasts, about 6 oz each
2 tbsp sunflower oil
1 tbsp red wine vinegar
1 tsp sugar
1 tsp red wine
1 tsp *crème de cassis* (black currant liqueur)
4 oz fresh blueberries
1 tbsp fresh mint, chopped
salt and freshly ground black pepper
fresh mint sprigs, to garnish
mixed green vegetables, steamed, to serve

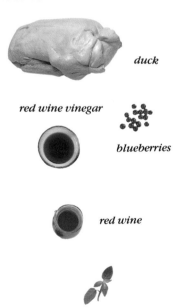

duck

red wine vinegar

blueberries

red wine

mint

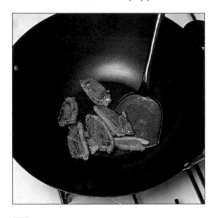

1 Cut the duck breasts into neat slices. Season well with salt and pepper.

2 Heat the wok, then add the oil. When the oil is hot, stir-fry the duck for 3 minutes.

3 Add the red wine vinegar, sugar, red wine and *crème de cassis*. Bubble for 3 minutes, to reduce to a thick syrup.

4 Stir in the blueberries, sprinkle over the mint and serve garnished with sprigs of fresh mint.

Stir-fried Sweet and Sour Chicken

There are few cooking concepts that are better suited to today's busy lifestyle than the all-in-one stir-fry. This one has a South-east Asian influence.

Serves 4

INGREDIENTS
10 oz Chinese egg noodles
2 tbsp vegetable oil
3 scallions, chopped
1 garlic clove, crushed
1 in fresh ginger root, peeled and grated
1 tsp hot paprika
1 tsp ground coriander
3 boneless chicken breasts, sliced
1 cup sugar-snap peas, topped and tailed
4 oz baby corn, halved
8 oz fresh bean sprouts
1 tbsp cornstarch
3 tbsp soy sauce
3 tbsp lemon juice
1 tbsp sugar
3 tbsp chopped fresh cilantro or scallion tops, to garnish

COOK'S TIP

Large wok lids are cumbersome and can be difficult to store in a small kitchen. Consider placing a circle of waxed paper against the food surface to keep cooking juices in.

chicken breasts
garlic
scallions
paprika
soy sauce
egg noodles
sugar-snap peas
ginger

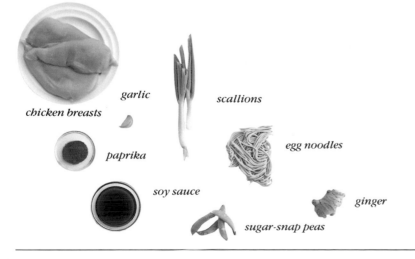

1 Bring a large saucepan of salted water to a boil. Add the noodles and cook according to the package instructions. Drain, cover and keep warm.

2 Heat the oil. Add the scallions and cook over a gentle heat. Mix in the next five ingredients, then stir-fry for 3–4 minutes. Add the next three ingredients and steam briefly. Add the noodles.

3 Combine the cornstarch, soy sauce, lemon juice and sugar in a small bowl. Add to the wok and simmer briefly to thicken. Serve garnished with chopped cilantro or scallion tops.

Chicken Liver Stir-fry

The final sprinkling of lemon, parsley and garlic granita gives this dish a delightful fresh flavor and wonderful aroma.

Serves 4

INGREDIENTS
1¼ lb chicken livers
6 tbsp butter
6 oz field mushrooms
2 oz chanterelle mushrooms
3 cloves garlic, finely chopped
2 shallots, finely chopped
⅔ cup medium sherry
3 fresh rosemary sprigs
2 tbsp fresh parsley, chopped
rind of 1 lemon, grated
salt and freshly ground pepper
fresh rosemary sprigs, to garnish
4 thick slices of white toast, to serve

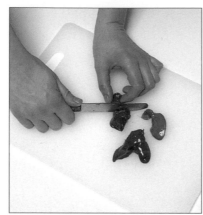

1 Clean and trim the chicken livers to remove any gristle or muscle.

2 Season the livers generously with salt and freshly ground black pepper, tossing well to coat thoroughly.

chanterelle mushrooms

field mushroom

lemon

rosemary

3 Heat the wok and add 1 tbsp of the butter. When melted, add the livers in batches (melting more butter where necessary but reserving 2 tbsp for the vegetables) and flash-fry until golden brown. Drain with a slotted spoon and transfer to a plate, then place in a low oven to keep warm.

4 Cut the field mushrooms into thick slices and, depending on the size of the chanterelles, cut in half.

5 Heat the wok and add the remaining butter. When melted, stir in two-thirds of the chopped garlic and the shallots and stir-fry for 1 minute until golden brown. Stir in the mushrooms and continue to cook for a further 2 minutes.

6 Add the sherry, bring to a boil and simmer for 2–3 minutes until syrupy. Add the rosemary, salt and pepper and return livers to the pan. Stir-fry for 1 minute. Garnish with extra sprigs of rosemary, and serve sprinkled with a mixture of lemon, parsley and the remaining chopped garlic, with slices of toast.

Indonesian-style Satay Chicken

Use boneless chicken thighs to give a good flavor to these satays.

Serves 4

INGREDIENTS
½ cup raw peanuts
3 tbsp vegetable oil
1 small onion, finely chopped
1 in piece ginger root, peeled and
    finely chopped
1 clove garlic, crushed
1½ lb chicken thighs, skinned and cut
    into cubes
3½ oz creamed coconut, chopped
1 tbsp chili sauce
4 tbsp chunky peanut butter
1 tsp soft dark brown sugar
⅔ cup milk
¼ tsp salt

creamed coconut

peanuts

chili sauce

peanut butter

COOK'S TIP
Soak bamboo skewers in cold water for at least 2 hours, or preferably overnight, so they do not char when keeping the threaded chicken warm in the oven.

1 Shell and rub the skins from the peanuts, then soak them in enough water to cover, for 1 minute. Drain the nuts and cut them into slivers.

2 Heat the wok and add 1 tsp oil. When the oil is hot, stir-fry the peanuts for 1 minute until crisp and golden. Remove with a slotted spoon and drain on paper towels.

3 Add the remaining oil to the hot wok. When the oil is hot, add the onion, ginger and garlic and stir-fry for 2–3 minutes until softened but not browned. Remove with a slotted spoon and drain on paper towels.

4 Add the chicken pieces and stir-fry for 3–4 minutes until crisp and golden on all sides. Thread on to pre-soaked bamboo skewers and keep warm.

5 Add the creamed coconut to the hot wok in small pieces and stir-fry until melted. Add the chili sauce, peanut butter and cooked ginger and garlic, and simmer for 2 minutes. Stir in the sugar, milk and salt, and simmer for a further 3 minutes. Serve the skewered chicken hot, with a dish of the hot dipping sauce sprinkled with the roasted peanuts.

Glazed Chicken with Cashew Nuts

Hoisin sauce lends a sweet yet slightly hot note to this chicken dish, while cashew nuts add a pleasing contrast of texture.

VARIATION
Use blanched almonds instead of cashew nuts if you prefer.

Serves 4

INGREDIENTS
¾ cup cashew nuts
1 red bell pepper
1 lb skinless and boneless
   chicken breasts
3 tbsp peanut oil
4 garlic cloves, finely chopped
2 tbsp Chinese rice wine or
   medium-dry sherry
3 tbsp hoisin sauce
2 tsp sesame oil
5–6 scallions,
   green parts only,
   cut into 1-in lengths

scallions

chicken

red pepper

cashew nuts

Chinese rice wine

garlic

peanut oil

hoisin sauce

sesame oil

1 Heat a wok until hot, add the cashew nuts and stir-fry over low to medium heat for 1–2 minutes, until golden brown. Remove and set aside.

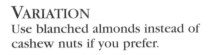

2 Halve the pepper and remove the seeds. Slice the pepper and chicken into finger-length strips.

3 Heat the wok again until hot, add the oil and swirl it around. Add the garlic and let it sizzle in the oil for a few seconds. Add the pepper and chicken and stir-fry for 2 minutes.

4 Add the rice wine or sherry and hoisin sauce. Continue to stir-fry until the chicken is tender and all the ingredients are evenly glazed.

5 Stir in the sesame oil, toasted cashew nuts and scallion tips. Serve immediately with rice or noodles.

Chicken Liver Kebabs

These may be barbecued outdoors and served with salad and baked potatoes, or broiled indoors and served with rice and broccoli.

Serves 4

INGREDIENTS
4 oz (roughly 6) lean bacon rashers
12 oz trimmed chicken livers
12 large, ready-to-eat pitted prunes
12 cherry tomatoes
8 button mushrooms
2 tbsp olive oil

prunes

olive oil

tomatoes

mushrooms

bacon

chicken livers

1 Cut each rasher of bacon into two pieces, wrap a piece around each chicken liver and secure in position with wooden toothpicks.

2 Wrap the pitted prunes around the cherry tomatoes.

3 Thread the bacon-wrapped livers onto metal skewers with the tomatoes and prunes. Brush with oil. Cover the tomatoes and prunes with foil to protect them while broiling or barbecuing. Cook for 5 minutes on each side.

4 Remove the toothpicks and serve the kebabs immediately.

Chicken Teriyaki

A bowl of boiled rice is the ideal accompaniment to this Japanese-style chicken dish.

Serves 4

INGREDIENTS
1 lb boneless, skinless chicken breasts

FOR THE MARINADE
1 tsp sugar
1 tbsp sake or rice wine
1 tbsp rice wine or dry sherry
2 tbsp dark soy sauce
rind of 1 orange, grated
orange segments and cress,
   to garnish

orange

rice wine

soy sauce

chicken breast

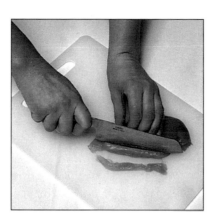

1 Finely slice the chicken.

2 Mix all the marinade ingredients together in a bowl.

3 Place the chicken in a bowl, pour over the marinade and leave to marinate for 15 minutes.

4 Heat the wok, add the chicken and marinade and stir-fry for 4–5 minutes. Serve garnished with orange segments and cress.

COOK'S TIP

Make sure the marinade is brought to a boil and cooked for 4–5 minutes, because it has been in contact with raw chicken.

Grilled Chicken with Pica de Gallo Salsa

This dish originates from Mexico. Its hot fruity flavors form the essence of Tex-Mex Cooking.

Serves 4

INGREDIENTS
4 chicken breasts
pinch of celery salt and cayenne
   pepper combined
2 tbsp vegetable oil
corn chips, to serve

FOR THE SALSA
10 oz watermelon
6 oz canteloupe melon
1 small red onion
1–2 green chilies
2 tbsp lime juice
4 tbsp chopped fresh cilantro
pinch of salt

COOK'S TIP
To capture the spirit of Tex-Mex food, cook the chicken over a barbecue and eat shaded from the hot summer sun.

green chilies

chicken breasts

red onion

lime

cilantro

canteloupe melon

watermelon

1 Preheat a moderate broiler. Slash the chicken breasts deeply to speed up the cooking time.

2 Season the chicken with celery salt and cayenne, brush with oil and broil for about 15 minutes.

3 To make the salsa, remove the rind and as many seeds as you can from the melons. Finely dice the flesh and put it into a bowl.

4 Finely chop the onion, split the chilies (discarding the seeds which contain most of the heat) and chop. Take care not to touch sensitive skin areas when handling cut chilies. Mix with the melon.

5 Add the lime juice and chopped cilantro, and season with a pinch of salt. Turn the salsa into a small bowl.

6 Arrange the grilled chicken on a plate and serve with the salsa and a handful of corn chips.

Thai Fried Rice

This hot and spicy dish is easy to prepare and makes a meal in itself.

Serves 4

INGREDIENTS
8 oz Thai jasmine rice
3 tbsp vegetable oil
1 onion, chopped
1 small red bell pepper, seeded
  and cut into ¾-in cubes
12 oz skinless and boneless
  chicken breasts, cut into
  ¾-in cubes
1 garlic clove, crushed
1 tbsp mild curry paste
½ tsp paprika
½ tsp ground turmeric
2 tbsp Thai fish sauce
  (*nam pla*)
2 eggs, beaten
salt and ground black pepper
fried basil leaves, to garnish

rice

Thai fish sauce

chicken

curry paste

onion

egg

red pepper

paprika

turmeric

vegetable oil

VARIATION
Add 2 oz frozen peas to the chicken in step 3, if you wish.

1 Put the rice in a sieve and wash thoroughly under cold running water. Then put the rice in a heavy-bottomed pan and add 6¼ cups boiling water. Return to a boil, then simmer, leaving the pan uncovered, for 8–10 minutes; drain well. Spread out the grains on a tray and set aside to cool.

2 Heat a wok until hot, add 2 tbsp of the oil and swirl it around. Add the onion and red pepper and stir-fry for 1 minute.

3 Add the chicken, garlic, curry paste and spices and stir-fry for 2–3 minutes.

4 Reduce the heat to medium, add the cooled rice, fish sauce and seasoning. Stir-fry for 2–3 minutes, until the rice is very hot.

5 Make a well in the center of the rice and add the remaining oil. When hot, add the beaten eggs, allow to cook for about 2 minutes until lightly set, then stir into the rice.

6 Sprinkle over the fried basil leaves and serve at once.

Stir-fried Turkey with Broccoli and Mushrooms

This is a really easy, tasty supper dish which works well with chicken too.

Serves 4

INGREDIENTS
4 oz broccoli florets
4 scallions
1 tsp cornstarch
3 tbsp oyster sauce
1 tbsp dark soy sauce
½ cup chicken stock,
    or bouillon cube
    and water
2 tsp lemon juice
3 tbsp peanut oil
1 lb turkey fillets, cut into
    strips, about ¼ x 2 in
1 small onion, chopped
2 garlic cloves, crushed
2 tsp fresh ginger,
    finely grated
4 oz fresh shiitake
    mushrooms, sliced
3 oz canned baby corn,
    halved lengthwise
1 tbsp sesame oil
salt and ground black pepper
egg noodles, to serve

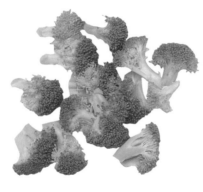

onion

broccoli

scallion

oyster sauce   *turkey*   *mushrooms*

lemon

dark soy sauce

peanut oil

baby corn

garlic

chicken stock

1 Divide the broccoli florets into smaller sprigs and cut the stalks into thin diagonal slices.

2 Finely chop the white parts of the scallions and slice the green parts into thin shreds.

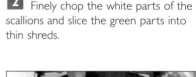

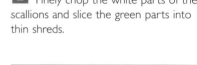

3 In a bowl, blend together the cornstarch, oyster sauce, soy sauce, stock and lemon juice. Set aside.

4 Heat a wok until hot, add 2 tbsp of the peanut oil and swirl it around. Add the turkey and stir-fry for about 2 minutes, until golden and crispy at the edges. Remove the turkey from the wok and keep warm.

5 Add the remaining peanut oil to the wok and stir-fry the chopped onion, garlic and ginger over medium heat for about 1 minute. Increase the heat to high, add the broccoli, mushrooms and corn and stir-fry for 2 minutes.

6 Return the turkey to the wok, then add the sauce with the chopped scallion and seasoning. Cook, stirring, for about 1 minute, until the sauce has thickened. Then stir in the sesame oil. Serve immediately on a bed of egg noodles with the finely shredded scallion sprinkled on top.

Fish is the **ideal** choice when time is short, as it needs little preparation and cooks very **quickly**. In fact, the biggest danger when it comes to preparing fish is overcooking, which ruins the **flavor** and texture. Cook it until the flesh turns opaque, but is still beautifully moist. When tested with the tip of a knife, the flesh should flake **easily**.

Some of the most **delicious** fish dishes are also the **easiest**: try Cajun-style Cod, Salmon Risotto with Cucumber and Tarragon, or Spiced Scallops in their Shells, and find out why they call it fishing for **compliments!**

FISH

Cajun-style Cod

This recipe works equally well with any firm-fleshed fish such as swordfish, shark, tuna or halibut.

Serves 4

INGREDIENTS

4 cod steaks, each weighing
   about 6 oz
2 tbsp plain low fat yogurt
1 tbsp lime or lemon juice
1 garlic clove, crushed
1 tsp ground cumin
1 tsp paprika
1 tsp mustard powder
½ tsp cayenne pepper
½ tsp dried thyme
½ tsp dried oregano
baby potatoes and a mixed salad,
   to serve

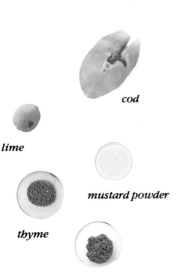

cod

lime

mustard powder

thyme

paprika

1 Pat the fish dry on absorbent paper towels. Mix together the yogurt and lime or lemon juice and brush lightly over both sides of the fish.

2 Mix together the garlic clove, spices and herbs. Coat both sides of the fish with the seasoning mix, rubbing in well.

COOK'S TIP

If you don't have a ridged broiler pan, heat several metal skewers under a broiler until red hot. Holding the ends with a cloth, press onto the seasoned fish before cooking to give a seared appearance.

3 Spray a ridged broiler pan or heavy-based frying pan with non-stick cooking spray. Heat until very hot. Add the fish and cook over a high heat for 4 minutes, or until the underside is well browned.

4 Turn over and cook for a further 4 minutes, or until the steaks have cooked through. Serve immediately accompanied with baby potatoes and a mixed salad.

Thick Cod Fillet with Fresh Mixed-herb Crust

Mixed fresh herbs make this a delicious crust. Season well and serve with large lemon wedges.

Serves 4

INGREDIENTS
2 tbsp butter
1 tbsp fresh chervil
1 tbsp fresh parsley
1 tbsp fresh chives
3 cups wholewheat bread
    crumbs
4 × 8 oz thickly cut cod fillets,
    skinned
1 tbsp olive oil
lemon wedges, to garnish
salt and freshly ground black pepper

chives

butter

bread crumbs

parsley

cod fillets

chervil

lemon

1 Preheat the oven to 400°F. Melt the butter and chop the fresh herbs finely.

2 Mix the butter with the bread crumbs, herbs and seasoning.

3 Press a quarter of the mixture on top of each fillet. Place on a baking sheet and drizzle over the olive oil. Bake in the preheated oven for 15 minutes until the fish flesh is firm and the top turns golden. Serve garnished with lemon wedges.

Jamaican Spiced Cod Steaks with Pumpkin Ragout

Spicy hot from Kingston town, this fast fish dish is guaranteed to appeal. The term 'ragout' is taken from the old French verb *ragouter*, which means to stimulate the appetite.

Serves 4

INGREDIENTS
finely grated zest of ½ orange
2 tbsp black peppercorns
1 tbsp allspice berries or Jamaican
   pepper
½ tsp salt
4 × 6 oz cod steaks
groundnut oil, for frying
new potatoes, to serve (optional)
3 tbsp chopped fresh parsley,
   to garnish

FOR THE RAGOUT
2 tbsp groundnut oil
1 medium onion, chopped
1 in fresh ginger root, peeled and
   grated
1 lb fresh pumpkin, peeled, deseeded
   and chopped
3–4 shakes of Tabasco sauce
2 tbsp soft brown sugar
1 tbsp vinegar

pumpkin

cod steaks

ginger

COOK'S TIP
This recipe can be adapted using any types of firm pink or white fish that is available, such as haddock, whiting, monkfish, halibut or tuna.

1 To make the ragout, heat the oil in a heavy saucepan and add the onion and ginger. Cover and cook, stirring, for 3–4 minutes until soft.

2 Add the chopped pumpkin, Tabasco sauce, brown sugar and vinegar, cover and cook over a low heat for 10–12 minutes until softened.

3 Combine the orange zest, peppercorns, allspice or Jamaican pepper and salt, then crush coarsely using a pestle and mortar. (Alternatively, coarsely grind the peppercorns in a pepper mill and combine with the zest and seasoning.)

4 Scatter the spice mixture over both sides of the fish and moisten with a sprinkling of oil.

5 Heat a large frying pan and fry the cod steaks for 12 minutes, turning once.

6 Serve the cod steaks with a spoonful of pumpkin ragout and new potatoes, if desired, and garnish the ragout with chopped fresh parsley.

Grilled Snapper with Hot Mango Salsa

A ripe mango provides the basis for a deliciously rich fruity salsa. The dressing needs no oil and features the tropical flavors of cilantro, ginger and chili.

VARIATION

If fresh mangoes are unavailable, use the canned variety and drain well. Sea bass are also good served with the hot mango salsa.

Serves 4

INGREDIENTS

12 oz new potatoes
3 eggs
4 oz green beans, topped, tailed and halved
4 × 12 oz red snapper, scaled and gutted
2 tbsp olive oil
6 oz mixed lettuce leaves, such as frisée or oak leaf
2 cherry tomatoes
salt and freshly ground black pepper

FOR THE SALSA

3 tbsp chopped fresh cilantro
1 medium sized ripe mango, peeled, pitted and diced
½ red chili, deseeded and chopped
1 in fresh ginger root, grated
juice of 2 limes
generous pinch of celery salt

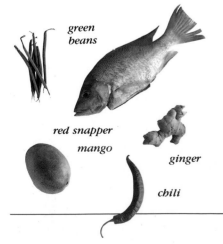

green beans

red snapper

mango

ginger

chili

1 Bring the potatoes to a boil in a large saucepan of salted water and simmer for 15–20 minutes. Drain.

2 Bring a second large saucepan of salted water to a boil. Put in the eggs and boil for 4 minutes, then add the beans and cook for a further 6 minutes, so that the eggs have had a total of 10 minutes. Remove the eggs from the pan, cool, peel and cut into quarters.

3 Preheat a moderate broiler. Slash each snapper three times on either side, moisten with oil and cook for 12 minutes, turning once.

6 Arrange the snapper over the lettuce and season to taste. Halve the new potatoes and tomatoes, and distribute them with the beans and quartered hard-boiled eggs over the salad. Serve with the salsa dressing.

4 To make the dressing, place the cilantro in a food processor. Add the mango, chili, ginger, lime juice and celery salt and process smoothly.

5 Moisten the lettuce leaves with olive oil, and distribute them between four large plates.

Red Snapper with Ginger and Scallions

This is a classic Chinese way of cooking fish. Pouring the oil slowly over the scallions and ginger allows it to partially cook them, enhancing their flavor.

Serves 2-3

INGREDIENTS
1 red snapper, about
  1½–2 lb, cleaned and scaled
  with head left on
1 bunch scallions, cut into thin
  shreds
1-in piece fresh ginger, cut into
  thin shreds
¼ tsp salt
¼ tsp sugar
3 tbsp peanut oil
1 tsp sesame oil
2–3 tbsp light soy sauce
scallion brushes, to garnish

scallions

ginger

peanut oil

sesame oil

red snapper

sugar

light soy sauce

COOK'S TIP
If the fish is too big to fit inside the steamer, cut off the head and place it alongside the body, which can then be reassembled after it is cooked for serving.

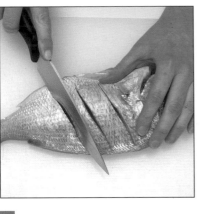

1 Rinse the fish, then pat dry with paper towels. Slash the flesh diagonally, three times on each side. Set the fish on a heatproof oval plate that will fit inside your bamboo steamer.

2 Tuck about one-third of the scallions and ginger inside the body cavity. Place the plate inside the steamer, cover with its lid, then place in a wok.

3 Steam over medium heat for 10–15 minutes, until the fish flakes easily when tested with the tip of a knife.

4 Carefully remove the plate from the steamer. Sprinkle over the salt, sugar and remaining scallions and ginger.

5 Heat the oils in a small pan until very hot, then slowly pour over the fish.

6 Drizzle over the soy sauce and serve at once, garnished with scallion brushes.

Pan-fried Red Snapper with Lemon

This dish, which is spectacularly attractive and delicious, is also quick and easy to make.

Serves 4

INGREDIENTS
1 large bulb fennel
1 lemon
12 red snapper fillets, skin left intact
3 tbsp fresh marjoram, chopped
3 tbsp olive oil
8 oz/3 cups lamb's lettuce or
  Bibb lettuce
salt and freshly ground black pepper

FOR THE VINAIGRETTE
generous ¾ cup peanut oil
1 tbsp white wine vinegar
1 tbsp sherry vinegar
salt and freshly ground black pepper,
  to taste

FOR THE SAUCE
1½ oz black olives, pitted
1 tbsp unsalted butter
1 tbsp capers

fennel

red snapper

marjoram

lamb's lettuce

1 Trim the fennel bulb and cut it into fine matchsticks. Peel the lemon. Remove any excess pith from the peel, then cut it into fine strips. Blanch the rind and refresh it immediately in cold water. Drain.

2 Make the vinaigrette by placing all the ingredients in a small bowl and lightly whisking until well mixed.

3 Sprinkle the red snapper fillets with salt, pepper and marjoram.

4 Heat the wok and add the olive oil. When the oil is very hot, add the fennel and stir-fry for 1 minute, then drain and remove.

5 Reheat the wok and, when the oil is hot, stir-fry the red snapper fillets, cooking them skin-side down first for 2 minutes, then flipping them over for 1 further minute. Drain well on paper towels and wipe the wok clean with paper towels.

6 For the sauce, cut the olives into slivers. Heat the wok and add the butter. When the butter is hot, stir-fry the capers and olives for about 1 minute. Toss the lettuce in the dressing. Arrange the fillets on a bed of lettuce, topped with the fennel and lemon, and serve with the olive and caper sauce.

Fish Parcels

Sea bass is good for this recipe, but you could also use small whole trout, or white fish fillet such as cod or haddock.

COOK'S TIP
These parcels can also be baked in the oven: place them on a baking sheet and cook at 400°F for 15–20 minutes.

Serves 4

4 pieces sea bass fillet or
   4 whole small sea bass,
   about 1 lb each
oil for brushing
2 shallots, thinly sliced
1 garlic clove, chopped
1 tbsp capers
6 sun-dried tomatoes, finely
   chopped
4 black olives, pitted and thinly
   sliced
grated rind and juice of
   1 lemon
1 tsp paprika
salt and freshly ground black
   pepper

1 Clean the fish if whole. Cut four large squares of double-thickness foil, large enough to enclose the fish; brush with a little oil.

2 Place a piece of fish in the center of each piece of foil and season well with salt and pepper.

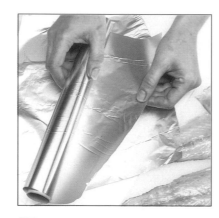

3 Scatter over the shallots, garlic, capers, tomatoes, olives and grated lemon rind. Sprinkle with the lemon juice and paprika.

paprika

shallots

lemon

garlic

sun-dried tomatoes

capers

black olives

sea bass fillets

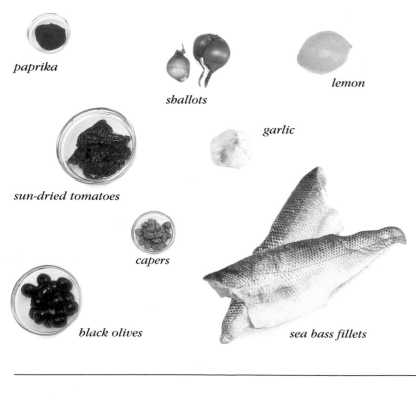

4 Fold the foil over to enclose the fish loosely, sealing the edges firmly so none of the juices can escape. Place on a moderately-hot barbecue and cook for 8–10 minutes. Then open up the tops of the parcels and serve.

Sea Bass with Chinese Chives

Chinese chives are widely available in Oriental supermarkets but if you are unable to buy them, use half a large Spanish onion, finely sliced, instead.

Serves 4

INGREDIENTS
4 sea bass fillets, about 1 lb in all
1 tsp cornstarch
3 tbsp vegetable oil
6 oz/2 cups Chinese chives
1 tbsp rice wine
1 tsp superfine sugar
salt and freshly ground black pepper
Chinese chives with flowerheads,
   to garnish
mixed lettuce salad, to serve

sea bass

cornstarch

rice wine

Chinese chives

1 Remove the scales from the bass by scraping the fillets with the back of a knife, working from tail end to head end.

2 Cut the fillets into large chunks and dust them lightly with cornstarch, salt and pepper.

3 Heat the wok, then add 2 tbsp of the oil. When the oil is hot, toss the chunks of fish in the wok briefly to seal, then set aside. Wipe out the wok with paper towels.

4 Cut the Chinese chives into 2 in lengths and discard the flowers. Heat the wok and add the remaining oil, then stir-fry the Chinese chives for 30 seconds. Add the fish and rice wine, then bring to a boil and stir in the sugar. Simmer until the fish is cooked through. Serve hot, with some flowering Chinese chives. Add a garnish of salad greens.

Smoked Haddock Fillets with Quick Parsley Sauce

Make any herb sauce with this method, making sure it is thickened and seasoned well to complement the smoky flavor of the fish.

Serves 4

INGREDIENTS
4 × 8 oz smoked haddock fillets
6 tbsp butter, softened
2 tbsp flour
1¼ cups milk
salt and freshly ground black pepper
4 tbsp chopped fresh parsley

flour   *butter*

smoked haddock fillets

parsley

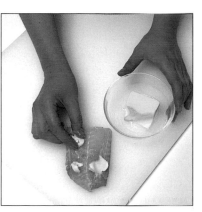

1 Smear the fish fillets liberally on both sides with 4 tbsp butter and preheat the broiler.

2 Beat the remaining butter and flour together to make a thick paste.

3 Broil the fish for 10–15 minutes turning when necessary. Meanwhile, heat the milk until just below boiling point. Add the flour mixture in small batches whisking constantly over the heat, until the sauce is smooth and thick.

4 Stir in the seasoning and parsley and serve poured over the fillets.

Fillets of Pink Trout with Tarragon Cream Sauce

If you do not like the idea of cooking and serving trout on the bone, ask your fishmonger to fillet and skin the fish. Serve two fillets per person.

Serves 4

INGREDIENTS
2 tbsp butter
4 fresh trout, filleted and skinned
salt and freshly ground black pepper
new potatoes, to serve
wax beans, to serve

FOR THE CREAM SAUCE
2 large scallions, white part only, chopped
½ cucumber, peeled, deseeded and cut into short sticks
1 tsp cornstarch
⅔ cup light cream
¼ cup dry sherry
2 tbsp chopped fresh tarragon
1 tomato, chopped and deseeded

VARIATION
This recipe can also be made with salmon fillets and the dry sherry may be substituted with white wine.

1 Melt the butter in a large frying pan, season the fillets and cook for 6 minutes, turning once. Transfer to a plate, cover and keep warm.

2 To make the sauce, add the scallions and cucumber to the pan, and cook over a gentle heat, stirring occasionally, until soft but not colored.

3 Remove the pan from the heat and stir in the cornstarch.

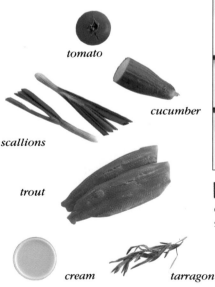

tomato

cucumber

scallions

trout

cream   tarragon

4 Return to the heat and pour in the cream and sherry. Simmer to thicken, stirring continuously.

5 Add the chopped tarragon and tomato, and season to taste.

6 Spoon the sauce over the fillets and serve with buttered new potatoes and wax beans.

Dover Sole in a Green Parsley Jacket

Quick to prepare and absolutely delicious, nothing compares with the rich sweetness of a Dover sole. Here, this fine fish sports a green parsley jacket trimmed with lemon and a hint of garlic.

Serves 2

INGREDIENTS
12 oz baking potatoes, peeled and finely chopped
1¼ cups milk, or as required
pinch of grated nutmeg
2 × Dover sole, skinned
2 tbsp butter
salt and freshly ground black pepper
lemon wedges, to serve

FOR THE PARSLEY JACKET
½ cup fresh parsley
1 oz crustless white bread, cubed
3 tbsp milk
2 tbsp olive oil
finely grated zest of ½ small lemon
1 small garlic clove, crushed

1 In a non-stick saucepan, cover the potatoes with the milk, add salt to taste, and the nutmeg, and bring to a boil. Simmer, uncovered, for 15 minutes until the potatoes have absorbed the milk. Mash, cover and keep warm.

Dover sole

lemon

parsley

2 To make the parsley jacket, chop the parsley in a food processor. Add the bread, milk, olive oil, lemon zest and garlic, then process to a fine paste.

3 Preheat a moderate broiler. Season the sole, dot with butter and broil for 5 minutes. Turn and allow 2 minutes on the other side. Spread with the parsley mixture, return to the broiler and continue to cook for a further 5 minutes. Serve with the mashed potatoes and wedges of lemon.

VARIATION
The same parsley mixture can be used to cover fillets of cod, haddock, whiting or flounder.

Grilled Porgy with Fennel, Mustard and Orange

Porgy is a revelation to anyone unfamiliar with its creamy rich flavor. The fish has a firm white flesh that partners well with a rich butter sauce, sharpened here with a dash of frozen orange juice concentrate.

Serves 2

INGREDIENTS
2 baking potatoes
2 × 12 oz porgies, scaled and
  gutted
2 tsp Dijon mustard
1 tsp fennel seeds
2 tbsp olive oil
2 oz watercress
6 oz mixed lettuce leaves, such as
  curly endive or frisée

FOR THE SAUCE
2 tbsp frozen orange juice
  concentrate
¾ cup unsalted butter,
  diced
salt and cayenne pepper

COOK'S TIP
For speedy baked potatoes, microwave small potatoes on 100% high power for 8 minutes, then crisp in a hot oven preheated to 400°F for a further 10 minutes. Split, butter and serve hot.

1 Cook the potatoes according to the tip at the beginning of this recipe. Preheat a moderate broiler. Slash the porgies four times on either side. Combine the mustard and fennel seeds, then spread over both sides of the fish. Moisten with oil and broil for 12 minutes, turning once.

2 Place the orange juice concentrate in a bowl and heat over 1 in of boiling water. Remove the pan from the stove, and gradually whisk the butter until creamy. Season, cover and set aside.

3 Moisten the watercress and lettuce leaves with the remaining olive oil, arrange the fish on two large plates and put the leaves to one side. Spoon over the sauce and serve with the potatoes.

Dijon mustard

orange juice

cayenne pepper

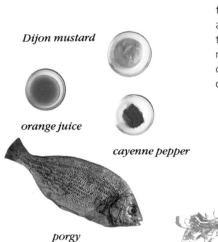

porgy

lettuce

Salmon Risotto with Cucumber and Tarragon

Any rice can be used for risotto. The creamiest ones are made with short-grain Arborio and Carnaroli rice but they do take more time. Fresh tarragon and cucumber bring out the flavor of the salmon.

Serves 4

INGREDIENTS
2 tbsp butter
1 small bunch scallions, white part
  only, chopped
½ cucumber, peeled, deseeded
  and chopped
2 cups rice
3¾ cups fresh or canned chicken or
  fish stock
⅔ cup dry white wine
1 lb salmon fillet, skinned
  and diced
3 tbsp chopped fresh tarragon

salmon
fillet

butter

cucumber

rice

tarragon

scallions

1 Heat the butter in a large saucepan, and add the scallions and cucumber. Cook for 2–3 minutes without coloring.

2 Add the rice, stock and wine, return to a boil and simmer uncovered for 10 minutes, stirring occasionally.

3 Stir in the diced salmon and tarragon. Continue cooking for a further 5 minutes, then switch off the heat. Cover and leave to stand for 5 minutes before serving.

VARIATION

Long-grain rice can also be used. Choose grains that have not been pre-cooked and reduce the stock to 3⅔ cups, per 2 cups of rice.

Pickled Herrings with Beet and Apple Relish

Soused or pickled herrings are delicious with cooked beets. Serve with buttered rye bread and a sweet and sour apple relish.

Serves 4

INGREDIENTS
2 eggs
8 pickled herrings
9 oz cooked baby beet
fresh flat-leaf parsley, to garnish
4 slices buttered rye bread, to serve
⅔ cup sour cream, to serve
    (optional)

FOR THE RELISH
2 tbsp vegetable oil
2 large apples, peeled, cored and
    finely chopped
1 medium onion, chopped
1 tbsp sugar
1 tbsp cider vinegar
1 tsp hot mustard
pinch of salt

pickled herrings *eggs*

baby beets

onion *apples*

1 Bring a saucepan of water to a boil, gently lower in the eggs and cook for 10 minutes. Cool under running water and peel. Cut into quarters.

2 To make the relish, heat the oil in a saucepan and add the apple and onion. Cook over a gentle heat for 3–4 minutes without coloring. Add the sugar, vinegar and mustard, then season with salt.

3 Divide the herrings between four plates. Slice the beets and arrange to one side with the relish. Decorate with egg quarters and garnish with parsley. Serve with buttered rye bread, and a spoonful of sour cream if you wish.

COOK'S TIP
Choose full-flavored green or red apples for the best results.

Thai Fish Stir-fry

This is a substantial dish: it is best served with chunks of fresh crusty white bread, for mopping up all the delicious, spicy juices.

Serves 4

INGREDIENTS
1½ lb mixed seafood (for example, red snapper, cod, raw shrimp), filleted and skinned
1¼ cups coconut milk
1 tbsp vegetable oil
salt and freshly ground black pepper

FOR THE SAUCE
2 large red chilies
1 onion, roughly chopped
2 in piece ginger root, peeled and sliced
2 in piece lemon grass, outer leaf discarded, roughly sliced
2 in piece galingale, peeled and sliced
6 blanched almonds, chopped
½ tsp turmeric
½ tsp salt

chili

onion

ginger

shrimp

1 Cut the filleted fish into large chunks. Peel the shrimp, keeping their tails intact.

2 Carefully remove the seeds from the chilies and chop roughly, wearing rubber gloves to protect your hands if necessary. Then, make the sauce by putting the chilies and the other sauce ingredients in the food processor with 3 tbsp of the coconut milk. Blend until smooth.

3 Heat the wok, then add the oil. When the oil is hot, stir-fry the seafood for 2–3 minutes, then remove.

4 Add the sauce and the remaining coconut milk to the wok, then return the seafood. Bring to the boil, season well and serve with crusty bread.

Spiced Scallops in their Shells

Scallops are excellent steamed. When served with this spicy sauce, they make a delicious yet simple appetizer. Each person spoons sauce onto the scallops before eating them.

Serves 4

INGREDIENTS
8 scallops, shelled (the shells are available in cooking ware stores and some good fish markets)
2 slices fresh ginger, finely shredded
½ garlic clove, shredded
2 scallions, green parts only, shredded
salt and pepper

FOR THE SAUCE
1 garlic clove, crushed
1 tbsp fresh ginger, finely grated
2 scallions, white parts only, chopped
1–2 fresh green chilies, seeded and finely chopped
1 tbsp light soy sauce
1 tbsp dark soy sauce
2 tsp sesame oil

scallops

ginger

scallions

garlic

light soy sauce

green chili

dark soy sauce

sesame oil

1 Remove the dark beard-like fringe and tough muscle from the scallops.

2 Place 2 scallops in each shell. Season lightly with salt and pepper, then sprinkle the ginger, garlic and scallions on top. Place the shells in a bamboo steamer and steam for about 6 minutes, until the scallops look opaque (you may have to do this in batches).

3 Meanwhile, mix together all the sauce ingredients and pour into a small serving bowl.

4 Carefully remove each shell from the steamer, taking care not to spill the juices, and arrange them on a serving plate with the sauce bowl in the center. Serve at once.

Nasi Goreng

This dish is originally from Thailand, but can easily be adapted by adding any cooked ingredients you have to hand. Crispy shrimp crackers make an ideal accompaniment.

Serves 4

INGREDIENTS
8 oz long grain rice
2 large eggs
2 tbsp vegetable oil
1 green chili
2 scallions, roughly chopped
2 cloves garlic, crushed
8 oz cooked chicken
8 oz cooked shrimp
3 tbsp dark soy sauce
shrimp crackers, to serve

rice

soy sauce

egg

chili

shrimp

1 Rinse the rice and then cook for 10–12 minutes in 2 cups water in a saucepan with a tight-fitting lid. When cooked, refresh under cold water.

2 Lightly beat the eggs. Heat 1 tbsp of oil in a small frying pan and swirl in the beaten egg. When cooked on one side, flip over and cook on the other side, remove from the pan and leave to cool. Cut the omelet into strips.

3 Carefully remove the seeds from the chili and chop finely, wearing rubber gloves to protect your hands if necessary. Place the scallions, chili and garlic in a food processor and blend to a paste.

4 Heat the wok, and then add the remaining oil. When the oil is hot, add the paste and stir-fry for 1 minute.

5 Add the chicken and shrimp.

6 Add the rice and stir-fry for 3–4 minutes. Stir in the soy sauce and serve with shrimp crackers.

Spiced Shrimp with Coconut

This spicy dish is based on *Sambal Goreng Udang*, which is Indonesian in origin. It is best served with plain boiled rice.

Serves 3-4

INGREDIENTS
2-3 fresh red chilies, seeded
  and chopped
3 shallots, chopped
1 lemongrass stalk, chopped
2 garlic cloves, chopped
thin sliver of dried shrimp paste
½ tsp ground galangal
1 tsp ground turmeric
1 tsp ground coriander
1 tbsp peanut oil
1 cup water
2 fresh kaffir lime leaves
1 tsp light brown sugar
2 tomatoes, peeled, seeded
  and chopped
1 cup coconut milk
1½ lb large raw shrimp,
  peeled and deveined
squeeze of lemon juice
salt, to taste
shredded scallions and
  flaked coconut, to garnish

1 In a mortar pound the chilies, shallots, lemongrass, garlic, shrimp paste, galangal, turmeric and coriander with a pestle until it forms a paste.

lemongrass

garlic

dried shrimp paste

red chilies

turmeric

shrimp

coriander

peanut oil

galangal

coconut milk   *sugar*

tomatoes

shallots

kaffir lime leaves

COOK'S TIP
Dried shrimp paste, much used in Southeast Asia, is available at Asian stores.

2 Heat a wok until hot, add the oil and swirl it around. Add the spiced paste and stir-fry for about 2 minutes. Pour in the water and add the kaffir lime leaves, sugar and tomatoes. Simmer for 8–10 minutes, until most of the liquid has evaporated.

3 Add the coconut milk and shrimp and cook gently, stirring, for about 4 minutes until the shrimp are pink. Taste and adjust the seasoning with salt and a squeeze of lemon juice. Serve at once, garnished with shredded scallions and toasted flaked coconut.

Spicy Crab and Coconut

This spicy dish is delicious served with plain warm Naan bread.

Serves 4

INGREDIENTS

1½ oz dried unsweetened shredded coconut
2 cloves garlic
2 in piece ginger root, peeled and grated
½ tsp cumin seeds
1 small stick cinnamon
½ tsp ground turmeric
2 dried red chilies
1 tbsp coriander seeds
½ tsp poppy seeds
1 tbsp vegetable oil
1 medium onion, sliced
1 small green pepper, cut into strips
16 crab claws
fresh coriander sprigs, crushed, to garnish
⅔ cup natural low-fat yogurt, to serve

pepper

cumin seeds

cinnamon

crab claw

1 Place the shredded coconut, garlic, ginger, cumin seeds, cinnamon, turmeric, red chilies, coriander and poppy seeds into a food processor and process until well blended.

2 Heat the oil in the wok and fry the onion until soft, but not colored.

3 Stir in the green pepper and stir-fry for 1 minute.

4 Remove the vegetables with a slotted spoon and heat the wok. Add the crab claws, stir-fry for 2 minutes, then briefly return all the spiced vegetables to the wok. Garnish with fresh coriander sprigs and serve with the cooling yogurt.

Steaming Mussels with a Spicy Dipping Sauce

In this recipe, the mussel juices are thickened with split red lentils and spiced with curry.

Serves 4

INGREDIENTS
5 tbsp red lentils
2 loaves French bread
4 pints live mussels
5 tbsp white wine

FOR THE DIPPING SAUCE
2 tbsp vegetable oil
1 small onion, finely chopped
½ celery stalk, finely chopped
1 large garlic clove, crushed
1 tsp medium-hot curry paste

curry paste

French bread

garlic

red lentils

onion

celery

mussels

1 Soak the lentils in plenty of cold water until they are required. Preheat the oven to 300°F and put the bread in to warm. Clean the mussels in plenty of cold water and pull off any stray beards. Discard any that are damaged.

2 Place the mussels in a large saucepan. Add the white wine, cover and steam the mussels for 8 minutes.

3 Transfer the mussels to a colander over a bowl to collect the juices. Keep warm until required.

4 To make the dipping sauce, heat the vegetable oil in a second saucepan, add the onion and celery, and cook for 3–4 minutes to soften without coloring. Strain the mussel juices into a measuring cup to remove any sand or grit. There will be approximately 1⅔ cups of liquid.

5 Add the mussel juices to the saucepan, then add the garlic, curry paste and lentils. Bring to a boil and simmer for 10–12 minutes or until the lentils have fallen apart.

6 Turn the mussels out onto four serving plates and bring to the table with the dipping sauce, the warm French bread and a bowl to put the empty shells in.

Stir-fried Squid with Black Bean Sauce

If you cannot buy fresh squid you will certainly find small or baby frozen squid, skinned, boned and with heads removed, at your local fishmonger.

Serves 4

INGREDIENTS
½ lb fresh or frozen squid
1 red chili
2 tsp peanut oil
1 clove garlic, crushed
2 tbsp black bean sauce
4 tbsp water
fresh parsley sprigs, to garnish
steamed rice, to serve

black bean sauce

garlic

squid

chilies

1 Carefully remove the skin from the squid and discard.

2 Cut off the head of each squid just below the eye, and discard.

3 Remove the bone from the squid and discard.

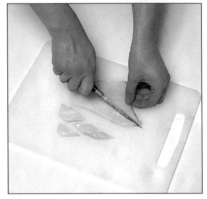

4 Cut the squid into bite-size pieces and score the flesh in a criss-cross pattern with a sharp knife.

5 Carefully deseed the chili and chop it finely. Wear rubber gloves to protect your hands if necessary.

6 Heat the wok, then add the oil. When the oil is hot, add the garlic and cook until it starts to sizzle but does not color. Stir in the squid and fry until the flesh starts to stiffen and turn white. Quickly stir in the black bean sauce, water and chili. Continue stirring until the squid is cooked and tender (not more than a minute). Garnish with parsley sprigs and the tentacles and serve with steamed rice.

A repertoire of rapid vegetarian dishes is extremely useful, not merely because **vegetarian** food is so **popular** with everyone these days, but also for those occasions when you've prepared a meat meal, only to find out that one of your guests is unable to **enjoy** it.

Being able to conjure up a **quick** and **delicious** alternative saves embarrassment and will earn you their respect and gratitude. **Classic** candidates would be Breaded Eggplant with Hot Vinaigrette, Creamy Cannellini Beans with Asparagus, or Red Bell Pepper Polenta with Sunflower Salsa.

VERITABLE VEGETARIAN

Risotto-stuffed Eggplants with Spicy Tomato Sauce

Eggplants are a challenge to the creative cook and allow for some unusual recipe ideas. Here, they are stuffed and baked with a cheese and pine nut topping.

Serves 4

INGREDIENTS
4 small eggplants
7 tbsp olive oil
1 small onion, chopped
scant 1 cup arborio rice
3⅔ cups ready-made or fresh
vegetable stock
1 tbsp white wine vinegar
8 fresh basil sprigs, to garnish

FOR THE TOPPING
¼ cup freshly grated Parmesan
cheese
1 tbsp pine nuts

FOR THE TOMATO SAUCE
1¼ cups crushed tomatoes or
tomato purée
1 tsp mild curry paste
pinch of salt

1 Preheat the oven to 400°F. Cut the eggplants in half lengthwise and take out their flesh with a small knife. Brush with 2 tbsp of the oil, place on a baking sheet and cook in the preheated oven for 6–8 minutes.

2 Chop the reserved eggplant flesh and heat the remainder of the olive oil in a medium saucepan. Add the eggplant flesh and the onion and cook over a gentle heat for 3–4 minutes until soft.

3 Add the rice, stir in the stock and simmer uncovered for a further 15 minutes. Stir in the vinegar.

COOK'S TIP

Don't be put off by the amount of oil eggplants absorb when cooking. Use olive oil and remember that good oils are low in saturated fat and are believed to fight against heart disease.

onion

eggplants

pine nuts

Parmesan cheese

tomato purée

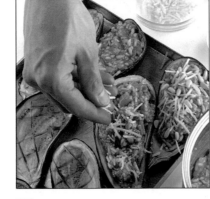

4 Increase the oven temperature to 450°F. Spoon the rice into the eggplant skins, top with cheese and pine nuts, and return to the oven to brown for 5 minutes.

5 To make the sauce, combine the crushed tomatoes or tomato purée with the curry paste, heat and add salt to taste.

6 Spoon the sauce onto four large serving plates and position two eggplant halves on each. Garnish with basil sprigs.

Creamy Cannellini Beans with Asparagus

Cannellini beans in a creamy sauce contrast with tender asparagus in this tasty toast topper.

Serves 2

INGREDIENTS
2 tsp butter
1 small onion, finely chopped
1 small carrot, grated
1 tsp fresh thyme leaves
14 oz can cannellini beans, drained
$^{2}/_{3}$ cup light cream
4 oz young asparagus spears, trimmed
2 slices of fresh sliced whole wheat bread
salt and freshly ground black pepper

whole wheat bread

carrot

thyme

butter

asparagus spears

light cream

onion

cannellini beans

parsley

1 Melt the butter in a pan. Add the onion and carrot, and fry over a moderate heat for 4 minutes until soft. Add the thyme leaves.

2 Rinse the cannellini beans under cold running water. Drain thoroughly. Then add to the onion and carrot. Mix lightly.

3 Pour in the cream, and heat slowly to just below boiling point, stirring occasionally. Remove the pan from the heat, and add salt and pepper to taste. Preheat the broiler.

4 Place the asparagus spears in a saucepan. Pour over just enough boiling water to cover. Poach for 3–4 minutes until the spears are just tender.

5 Meanwhile, toast the bread under the broiler until both sides are golden.

6 Place the toast on individual plates. Drain the asparagus, and divide the spears between the slices of toast. Spoon the bean mixture over each portion, and serve.

Spring Vegetable Stir-fry

A colorful, dazzling medley of fresh and sweet young vegetables.

Serves 4

INGREDIENTS

1 tbsp peanut oil
1 garlic clove, sliced
1 in piece of fresh ginger root, finely
  chopped
4 oz baby carrots
4 oz patty pan squash
4 oz baby corn
4 oz green beans, topped and tailed
4 oz sugar-snap peas, topped and
  tailed
4 oz young asparagus, cut into 3 in
  pieces
8 scallions, trimmed and cut into 2 in
  pieces
4 oz cherry tomatoes

FOR THE DRESSING

juice of 2 limes
1 tbsp honey
1 tbsp soy sauce
1 tsp sesame oil

1 Heat the peanut oil in a wok or large frying pan.

2 Add the garlic and ginger and stir-fry over a high heat for 1 minute.

3 Add the carrots, patty pan squash, baby corn and beans and stir-fry for another 3–4 minutes.

4 Add the sugar-snap peas, asparagus, scallions and cherry tomatoes and stir-fry for a further 1–2 minutes.

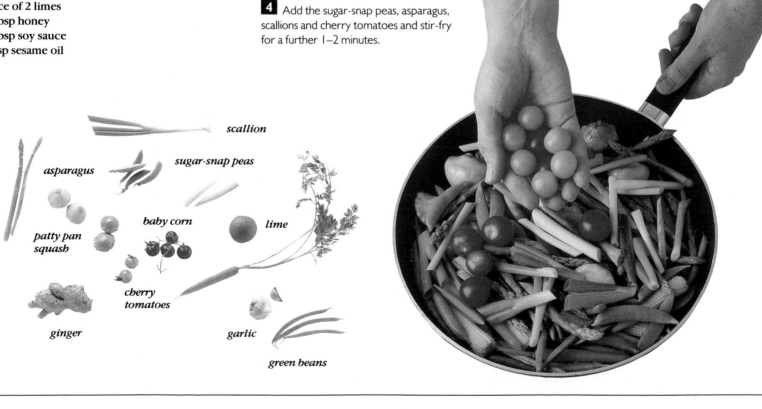

scallion

asparagus

sugar-snap peas

patty pan
squash

baby corn

lime

ginger

cherry
tomatoes

garlic

green beans

5 Mix the dressing ingredients together and add to the pan.

6 Stir well then cover the pan. Cook for 2–3 minutes more until the vegetables are just tender but still crisp.

COOK'S TIP
Stir-fries take only moments to cook so prepare this dish at the last minute.

Stir-fried Chickpeas

Buy canned chickpeas and you will save all the time needed for soaking and then thoroughly cooking dried chickpeas. Served with a crisp green salad, this dish makes a filling vegetarian main course for two, or could be served in smaller quantities as a starter or side dish.

Serves 2–4 as an
accompaniment

INGREDIENTS
2 tbsp sunflower seeds
1 × 14 oz can chickpeas, drained
   and rinsed
1 tsp chili powder
1 tsp paprika
2 tbsp vegetable oil
1 clove garlic, crushed
7 oz canned chopped tomatoes
8 oz fresh spinach, well washed and
   coarse stalks removed
salt and freshly ground black pepper
2 tsp chili oil

spinach

garlic

sunflower seeds

chickpeas

1 Heat the wok, and then add the sunflower seeds. Dry-fry until the seeds are golden and toasted.

2 Remove the sunflower seeds and set aside. Toss the chickpeas in chili powder and paprika. Remove and reserve.

3 Heat the wok, then add the oil. When the oil is hot, stir-fry the garlic for 30 seconds, add the chickpeas and stir-fry for 1 minute.

4 Stir in the tomatoes and stir-fry for 4 minutes. Toss in the spinach, season well and stir-fry for 1 minute. Drizzle chili oil and scatter sunflower seeds over the vegetables, then serve.

Gorgonzola, Cauliflower and Walnut Gratin

This cauliflower dish is covered with a bubbly blue cheese sauce topped with chopped walnuts and cooked under the broiler.

Serves 4

INGREDIENTS

1 large cauliflower, broken into florets
2 tbsp butter
1 medium onion, finely chopped
3 tbsp flour
scant 2 cups milk
5 oz Gorgonzola or other blue cheese, cut into pieces
½ tsp celery salt
pinch of cayenne papper
¾ cup chopped walnuts
pinch of salt
fresh parsley, to garnish
4 oz green salad, to serve

1 Bring a large saucepan of salted water to a boil and cook the cauliflower for 6 minutes. Drain and place in a flameproof gratin dish.

onion

butter

Gorgonzola

walnuts

cauliflower

2 Heat the butter in a heavy saucepan. Add the onion and cook over a gentle heat to soften without coloring. Stir in the flour, then remove from the heat. Stir in the milk a little at a time until absorbed by the flour, stirring continuously. Add the cheese, celery salt and cayenne pepper. Simmer and stir to thicken.

3 Preheat a moderate broiler. Spoon the sauce over the cauliflower, scatter with chopped walnuts and broil until golden. Garnish with the parsley and serve with a crisp green salad.

VARIATION

For a delicious alternative, substitute cauliflower with 2½ lb fresh broccoli or combine both together.

Lemon and Ginger Spicy Beans

An extremely quick delicious meal, made with canned beans for speed. You probably won't need extra salt as canned beans tend to be already salted.

Serves 4

INGREDIENTS
2 tbsp roughly chopped fresh ginger
  root
3 garlic cloves, roughly chopped
1 cup cold water
1 tbsp sunflower oil
1 large onion, thinly sliced
1 fresh red chili, seeded and finely
  chopped
¼ tsp cayenne pepper
2 tsp ground cumin
1 tsp ground coriander
½ tsp ground turmeric
2 tbsp lemon juice
⅓ cup chopped fresh cilantro
14 oz can black-eyed beans,
  drained and rinsed
14 oz can adzuki beans, drained
  and rinsed
14 oz can navy beans, drained
  and rinsed
freshly ground black pepper

1 Place the ginger, garlic and 4 tbsp of the cold water in a blender and mix until smooth.

2 Heat the oil in a pan. Add the onion and chili and cook gently for 5 minutes until softened.

3 Add the cayenne pepper, cumin, ground coriander and turmeric and stir-fry for 1 minute.

4 Stir in the ginger and garlic paste from the blender and cook for another minute.

garlic

red chilli

ginger

ground coriander

ground turmeric

ground cumin

adzuki beans

black-eyed beans

navy beans

onion

5 Add the remaining water, lemon juice and fresh cilantro, stir well and bring to a boil. Cover the pan tightly and cook for 5 minutes.

6 Add all the beans and cook for a further 5–10 minutes. Season with pepper to taste and serve.

Bengali-style Vegetables

A hot, dry curry using spices that do not require long, slow cooking.

Serves 4

INGREDIENTS

½ cauliflower, broken into
  small florets
1 large potato, peeled and cut into
  1 in dice
4 oz green beans, trimmed
2 zucchini, halved lengthwise
  and sliced
2 green chilies
1 in piece of fresh ginger, peeled
½ cup plain yogurt
2 tsp ground coriander
½ tsp ground turmeric
2 tbsp ghee or vegetable oil
½ tsp garam masala
1 tsp cumin seeds
2 tsp sugar
pinch each of ground cloves,
  ground cinnamon and
  ground cardamom
salt and freshly ground black pepper

1 Bring a large pan of water to a boil. Add the cauliflower and potato, and cook for 5 minutes. Add the beans and zucchini, and cook for 2–3 minutes.

2 Meanwhile, cut the chilies in half, remove the seeds, and coarsely chop the flesh. Finely chop the ginger. Mix the chilies and ginger in a small bowl.

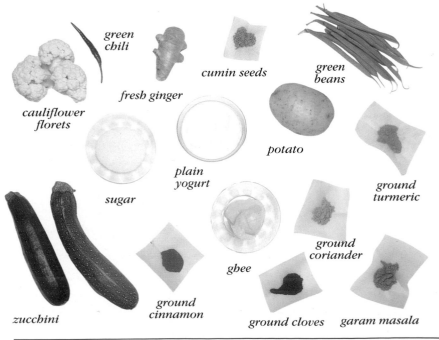

green chili

cumin seeds

green beans

fresh ginger

cauliflower florets

plain yogurt

potato

sugar

ground turmeric

zucchini

ghee

ground cinnamon

ground coriander

ground cloves

garam masala

3 Drain the vegetables, and turn them into a bowl. Add the chili and ginger mixture, with the yogurt, ground coriander and turmeric. Season with plenty of salt and pepper, and mix well.

4 Heat the ghee or oil in a large frying pan. Add the vegetable mixture, and cook over a high heat for 2 minutes, stirring from time to time.

5 Stir in the garam masala and cumin seeds, and cook for 2 minutes.

6 Stir in the sugar and remaining spices, and cook for 1 minute or until all the liquid has evaporated.

COOK'S TIP

If ghee is not available, you can clarify your own butter. Melt ¼ cup butter slowly in a small pan. Remove from the heat, and leave for about 5 minutes. Then pour off the clear yellow clarified butter, leaving the sediment in the pan.

Red Bean and Mushroom Burgers

Vegetarians, vegans and even meat-eaters can all enjoy these healthy, low-fat veggie burgers. With salad, pita bread and yogurt, they make a substantial meal.

COOK'S TIP

These burgers are not quite as firm as meat burgers, so handle them gently on the barbecue.

Serves 4

1 tbsp olive oil
1 small onion, finely chopped
1 garlic clove, crushed
1 tsp ground cumin
1 tsp ground coriander
$\frac{1}{2}$ tsp ground turmeric
$1\frac{1}{2}$ cups finely chopped mushrooms
14 oz can red kidney beans
2 tbsp chopped fresh cilantro
whole-wheat flour (optional)
olive oil for brushing
salt and black pepper
yogurt, to serve

onion

mushrooms

whole-wheat flour

red kidney beans

garlic

olive oil   *cilantro*

cumin   *turmeric*

ground coriander

1 Heat the oil in a wide pan and fry the onion and garlic over a moderate heat, stirring, until softened. Add the spices and cook for a minute more, stirring continuously.

2 Add the mushrooms and cook, stirring, until softened and dry. Remove from the heat.

3 Drain the beans thoroughly and then mash them with a fork.

4 Stir into the pan, with the fresh cilantro, mixing thoroughly. Season well with salt and pepper.

5 Using floured hands, form the mixture into four flat burger shapes. If the mixture is too sticky to handle, mix in a little flour.

6 Brush the burgers with oil and cook on a hot barbecue for 8–10 minutes, turning once, until golden brown. Serve with a spoonful of yogurt and a crisp green salad.

Mushroom and Okra Curry with Fresh Mango Relish

This simple but delicious curry with its fresh gingery mango relish is best served with plain basmati rice.

Serves 4

INGREDIENTS
4 garlic cloves, roughly chopped
1 in piece of fresh ginger root, peeled and roughly chopped
1–2 red chillies, seeded and chopped
¾ cup cold water
1 tbsp sunflower oil
1 tsp coriander seeds
1 tsp cumin seeds
1 tsp ground cumin
2 green cardamom pods, seeds removed and ground
pinch of ground turmeric
1 × 14 oz can chopped tomatoes
1 lb mushrooms, halved or quartered if large
8 oz okra, trimmed and cut into ½ in slices
2 tbsp chopped fresh coriander
basmati rice, to serve

FOR THE MANGO RELISH
1 large ripe mango, about 1¼ lb in weight
1 small garlic clove, crushed
1 onion, finely chopped
2 tsp grated fresh ginger root
1 fresh red chilli, seeded and finely chopped
pinch of salt and sugar

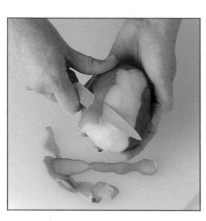

1 For the mango relish, peel the mango and cut off the flesh from the pit.

2 In a bowl mash the mango flesh with a fork or pulse in a food processor, and mix in the rest of the relish ingredients. Set to one side.

3 Place the garlic, ginger, chilli and 3 tbsp of the water into a blender and blend until smooth.

4 Heat the sunflower oil in a large pan. Add the whole coriander and cumin seeds and allow them to sizzle for a few seconds. Add the ground cumin, ground cardamom and turmeric and cook for 1 minute more.

onion
garlic
ginger
coriander seeds
mushrooms
mango
okra
red chillies
chopped tomatoes
cumin seeds
turmeric
cardamom pods

5 Add the paste from the blender, the tomatoes, remaining water, mushrooms and okra. Stir to mix well and bring to a boil. Reduce the heat, cover, and simmer for 5 minutes.

6 Remove the cover, turn up the heat slightly and cook for another 5–10 minutes until the okra is tender. Stir in the fresh coriander and serve with rice and the mango relish.

Vedgeree with Green Beans and Mushrooms

Crunchy green beans and mushrooms are the star ingredients in this vegetarian version of an old favorite.

Serves 2

INGREDIENTS
³/₄ cup basmati rice
1¹/₄ cups cold water
3 eggs
6 oz green beans, trimmed
¹/₄ cup butter
1 onion, finely chopped
8 oz crimini mushrooms, quartered
2 tbsp light cream
1 tbsp chopped fresh parsley
salt and freshly ground black pepper

light cream *crimini mushrooms* *parsley*

onion

butter

green beans

eggs

basmati rice

1 Wash the rice several times under cold running water. Drain thoroughly. Bring a pan of water to a boil. Add the rice, and cook for 10–12 minutes until tender. Drain thoroughly.

2 Half fill a second pan with water. Add the eggs, and bring to a boil. Lower the heat, and simmer for 8 minutes. Drain the eggs, and cool them under cold water. Remove the shells.

3 Bring another pan of water to a boil, and cook the green beans for 5 minutes. Drain, and refresh under cold running water. Then drain again.

4 Melt the butter in a large frying pan. Add the onions and mushrooms. Cook for 2–3 minutes over a moderate heat.

5 Add the green beans and rice to the onion mixture. Stir lightly to mix. Cook for 2 minutes. Cut the hard-boiled eggs in wedges, and add them to the pan.

6 Stir in the cream and parsley, taking care not to break up the eggs. Reheat the kedgeree, but do not allow it to boil. Serve at once.

Nutty Rice and Mushroom Stir-fry

This delicious and substantial supper dish can be eaten hot or cold with salads.

Serves 4–6

INGREDIENTS

12 oz long grain rice
3 tbsp sunflower oil
1 small onion, roughly chopped
8 oz field mushrooms, sliced
½ cup hazelnuts, roughly chopped
½ cup pecans, roughly chopped
½ cup almonds, roughly chopped
4 tbsp fresh parsley, chopped
salt and freshly ground black pepper

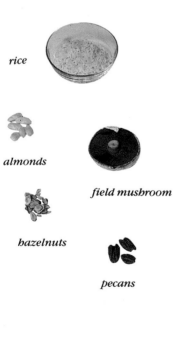

rice

almonds

field mushroom

hazelnuts

pecans

1 Rinse the rice, then cook for about 10–12 minutes in 2½–3 cups water in a saucepan with a tight-fitting lid. When cooked, refresh under cold water. Heat the wok, then add half the oil. When the oil is hot, stir-fry the rice for 2–3 minutes. Remove and set aside.

2 Add the remaining oil and stir-fry the onion for 2 minutes until softened.

3 Mix in the field mushrooms and stir-fry for 2 minutes.

4 Add all the nuts and stir-fry for 1 minute. Return the rice to the wok and stir-fry for 3 minutes. Season with salt and pepper. Stir in the parsley and serve.

Grilled Mixed Peppers with Feta and Green Salsa

Soft, smoky grilled peppers make a lovely combination with the slightly tart salsa.

Serves 4

INGREDIENTS

4 medium peppers in different colors
3 tbsp chopped fresh flat-leaf parsley
3 tbsp chopped fresh dill
3 tbsp chopped fresh mint
½ small red onion, finely chopped
1 tbsp capers, coarsely chopped
¼ cup Greek olives, pitted and sliced
1 fresh green chilli, seeded and finely chopped
4 tbsp pistachios, chopped
5 tbsp extra-virgin olive oil
3 tbsp fresh lime juice
½ cup medium-fat feta cheese, crumbled
1 oz cornichons, finely chopped

olives
feta cheese
green chilli
mint
pistachios
peppers
cornichons
red onion

1 Preheat the broiler. Place the whole peppers on a tray and broil until charred and blistered.

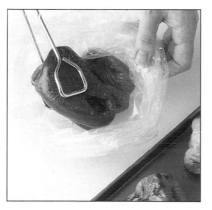

2 Place the peppers in a plastic bag and leave to cool.

COOK'S TIP

Feta cheese is quite salty so if preferred, soak in cold water and drain well before using.

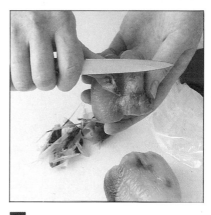

3 Peel, seed and cut the peppers into even strips.

4 Mix all the remaining ingredients together, and stir in the pepper strips.

Red Bell Pepper Polenta with Sunflower Salsa

This recipe is inspired by Italian and Mexican cookery. Cornmeal polenta is a staple food in Italy, served with brightly colored vegetables. Mexican *Pipian* is a salsa made from sunflower seeds, chili and lime.

Serves 4

INGREDIENTS
3 young zucchinis
oil, for greasing
5 cups light vegetable
   stock
2 cups fine polenta or
   cornmeal
1 × 7 oz jar red peppers, drained
   and sliced
4 oz green salad, to serve

FOR THE SUNFLOWER SALSA
3 oz sunflower seeds, toasted
1 cup crustless white
   bread
scant 1 cup vegetable
   stock
1 garlic clove, crushed
½ red chili, deseeded and chopped
2 tbsp chopped fresh cilantro
1 tsp sugar
1 tbsp lime juice
pinch of salt

polenta

sunflower seeds

zucchini

limes

red chilies

red bell peppers

cilantro

white bread

1 Bring a saucepan of salted water to a boil. Add the zucchinis and simmer over a low heat for 2–3 minutes. Refresh under cold running water and drain. When they are cool, cut into strips.

2 Lightly oil a 9 in loaf pan and line with a single sheet of waxed paper.

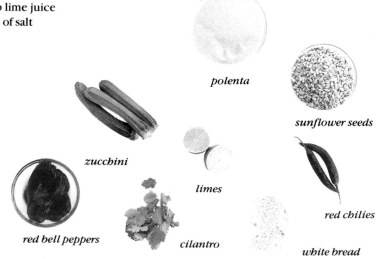

3 Bring the vegetable stock to a simmer in a heavy saucepan. Add the polenta in a steady stream, stirring continuously for about 2–3 minutes until thickened.

4 Partly fill the lined pan with the polenta mixture. Layer the sliced zucchinis and peppers over the polenta. Fill the pan with the remaining polenta and leave to set for about 10–15 minutes. Polenta should be served warm or at room temperature.

Cook's Tip
Sunflower salsa will keep for up to 10 days in the refrigerator. It is delicious poured over a simple dish of pasta.

5 To make the salsa, grind the sunflower seeds to a thick paste in a food processor. Add the remaining ingredients and combine thoroughly.

6 Turn the warm polenta out onto a board, remove the paper and cut into thick slices with a large wet knife. Serve with the salsa and a green salad.

Zucchini and Asparagus en Papillote

An impressive dinner party accompaniment, these puffed paper parcels should be broken open at the table by each guest, so that the wonderful aroma can be fully appreciated.

Serves 4

INGREDIENTS
2 medium zucchini
1 medium leek
8 oz young asparagus, trimmed
4 tarragon sprigs
4 whole garlic cloves, unpeeled
salt and freshly ground black pepper
1 egg, beaten

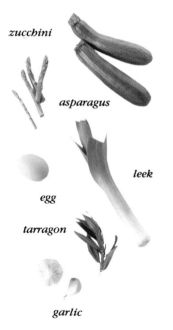

zucchini

asparagus

leek

egg

tarragon

garlic

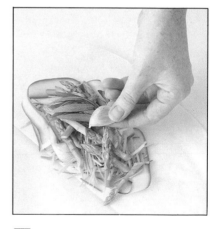

1 Preheat the oven to 400°F. Using a potato peeler slice the zucchini lengthwise into thin strips.

2 Cut the leek into very fine julienne strips and cut the asparagus evenly into 2 in lengths.

3 Cut out 4 sheets of parchment paper 12 × 15 in in size and fold each in half. Draw a large curve to make a heart shape when unfolded. Cut along the inside of the line and open out.

4 Divide the zucchini, asparagus and leek evenly between each paper heart, positioning the filling on one side of the fold line, and topping each with a sprig of tarragon and an unpeeled garlic clove. Season to taste.

COOK'S TIP

Experiment with other vegetables and herbs such as sugar-snap peas and mint or baby carrots and rosemary. The possibilities are endless.

5 Brush the edges lightly with the beaten egg and fold over.

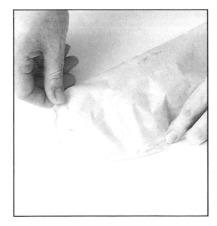

6 Pleat the edges together so that each parcel is completely sealed. Lay the parcels on a cookie sheet and cook for 10 minutes. Serve immediately.

Breaded Eggplant with Hot Vinaigrette

Crisp on the outside, beautifully tender within, these eggplant slices taste wonderful with a spicy dressing flavored with chili and capers.

COOK'S TIP
When serving a salad with a warm dressing, use robust leaves that will stand up to the heat.

Serves 2

INGREDIENTS
1 large eggplant
1/2 cup all-purpose flour
2 eggs, beaten
2 cups fresh white bread crumbs
vegetable oil for frying
1 head radicchio
salt and freshly ground black pepper

FOR THE DRESSING
2 tbsp olive oil
1 garlic clove, crushed
1 tbsp capers, drained
1 tbsp white wine vinegar
1 tbsp chili oil

eggplant
bread crumbs
eggs
all-purpose flour
radicchio
capers
white wine vinegar
garlic clove

1 Remove the ends from the eggplant. Cut it into 1/4 in slices. Set aside.

2 Season the flour with a generous amount of salt and black pepper. Spread out in a shallow dish. Pour the beaten eggs into a second dish. Spread out the bread crumbs in a third.

3 Dip the eggplant slices in the flour, then in the beaten egg and finally in the bread crumbs, patting them on to make an even coating.

4 Pour vegetable oil into a large frying pan to a depth of about 1/4 in. Heat the oil, then fry the eggplant slices for 3–4 minutes, turning once. Drain well on paper towels.

5 Heat the olive oil in a small pan. Add the garlic and the capers, and cook over gentle heat for 1 minute. Increase the heat, add the vinegar, and cook for 30 seconds. Stir in the chili oil, and remove the pan from the heat.

6 Arrange the radicchio leaves on two plates. Top with the hot eggplant slices. Drizzle over the vinaigrette, and serve.

Asparagus Rolls with Herb Butter Sauce

For a taste sensation, try tender asparagus spears wrapped in crisp filo pastry. The buttery herb sauce makes the perfect accompaniment.

Serves 2

INGREDIENTS
4 sheets of filo pastry
$1/4$ cup butter, melted
16 young asparagus spears, trimmed

FOR THE SAUCE
2 shallots, finely chopped
1 bay leaf
$2/3$ cup dry white wine
6 oz butter, softened
1 tbsp chopped fresh herbs
salt and freshly ground black pepper
chopped chives, to garnish

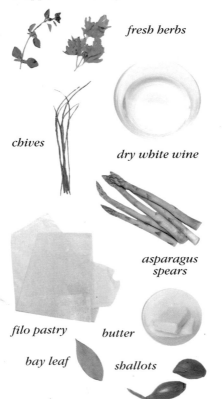

fresh herbs

chives

dry white wine

asparagus spears

filo pastry   *butter*

bay leaf   *shallots*

1 Preheat the oven to 400°F. Cut the filo sheets in half. Brush a half sheet with melted butter. Fold one corner of the sheet down to the bottom edge to give a wedge shape.

2 Lay 4 asparagus spears on top at the longest edge, and roll up toward the shortest edge. Using the remaining filo and asparagus spears, make three more rolls in the same way.

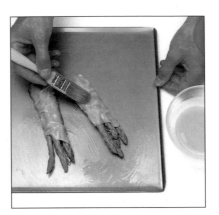

3 Lay the rolls on a greased baking sheet. Brush with the remaining melted butter. Bake in the oven for 8 minutes until golden.

4 Meanwhile, put the shallots, bay leaf and wine into a pan. Cover, and cook over a high heat until the wine is reduced to 3–4 tbsp.

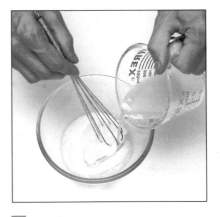

5 Strain the wine mixture into a bowl. Whisk in the butter, a little at a time, until the sauce is smooth and glossy.

6 Stir in the herbs, and add salt and pepper to taste. Return to the pan, and keep the sauce warm. Serve the rolls on individual plates with a salad garnish, if desired. Serve the sauce separately, sprinkled with a few chopped chives.

Deep-fried Zucchini with Chili Sauce

Crunchy coated zucchini are great served with a fiery tomato sauce.

Serves 2

INGREDIENTS
1 tbsp olive oil
1 onion, finely chopped
1 red chili, seeded and finely diced
2 tsp hot chili powder
14 oz can chopped tomatoes
1 vegetable bouillon cube
$1/4$ cup hot water
1 lb zucchini
$2/3$ cup milk
$1/2$ cup all-purpose flour
oil for deep-frying
salt and freshly ground black pepper

TO SERVE
lettuce leaves
watercress sprigs
slices of seeded bread
thyme sprigs, to garnish

zucchini

chopped tomatoes

onion

red chili

all-purpose flour

bouillon cube

milk

chili powder

1 Heat the oil in a pan. Add the onion, and cook for 2–3 minutes. Add the chili. Stir in the chili powder, and cook for 30 seconds.

2 Add the tomatoes. Crumble in the bouillon cube, and stir in the water. Cover and cook for 10 minutes.

3 Meanwhile, remove the ends from the zucchini. Cut them into $1/4$ in slices.

4 Pour the milk into one shallow dish, and spread out the flour in another. Dip the zucchini first in the milk, then into the flour, until well-coated.

5 Heat the oil for deep-frying to 350°F or until a cube of bread, when added to the oil, browns in 30–45 seconds. Add the zucchini slices in batches, and deep-fry for 3–4 minutes until crisp. Drain on paper towels.

6 Place two or three lettuce leaves on each serving plate. Add a few sprigs of watercress, and fan out the bread slices to one side. Season the sauce, spoon some on to each plate, top with the zucchini and garnish with the sprigs of thyme. Serve at once with a crisp salad and bread.

Stir-fried Spinach with Garlic and Sesame Seeds

The sesame seeds add a crunchy texture which contrasts well with the wilted spinach in this easy vegetable dish.

Serves 2

INGREDIENTS
8 oz fresh spinach, washed
1½ tbsp sesame seeds
2 tbsp peanut oil
¼ tsp sea salt flakes
2–3 garlic cloves, sliced

spinach

peanut oil

garlic

sesame seeds

1 Shake the spinach to get rid of any excess water, then remove the stalks and discard any yellow or damaged leaves. Lay several spinach leaves one on top of another, roll up tightly and cut crossways into wide strips. Repeat with the remaining leaves.

COOK'S TIP
Take care when adding the spinach to the hot oil, as it will spit furiously.

2 Heat a wok to medium heat, add the sesame seeds and dry-fry, stirring, for 1–2 minutes, until golden brown. Transfer to a small bowl and set aside.

3 Add the oil to the wok and swirl it around. When hot, add the salt, spinach and garlic and stir-fry for 2 minutes until the spinach just wilts and the leaves are coated with the oil.

4 Sprinkle over the sesame seeds and toss well. Serve at once.

Spiced Coconut Mushrooms

Here is a simple and delicious way to cook mushrooms. They may be served alongside almost any Asian meal, such as stir-fried chicken or pork.

Serves 3-4

INGREDIENTS

2 tbsp peanut oil
2 garlic cloves, finely chopped
2 fresh red chilies, seeded and sliced into rings
3 shallots, finely chopped
225 g/8 oz crimini or button mushrooms, thickly sliced
⅔ cup coconut milk
2 tbsp fresh cilantro, finely chopped
salt and ground black pepper

red chilies

coconut milk

mushrooms

peanut oil

cilantro

garlic

VARIATION
Use chopped fresh chives instead of cilantro if you wish.

1 Heat a wok until hot, add the oil and swirl it around. Add the garlic and chilies, then stir-fry for a few seconds.

2 Add the shallots and stir-fry for 2–3 minutes, until softened. Add the mushrooms and stir-fry for 3 minutes.

3 Pour in the coconut milk and bring to a boil. Boil rapidly over high heat until the liquid is reduced by half and coats the mushrooms. Taste and adjust the seasoning, if necessary.

4 Sprinkle over the cilantro and toss gently to mix. Serve at once.

Masala Okra

Okra, or "ladies' fingers" are a popular Indian vegetable. In this recipe they are stir-fried with a dry, spicy masala to make a delicious side dish.

Serves 4

INGREDIENTS
1 pound okra
½ teaspoon ground turmeric
1 teaspoon cayenne pepper
1 tablespoon ground cumin
1 tablespoon ground coriander
¼ teaspoon salt
¼ teaspoon sugar
1 tablespoon lemon juice
1 tablespoon dried coconut
2 tablespoons chopped cilantro
3 tablespoons oil
½ teaspoon cumin seeds
½ teaspoon black mustard seeds
chopped fresh tomatoes, to garnish
poppadums, to serve

black mustard seeds   lemon juice   ground coriander   cumin seeds

ground cumin

cayenne pepper

sugar

ground turmeric   okra

dried coconut

salt   cilantro

COOK'S TIP
When buying okra, choose firm, brightly colored, unblemished pods that are less than 4 inches long.

1 Wash, dry and trim the okra. In a bowl, mix together the turmeric, cayenne pepper, cumin, ground coriander, salt, sugar, lemon juice, dried coconut and the cilantro.

2 Heat the oil in a large frying pan. Add the cumin seeds and mustard seeds and fry for about 2 minutes, or until they begin to sputter.

3 Add the spice mixture and continue to fry for 2 minutes.

4 Add the okra, cover, and cook over low heat for 10 minutes, or until tender. Garnish with chopped fresh tomatoes and serve with poppadums.

Beet and Celeriac Gratin

Beautiful ruby-red slices of beets and celeriac make a stunning light accompaniment to any main course dish.

Serves 6

INGREDIENTS
12 oz raw beets
12 oz celeriac
4 thyme sprigs
6 juniper berries, crushed
salt and freshly ground black pepper
½ cup fresh orange juice
½ cup vegetable stock

celeriac

orange juice

juniper berries

beet

thyme

1 Preheat the oven to 375°F. Scrub, peel and slice the beets very finely. Scrub, quarter and peel the celeriac and slice very finely.

2 Fill a 10 in diameter, cast iron, ovenproof or flameproof frying pan with alternate layers of beet and celeriac slices, sprinkling with the thyme, juniper and seasoning between each layer.

3 Mix the orange juice and stock together and pour over the gratin. Place over a medium heat and bring to a boil. Boil for 2 minutes.

4 Cover with foil and place in the oven for 15–20 minutes. Remove the foil and raise the oven temperature to 400°F. Cook for a further 10 minutes until tender and bubbling.

Red Cabbage in Port and Red Wine

A sweet and sour, spicy red cabbage dish, with the added crunch of pears and walnuts.

Serves 6

INGREDIENTS
1 tbsp walnut oil
1 onion, sliced
2 whole star anise
1 tsp ground cinnamon
pinch of ground cloves
1 lb red cabbage, finely shredded
2 tbsp dark brown sugar
3 tbsp red wine vinegar
1¼ cups red wine
⅔ cup port
2 pears, cut into ½ in cubes
½ cup raisins
salt and freshly ground black pepper
½ cup walnut halves

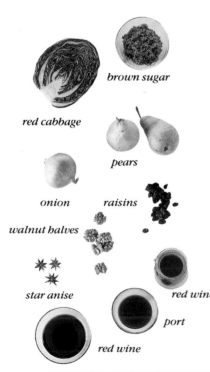

red cabbage

brown sugar

pears

onion

raisins

walnut halves

star anise

red wine vinegar

port

red wine

1 Heat the oil in a large pan. Add the onion and cook gently for about 5 minutes until softened.

2 Add the star anise, cinnamon, cloves and cabbage and cook for about 3 minutes more.

3 Stir in the sugar, vinegar, red wine and port. Cover the pan and simmer gently for 10 minutes, stirring occasionally.

4 Stir in the cubed pears and raisins and cook for a further 10 minutes or until the cabbage is tender. Season to taste. Mix in the walnut halves and serve.

Chinese Greens with Oyster Sauce

Here Chinese greens are prepared in a very simple way – stir-fried and served with oyster sauce. The combination makes a simple, quickly prepared, tasty accompaniment.

Serves 3-4

INGREDIENTS
1 lb Chinese greens
  (*bok choy*)
2 tbsp peanut oil
1-2 tbsp oyster sauce

Chinese greens

peanut oil

oyster sauce

VARIATION
You can replace the Chinese greens with Chinese flowering cabbage, or Chinese broccoli, which is also known by its Cantonese name *choi sam*. It has green leaves and tiny yellow flowers, which are also eaten along with the leaves and stalks. It is available at Asian markets.

1 Trim the Chinese greens, removing any discolored leaves and damaged stems. Tear into manageable pieces.

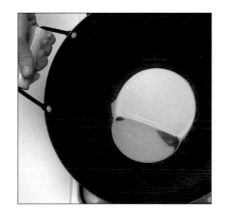

2 Heat a wok until hot, add the oil and swirl it around.

3 Add the Chinese greens and stir-fry for 2–3 minutes, until the greens have wilted a little.

4 Add the oyster sauce and continue to stir-fry a few seconds more until the greens are cooked but still slightly crisp. Serve immediately.

SNAPPY
SALADS

The sort of salad that used to be served as a **speedy** meal was often dreary in the extreme—a few lettuce leaves, some limp slices of cucumber and a wedge or two of tomato. Today's cooks are more **creative**, thanks to supermarkets and farm stands that stock a **superb** selection of salad greens and **fresh** young vegetables. The secret is in the assembly: a great salad first caresses the senses with its **good** looks, then satisfies the taste buds with its fabulous flavors. **Classic** combinations featured here include Arugula, Pear, and Parmesan Salad, and Tomato and Feta Cheese Salad.

Zucchini Puffs with Salad and Balsamic Dressing

This unusual salad consists of deep-fried zucchini, flavored with mint, and served warm on a bed of salad leaves with a balsamic dressing.

Serves 2

INGREDIENTS
1 lb zucchini
1½ cups fresh white bread crumbs
1 egg
pinch of cayenne pepper
1 tbsp chopped fresh mint
oil for deep-frying
3 tbsp balsamic vinegar
3 tbsp extra virgin olive oil
7 oz mixed salad leaves
salt and freshly ground black pepper

zucchini

white bread crumbs

balsamic vinegar

mixed salad leaves

egg

mint

1 Remove the ends from the zucchini. Coarsely grate them, and put into a colander. Squeeze out the excess water. Then put the zucchini into a bowl.

2 Add the bread crumbs, egg, cayenne, mint and seasoning. Mix well.

3 Shape the zucchini mixture into balls, about the size of walnuts.

4 Heat the oil for deep-frying to 350°F or until a cube of bread, when added to the oil, browns in 30–40 seconds. Deep-fry the zucchini balls in batches for 2–3 minutes. Drain on paper towels.

5 Whisk the vinegar and oil together, and season well.

6 Put the salad leaves in a bowl, and pour over the dressing. Add the zucchini puffs, and toss lightly together. Serve at once, while the puffs are still crisp.

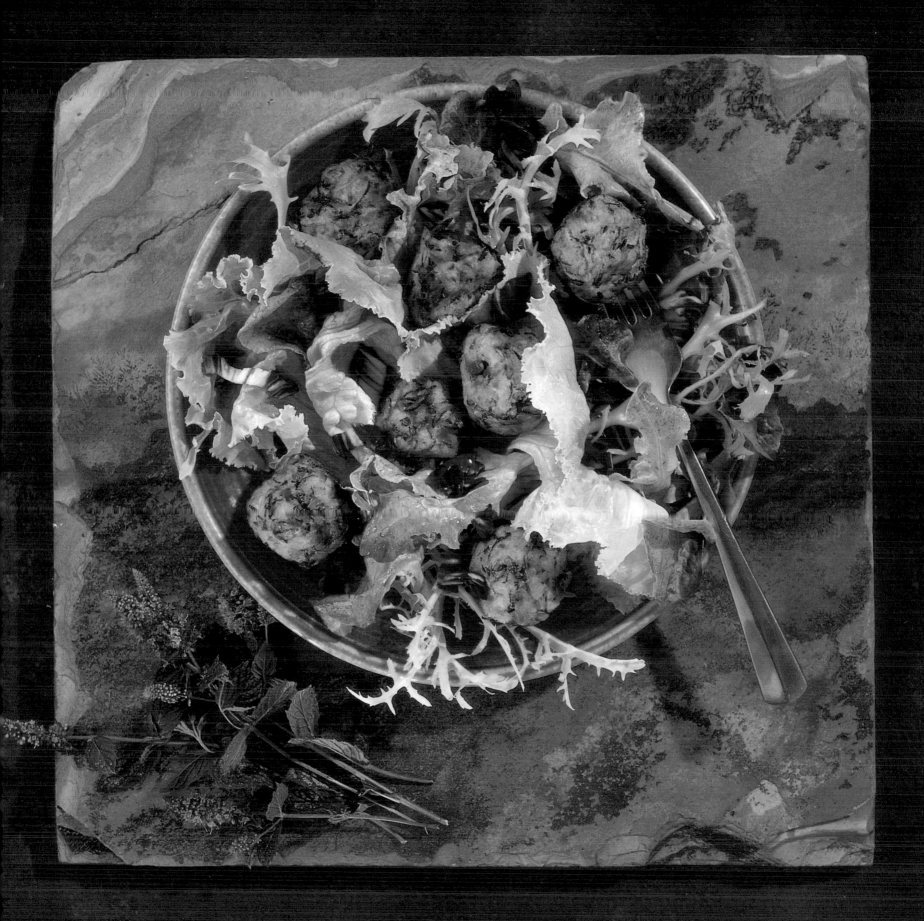

Arugula, Pear, and Parmesan Salad

For a sophisticated start to an elaborate meal, try this simple salad of honey-rich pears, fresh Parmesan, and aromatic leaves of arugula. Enjoy with a young Beaujolais or chilled Lambrusco wine.

Serves 4

INGREDIENTS
3 ripe pears, Williams or Packhams
2 tsp lemon juice
3 tbsp hazelnut or walnut oil
4 oz arugula
3 oz Parmesan cheese
black pepper
open-textured bread, to serve

arugula

Parmesan cheese

pears

1 Peel and core the pears and slice thickly. Toss with lemon juice to keep the flesh white.

2 Combine the nut oil with the pears. Add the arugula leaves and toss.

3 Transfer the salad to 4 small plates and top with shavings of Parmesan cheese. Season with freshly ground black pepper and serve.

COOK'S TIP
If you are unable to buy arugula easily, you can grow your own from early spring to late summer.

New Spring Salad

This chunky salad makes a satisfying meal. Use other spring vegetables, if you like.

Serves 4

INGREDIENTS

1½ lb small new potatoes, halved
14 oz can fava beans, drained
4 oz cherry tomatoes
½ cup walnut halves
2 tbsp white wine vinegar
1 tbsp whole-grain mustard
4 tbsp olive oil
pinch of sugar
8 oz young asparagus spears, trimmed
6 scallions, trimmed
salt and freshly ground black pepper
baby spinach leaves, to serve

asparagus spears

whole-grain mustard

fava beans

new potatoes

cherry tomatoes

scallions

walnut halves

1 Put the potatoes in a pan. Cover with cold water, and bring to a boil. Cook for 10–12 minutes, until tender. Meanwhile, turn the fava beans into a bowl. Cut the tomatoes in half, and add them to the bowl with the walnuts.

2 Put the white wine vinegar, mustard, olive oil and sugar into a jar. Add salt and pepper to taste. Close the jar tightly, and shake well.

3 Add the asparagus to the potatoes, and cook for 3 minutes more. Drain the cooked vegetables well. Cool under cold running water, and drain again. Thickly slice the potatoes, and cut the scallions into halves.

4 Add the asparagus, potatoes and scallions to the bowl containing the fava bean mixture. Pour the dressing over the salad, and toss well. Serve on a bed of baby spinach leaves.

Fresh Spinach and Avocado Salad

Young, tender spinach leaves make a change from lettuce and are delicious served with avocado, cherry tomatoes and radishes in a tofu sauce.

Serves 2–3

INGREDIENTS
1 large avocado
juice of 1 lime
8 oz fresh baby spinach leaves
4 oz cherry tomatoes
4 scallions, sliced
½ cucumber
2 oz radishes, sliced

FOR THE DRESSING
4 oz soft silken tofu
3 tbsp milk
2 tsp prepared mustard
½ tsp white wine vinegar
pinch of cayenne
salt and freshly ground black pepper

tofu   scallions

spinach leaves

cherry tomatoes

avocado

white wine vinegar

mustard

lime

cayenne

cucumber

radishes

milk

1 Cut the avocado in half, remove the pit, and strip off the skin. Cut the flesh into slices. Transfer to a plate, drizzle over the lime juice, and set aside.

2 Wash and dry the spinach leaves. Put them in a mixing bowl.

COOK'S TIP
Use soft silken tofu rather than the block variety. It can be found in most supermarkets in the vegetable or refrigerated sections.

3 Cut the larger cherry tomatoes in half, and add all the tomatoes to the mixing bowl, with the scallions. Cut the cucumber into chunks, and add to the bowl with the sliced radishes.

4 Make the dressing. Put the tofu, milk, mustard, wine vinegar and cayenne in a food processor or blender. Add salt and pepper to taste. Process for 30 seconds until smooth. Scrape the dressing into a bowl, and add a little extra milk if you like a thinner dressing. Sprinkle with a little extra cayenne, and garnish with radish roses and herb sprigs, if desired.

Roquefort and Walnut Pasta Salad

This is a simple earthy salad, relying totally on the quality of the ingredients. There is no real substitute for the Roquefort – a blue-veined ewe's-milk cheese from southwestern France.

Serves 4

INGREDIENTS

½ lb pasta shapes
selection of salad leaves (such as arugula, frisée, lamb's lettuce, baby spinach, radicchio, etc.)
2 tbsp walnut oil
4 tbsp sunflower oil
2 tbsp red-wine vinegar or sherry vinegar
salt and pepper
½ lb Roquefort cheese, roughly crumbled
1 cup walnut halves

pasta shapes

Roquefort cheese   *walnuts*

salad leaves

COOK'S TIP
Try toasting the walnuts under the broiler for a couple of minutes to release the flavor.

1 Cook the pasta in plenty of boiling salted water according to the manufacturer's instructions. Drain well and cool. Wash and dry the salad leaves and place in a bowl.

2 Whisk together the walnut oil, sunflower oil, vinegar, and salt and pepper to taste.

3 Pile the pasta in the center of the leaves, scatter over the crumbled Roquefort, and pour over the dressing.

4 Scatter over the walnuts. Toss just before serving.

Belgian Endive, Fruit and Nut Salad

Mildly bitter endive is wonderful with sweet fruit, and is especially delicious when complemented by a creamy curry sauce.

Serves 4

INGREDIENTS
3 tbsp mayonnaise
1 tbsp strained, plain yogurt
1 tbsp mild curry paste
6 tbsp light cream
$^1/_2$ iceberg lettuce
2 heads of Belgian endive
$^1/_2$ cup cashews
$1^1/_4$ cups flaked coconut
2 red apples
$^1/_2$ cup currants

currants

iceberg lettuce

curry paste   *mayonnaise*

cashews

red apples

light cream   *flaked coconut*

Belgian endive

1 Mix the mayonnaise, yogurt, curry paste and light cream in a small bowl. Cover, and chill until required.

2 Tear the iceberg lettuce into pieces, and put into a salad bowl.

3 Cut the root end off each head of Belgian endive, and discard. Slice the endive, and add it to the salad bowl.

4 Preheat the broiler. Toast the cashews for 2 minutes until they are golden. Turn into a bowl, and set aside. Spread out the coconut flakes on a baking sheet. Broil for 1 minute.

5 Quarter the apples, and cut out the cores. Slice the apples, and add to the lettuce with the cashews, flaked coconut, and currants.

COOK'S TIP
Watch the coconut and cashews very carefully when broiling, as they brown very fast.

6 Spoon the dressing over the salad. Toss lightly, and serve.

Avocado, Tomato, and Mozzarella Pasta Salad with Pine Nuts

A salad made from ingredients representing the colors of the Italian flag – a sunny cheerful dish!

Serves 4

INGREDIENTS
1½ cups pasta bows (farfalle)
6 ripe red tomatoes
½ lb mozzarella cheese
1 large ripe avocado
2 tbsp pine nuts, toasted
1 sprig fresh basil, to garnish

DRESSING
6 tbsp olive oil
2 tbsp wine vinegar
1 tsp balsamic vinegar (optional)
1 tsp whole-grain mustard
pinch of sugar
salt and pepper
2 tbsp chopped fresh basil

olive oil

avocado

tomatoes

basil

mozzarella cheese

pine nuts   *pasta bows*

1 Cook the pasta in plenty of boiling salted water according to the manufacturer's instructions. Drain well and cool.

4 Whisk all the dressing ingredients together in a small bowl.

2 Slice the tomatoes and mozzarella cheese into thin rounds.

5 Arrange the tomato, mozzarella, and avocado in overlapping slices around the edge of a flat plate.

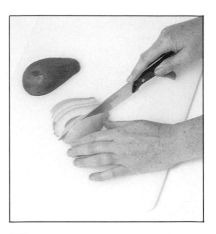

3 Halve the avocado, remove the pit, and peel off the skin. Slice the flesh lengthwise.

6 Toss the pasta with half the dressing and the chopped basil. Pile into the center of the plate. Pour over the remaining dressing, scatter over the pine nuts, and garnish with a sprig of fresh basil. Serve immediately.

Tomato and Feta Cheese Salad

Sweet sun-ripened tomatoes are rarely more delicious than when served with feta cheese and olive oil. This salad, popular in Greece and Turkey, is enjoyed as a light meal with pieces of crispy bread.

Serves 4

INGREDIENTS
2 lb tomatoes
7 oz feta cheese
½ cup olive oil, preferably Greek
12 black olives
4 sprigs fresh basil
black pepper

COOK'S TIP

Feta cheese has a strong flavor and can be salty. The least salty variety is imported from Greece and Turkey, and is available from specialty or gourmet stores.

tomatoes

basil

feta cheese

olives

1 Remove the tough cores from the tomatoes with a small knife.

2 Slice the tomatoes thickly and arrange in a shallow dish.

3 Crumble the cheese over the tomatoes, sprinkle with olive oil, then sprinkle over the olives and fresh basil. Season with freshly ground black pepper and serve at room temperature.

Potato Salad with Egg and Lemon Dressing

Potato salads are a popular addition to any salad spread and are enjoyed with an assortment of cold meats and fish. This recipe draws on the contrasting flavors of egg and lemon. Chopped parsley provides a fresh finish.

Serves 4

INGREDIENTS
2 lb new potatoes, scrubbed or
  scraped
salt and pepper
1 medium onion, finely chopped
1 egg, hard-cooked
1¼ cups mayonnaise
1 clove garlic, crushed
finely grated zest and juice of 1 lemon
4 tbsp chopped fresh parsley

COOK'S TIP

At certain times of the year potatoes are inclined to fall apart when boiled. This usually coincides with the end of a particular season when potatoes become starchy. Early-season varieties are therefore best for making salads.

egg

garlic

onion

lemon

new potatoes

1 Bring the potatoes to a boil in a saucepan of salted water. Simmer for 20 minutes. Drain and allow to cool. Cut the potatoes into large dice, season well, and combine with the onion.

2 Shell the hard-cooked egg and grate into a mixing bowl, then add the mayonnaise. Combine the garlic and lemon zest and juice in a small bowl and stir into the mayonnaise.

3 Fold in the chopped parsley, mix thoroughly into the potatoes, and serve.

Broiled Bell Pepper Salad

Broiled bell peppers are delicious served hot
with a sharp dressing. You can also eat them cold.

Serves 2

INGREDIENTS
1 red bell pepper
1 green bell pepper
1 yellow or orange bell pepper
½ radicchio, separated into leaves
½ frisée, separated into leaves
1½ tsp white wine vinegar
2 tbsp extra virgin olive oil
6 oz goat cheese
salt and freshly ground black pepper

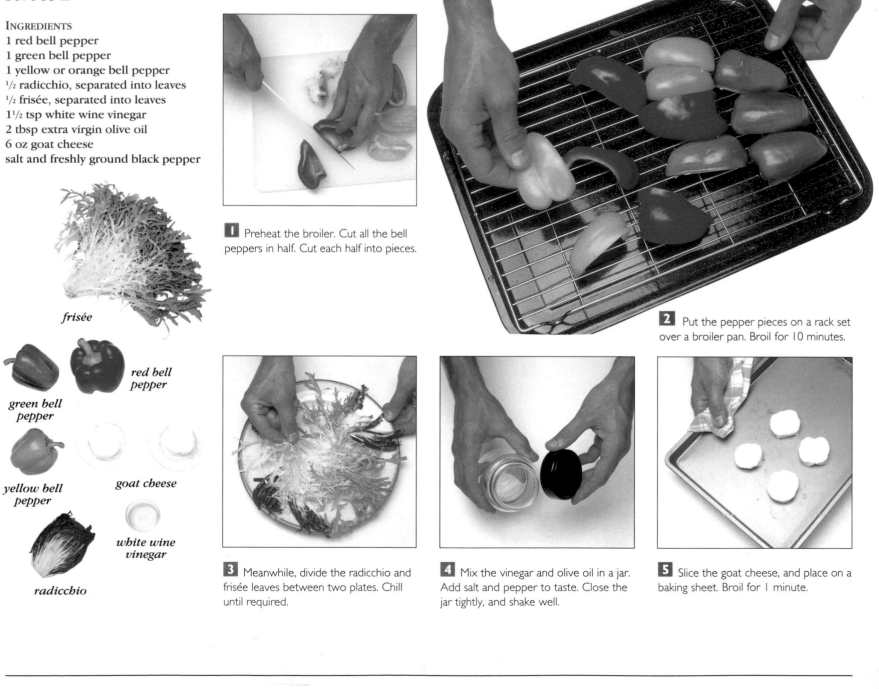

frisée

green bell pepper

red bell pepper

yellow bell pepper

goat cheese

white wine vinegar

radicchio

1 Preheat the broiler. Cut all the bell peppers in half. Cut each half into pieces.

2 Put the pepper pieces on a rack set over a broiler pan. Broil for 10 minutes.

3 Meanwhile, divide the radicchio and frisée leaves between two plates. Chill until required.

4 Mix the vinegar and olive oil in a jar. Add salt and pepper to taste. Close the jar tightly, and shake well.

5 Slice the goat cheese, and place on a baking sheet. Broil for 1 minute.

6 Arrange the peppers and broiled goat cheese on the salads. Pour over the dressing, and grind a little extra black pepper over each.

COOK'S TIP
Broil the bell peppers until they just start to blacken around the edges – don't let them burn.

Parmesan and Poached Egg Salad with Croûtons

Soft poached eggs, hot garlic croûtons and cool, crisp salad leaves make an unforgettable combination.

Serves 2

INGREDIENTS
1/2 small loaf white bread
5 tbsp extra virgin olive oil
2 eggs
4 oz mixed salad leaves
2 garlic cloves, crushed
1/2 tbsp white wine vinegar
1 oz Parmesan cheese

Parmesan cheese

mixed salad leaves

white bread

garlic cloves

eggs

1 Remove the crust from the bread. Cut the bread into 1 in cubes.

2 Heat 2 tbsp of the oil in a frying pan. Cook the bread for about 5 minutes, tossing the cubes occasionally, until they are golden brown.

3 Meanwhile, bring a pan of water to a boil. Carefully slide in the eggs, one at a time. Gently poach the eggs for 4 minutes until lightly cooked.

4 Divide the salad leaves between two plates. Remove the croûtons from the pan, and arrange them over the leaves. Wipe the pan clean with paper towels.

5 Heat the remaining oil in the pan, add the garlic and vinegar, and cook over high heat for 1 minute. Pour the warm dressing over each salad.

COOK'S TIP

Add a dash of vinegar to the water before poaching the eggs. This helps to keep the whites together. To make sure that a poached egg has a good shape, swirl the water with a spoon, whirlpool-fashion, before sliding in the egg.

6 Place a poached egg on each salad. Sprinkle with shavings of Parmesan and freshly ground black pepper, if desired.

Green Lentil and Cabbage Salad

This warm crunchy salad makes a satisfying meal if served with crusty French bread or wholemeal rolls.

Serves 4–6

INGREDIENTS
1 cup green lentils
6 cups cold water
1 garlic clove
1 bay leaf
1 small onion, peeled and studded
   with 2 cloves
1 tbsp olive oil
1 red onion, finely sliced
2 garlic cloves, crushed
1 tbsp thyme leaves
12 oz cabbage, finely shredded
finely grated rind and juice of 1 lemon
1 tbsp raspberry vinegar
salt and freshly ground black pepper

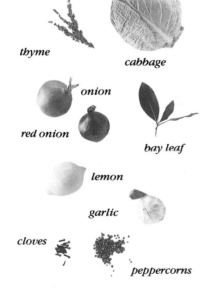

thyme

cabbage

onion

red onion

bay leaf

lemon

garlic

cloves

peppercorns

1 Rinse the lentils in cold water and place in a large pan with the water, peeled garlic clove, bay leaf and clove-studded onion. Bring to a boil and cook for 10 minutes. Reduce the heat, cover the pan and simmer gently for 15–20 minutes. Drain and remove the onion, garlic and bay leaf.

2 Heat the oil in a large pan. Add the red onion, garlic and thyme and cook for 5 minutes until softened.

3 Add the cabbage and cook for 3–5 minutes until just cooked but still crunchy.

4 Stir in the cooked lentils, lemon rind and juice and the raspberry vinegar. Season to taste and serve.

Whole-wheat Pasta, Asparagus, and Potato Salad with Parmesan

A meal in itself, this is a real treat when made with fresh asparagus just in season.

Serves 4

INGREDIENTS
½ lb whole-wheat pasta shapes
4 tbsp extra-virgin olive oil
salt and pepper
12 oz baby new potatoes
½ lb fresh asparagus
¼ lb piece fresh Parmesan cheese

olive oil

asparagus

pasta shapes

Parmesan cheese

new potatoes

1 Cook the pasta in boiling salted water according to the manufacturer's instructions. Drain well and toss with the olive oil, salt, and pepper while still warm.

2 Wash the potatoes and cook in boiling salted water for 12–15 minutes or until tender. Drain and toss with the pasta.

3 Trim any woody ends off the asparagus and halve the stalks if very long. Blanch in boiling salted water for 6 minutes until bright green and still crunchy. Drain. Plunge into cold water to stop them cooking and allow to cool. Drain and dry on paper towels.

4 Toss the asparagus with the potatoes and pasta, season, and transfer to a shallow bowl. Using a rotary vegetable peeler, shave the Parmesan cheese over the salad.

Caesar Salad

There are many stories about the origin of Caesar Salad. The most likely is that it was invented by an Italian, Caesar Cardini, who owned a restaurant in Mexico in the 1920s. Simplicity is the key to its success.

Serves 4

INGREDIENTS
3 slices day-old bread, ½ in thick
4 tbsp garlic oil
salt and pepper
2 oz piece Parmesan cheese
1 romaine lettuce

DRESSING
2 egg yolks, as fresh as possible
1 oz canned anchovies, roughly
    chopped
½ tsp Dijon mustard
½ cup olive oil, preferably Italian
1 tbsp white-wine vinegar

COOK'S TIP
The classic dressing for Caesar Salad is made with raw egg yolks. Ensure you use only the freshest eggs, bought from a reputable dealer. Expectant mothers, young children and the elderly are not advised to eat raw egg yolks. You could omit them from the dressing and grate hard-cooked yolks on top of the salad instead.

1 To make the dressing, combine the egg yolks, anchovies, mustard, oil, and vinegar in a screw-top jar and shake well.

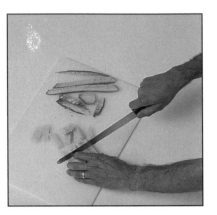

2 Remove the crusts from the bread with a serrated knife and cut into 1 in fingers.

3 Heat the garlic oil in a large skillet, add the pieces of bread, and fry until golden. Sprinkle with salt and leave to drain on paper towels.

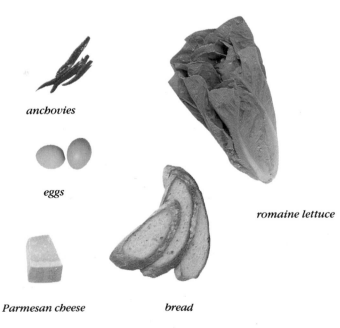

anchovies

eggs

romaine lettuce

Parmesan cheese *bread*

4 Cut thin shavings from the Parmesan cheese with a vegetable peeler.

5 Wash the salad leaves and spin dry. Smother with the dressing, and scatter with garlic croutons and Parmesan cheese. Season and serve.

Mediterranean Salad with Basil

A type of Salade Niçoise with pasta, conjuring up all the sunny flavors of the Mediterranean.

Serves 4

INGREDIENTS
½ lb chunky pasta shapes
6 oz fine green beans
2 large ripe tomatoes
2 oz fresh basil leaves
7 oz can tuna fish in oil, drained
2 hard-cooked eggs, shelled and sliced
   or quartered
2 oz can anchovies, drained
capers and black olives

DRESSING
6 tbsp extra-virgin olive oil
2 tbsp white-wine vinegar or lemon
   juice
2 garlic cloves, crushed
½ tsp Dijon mustard
2 tbsp chopped fresh basil
salt and pepper

tomatoes

olive oil

garlic

basil

pasta

egg

anchovies

green beans

tuna fish

1 Whisk all the ingredients for the dressing together and leave to infuse while you make the salad.

2 Cook the pasta in plenty of boiling salted water according to the manufacturer's instructions. Drain well and cool.

3 Trim the beans and blanch in boiling salted water for 3 minutes. Drain and refresh in cold water.

4 Slice or quarter the tomatoes and arrange on the bottom of a bowl. Toss with a little dressing and cover with a quarter of the basil leaves. Then cover with the beans. Toss with a little more dressing and cover with a third of the remaining basil.

5 Cover with the pasta tossed in a little more dressing, half the remaining basil and the roughly flaked tuna.

6 Arrange the eggs on top, then finally scatter over the anchovies, capers and black olives. Pour over the remaining dressing and garnish with the remaining basil. Serve immediately. Don't be tempted to chill this salad – all the flavor will be dulled.

Shrimp and Mint Salad

Shrimp make all the difference to this salad, as the flavors marinate well into the shrimp before cooking. Garnish with shavings of fresh coconut for a tropical topping.

Serves 4

INGREDIENTS
12 large shrimp
1 tbsp unsalted butter
1 tbsp fish sauce
juice of 1 lime
3 tbsp thin coconut milk
1 tsp sugar
1 garlic clove, crushed
1 in piece of ginger root, peeled and grated
2 fresh red chilies, seeded and finely chopped
freshly ground black pepper
2 tbsp fresh mint leaves
½ head light green lettuce leaves, to serve

lime

red chili

shrimp

fish sauce

coconut milk

mint

ginger

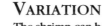
lettuce

1 Peel the shrimp leaving the tails intact.

2 Remove the vein.

3 Melt the butter in a large frying pan and toss in the shrimp until they turn pink.

4 Mix the fish sauce, lime juice, coconut milk, sugar, garlic, ginger, chilies and pepper together.

5 Toss the warm shrimp into the sauce with the mint leaves. Serve the shrimp mixture on a bed of green lettuce leaves.

VARIATION
The shrimp can be substituted with lobster tails if you are feeling extravagant.

Tuna Fish and Flageolet Bean Salad

Two cans of tuna fish form the basis of this delicious store cupboard salad.

Serves 4

INGREDIENTS
6 tbsp mayonnaise
1 tsp mustard
2 tbsp capers
3 tbsp chopped fresh parsley
pinch of celery salt
2 × 7 oz cans tuna fish in oil, drained
3 Bibb lettuces
1 × 14 oz can flageolet beans, drained
1 × 14 oz can baby artichoke hearts, halved
12 cherry tomatoes, halved
toasted sesame bread, to serve

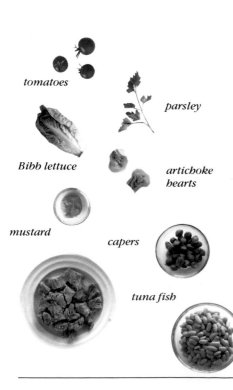

tomatoes

parsley

Bibb lettuce

artichoke hearts

mustard

capers

tuna fish

flageolet beans

1 Combine the mayonnaise, mustard, capers and parsley in a mixing bowl. Season to taste with celery salt. Flake the tuna into the dressing and toss gently.

2 Arrange the lettuce leaves on four plates, then spoon the tuna mixture onto the leaves.

3 Spoon the flageolet beans to one side, followed by the tomatoes and artichoke hearts. Serve with slices of toasted sesame bread.

VARIATION

Flageolet beans are taken from the under-developed pods of navy beans. They have a sweet creamy flavor and an attractive green color. If not available, use cannellini beans.

Thai Seafood Salad

This seafood salad with chili, lemongrass and fish sauce is light and refreshing.

Serves 4

INGREDIENTS
8 oz cleaned squid
8 oz raw large shrimp
8 sea scallops, whole
8 oz firm white fish
2–3 tbsp olive oil
small mixed lettuce leaves and
   cilantro sprigs, to serve

FOR THE DRESSING
2 small fresh red chilies, seeded
   and finely chopped
2-in piece lemongrass,
   finely chopped
2 fresh kaffir lime leaves,
   shredded
2 tbsp Thai fish sauce
   (*nam pla*)
2 shallots, thinly sliced
2 tbsp lime juice
2 tbsp rice vinegar
2 tsp sugar

white fish   *squid*

large shrimp
scallops
lemongrass

Thai fish sauce

shallots   *kaffir lime leaves*

1 Prepare the seafood: slit open the squid bodies, score the flesh with a sharp knife, then cut into square pieces. Halve the tentacles, if necessary. Peel and devein the shrimp. Cut the sea scallops in half (if using bay scallops, leave whole). Cube the white fish.

2 Heat a wok until hot. Add the oil and swirl it around, then add the shrimp and stir-fry for 2–3 minutes until pink. Transfer to a large bowl. Stir-fry the squid and scallops for 1–2 minutes, until opaque. Remove and add to the shrimp. Stir-fry the white fish for 2–3 minutes. Remove and add to the cooked seafood. Reserve any juices.

3 Put all the dressing ingredients in a small bowl with the reserved juices from the wok; mix well.

4 Pour the dressing over the seafood and toss gently. Arrange the salad leaves and cilantro sprigs on four individual plates, then spoon the seafood on top. Serve at once.

Avocado, Crab, and Cilantro Salad

The sweet richness of crab combines especially well with ripe avocado, fresh cilantro, and tomato.

Serves 4

INGREDIENTS
1½ lb small new potatoes
1 sprig fresh mint
2 lb boiled crabs, or 10 oz frozen
  crabmeat
1 Batavia or Bibb lettuce
6 oz lamb's lettuce or young spinach
1 large ripe avocado, peeled and
  sliced
6 oz cherry tomatoes
salt, pepper and nutmeg

DRESSING
5 tbsp olive oil, preferably Tuscan
1 tbsp lime juice
3 tbsp chopped fresh cilantro
½ tsp superfine sugar

1 Scrape or peel the potatoes. Cover with water, add a good pinch of salt, and a sprig of mint. Bring to a boil and simmer for 20 minutes. Drain, cover, and keep warm until needed.

2 Remove the legs and claws from each crab. Crack these open with the back of a chopping knife and then remove the white meat.

crab

avocado

mint

lamb's lettuce

cherry tomatoes

cilantro

new potatoes

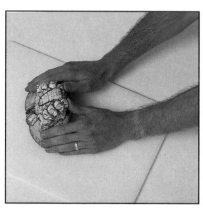

3 Turn the crab on its back and push the rear leg section away with the thumb and forefinger of each hand. Remove the flesh from inside the shell.

4 Discard the soft gills ('dead men's fingers'): the crab uses these gills to filter impurities in its diet. Apart from these and the shell, everything else is edible – white and dark meat.

5 Split the central body section open with a knife and remove the white and dark flesh with a pick or skewer.

COOK'S TIP

Young crabs offer the sweetest meat, but are more difficult to prepare than older, larger ones. The female crab carries more flesh than the male, which is considered to have a better overall flavor. The male crab, shown here, is identified by his narrow apron flap at the rear. The female has a broad flap under which she carries her eggs. Frozen crabmeat is a good alternative to fresh and retains much of its original sweetness.

6 Combine the dressing ingredients in a screw-top jar and shake. Wash and spin the lettuces, then dress them. Distribute between 4 plates. Top with avocado, crab, tomatoes, and warm new potatoes. Season with salt, pepper, and freshly grated nutmeg and serve.

Chicken Liver Salad

This salad may be served as a first course on individual plates.

Serves 4

INGREDIENTS
mixed salad leaves, e.g. frisée and
    oakleaf lettuce or radicchio
1 avocado, diced
2 pink grapefruits, segmented
12 oz trimmed chicken livers
2 tbsp olive oil
1 garlic clove, crushed
salt and freshly ground black pepper
crusty bread, to serve

FOR THE DRESSING
2 tbsp lemon juice
4 tbsp olive oil
½ tsp whole grain mustard
½ tsp honey
1 tbsp snipped fresh chives

chicken livers

grapefruit

olive oil

honey

avocado

mustard

lemon

chives

garlic

salad leaves

1 First prepare the dressing: put all the ingredients into a screw-topped jar and shake vigorously to emulsify. Taste and adjust the seasoning.

2 Wash and dry the salad. Arrange attractively on a serving plate with the avocado and grapefruit.

3 Dry the chicken livers on paper towels and remove any unwanted pieces. Cut the larger livers in half and leave the smaller ones whole.

4 Heat the oil in a large frying pan. Stir-fry the livers and garlic briskly until the livers are brown all over (they should be slightly pink inside).

5 Season with salt and freshly ground black pepper and drain on paper towels.

6 Place the liver on the salad and spoon over the dressing. Serve immediately with warm crusty bread.

Warm Stir-fried Salad

Warm salads are becoming increasingly popular because they are delicious and nutritious. Arrange the salad leaves on four individual plates, so the hot stir-fry can be served quickly on to them, ensuring the lettuce remains crisp and the chicken warm.

Serves 4

INGREDIENTS
1 tbsp fresh tarragon
2 boneless, skinless chicken breasts,
   about 8 oz each
2 in piece ginger root, peeled and
   finely chopped
3 tbsp light soy sauce
1 tbsp sugar
1 tbsp sunflower oil
1 Napa cabbage
½ chicory lettuce, torn into
   bite-size pieces
1 cup unsalted cashews
2 large carrots, peeled and cut into
   fine strips
salt and freshly ground black pepper

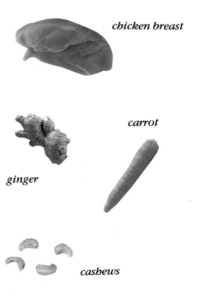

chicken breast

carrot

ginger

cashews

1 Chop the tarragon.

2 Cut the chicken into fine strips and place in a bowl.

3 To make the marinade, mix together in a bowl the tarragon, ginger, soy sauce, sugar and seasoning.

4 Pour the marinade over the chicken strips and leave for a few minutes.

5 Strain the chicken from the marinade. Heat the wok, then add the oil. When the oil is hot, stir-fry the chicken for 3 minutes, add the marinade and bubble for 2–3 minutes.

6 Slice the Napa cabbage and arrange on a plate with the chicory. Toss the cashews and carrots together with the chicken, pile on top of the bed of lettuce and serve immediately.

Chicken and Pasta Salad

This is a delicious way to use up left-over cooked chicken, and makes a filling meal.

Serves 4

INGREDIENTS
8 oz tri-colored pasta twists
2 tbsp bottied pesto sauce
1 tbsp olive oil
1 beefsteak tomato
12 pitted black olives
8 oz cooked green beans
12 oz cooked chicken, cubed
salt and freshly ground black pepper
fresh basil, to garnish

tomato

pesto sauce

green beans

basil

olive oil

pasta twists

chicken

black olives

1 Cook the pasta in plenty of boiling, salted water until *al dente* (for about 12 minutes or as directed on the package).

2 Drain the pasta and rinse in plenty of cold running water. Put into a bowl and stir in the pesto sauce and olive oil.

3 Skin the tomato by placing in boiling water for about 10 seconds and then into cold water, to loosen the skin.

4 Cut the tomato into small cubes and add to the pasta with the black olives, seasoning and green beans cut into 1½ in lengths. Add the cubed chicken. Toss gently together and transfer to a serving platter. Garnish with fresh basil.

Melon and Prosciutto Salad with Strawberry Salsa

Sections of cool fragrant melon wrapped with slices of air-dried ham make a delicious salad starter. If strawberries are in season, serve with a savory-sweet strawberry salsa and watch it disappear.

Serves 4

INGREDIENTS
1 large melon, cantaloupe, Spanish or
   charentais
6 oz prosciutto, thinly sliced

SALSA
½ lb strawberries
1 tsp superfine sugar
2 tbsp peanut or sunflower oil
1 tbsp orange juice
½ tsp finely grated orange zest
½ tsp finely grated fresh ginger
salt and black pepper

2 To make the salsa, hull the strawberries and cut them into large dice. Place in a small mixing bowl with the sugar and crush lightly to release the juices. Add the oil, orange juice, zest, and ginger. Season with salt and a generous twist of black pepper.

3 Arrange the melon on a serving plate, lay the ham over the top, and serve with a bowl of salsa.

1 Halve the melon and take the seeds out with a spoon. Cut the rind away with a paring knife, then slice the melon thickly. Chill until ready to serve.

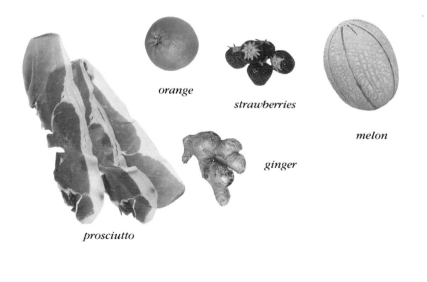

orange

strawberries

melon

ginger

prosciutto

Sweet Potato, Egg, Pork, and Beet Salad

A delicious way to use up leftover pork roast. Sweet flavors balance well with the bitterness of the salad leaves.

Serves 4

INGREDIENTS
2 lb sweet potato, peeled and diced
salt
4 heads Belgian endive
5 eggs, hard-cooked
1 lb pickled young beets
6 oz cold pork roast, sliced

DRESSING
5 tbsp peanut or sunflower oil
2 tbsp white-wine vinegar
2 tsp Dijon mustard
1 tsp fennel seeds, crushed

pork

sweet potato

eggs

beet

Belgian endive

1 Bring the sweet potato to a boil in salted water and cook for 10–15 minutes or until soft. Drain and allow to cool.

2 To make the dressing, combine the oil, vinegar, mustard, and fennel seeds in a screw-top jar and shake.

3 Separate the Belgian endive leaves and arrange around the edge of 4 serving plates.

4 Dress the sweet potato and spoon over the salad leaves.

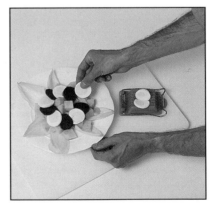

5 Shell the hard-cooked eggs. Slice the eggs and beets, and arrange to make an attractive border.

6 Cut the pork into 1½ in fingers, toss with dressing, and pile into the center. Season and serve.

Sesame Noodle Salad with Hot Peanuts

An orient-inspired salad with crunchy vegetables and a light soy dressing. The hot peanuts make a surprisingly successful union with the cold noodles.

Serves 4

INGREDIENTS
12 oz egg noodles
2 carrots, peeled and cut into fine
    julienne strips
½ cucumber, peeled and cut into
    ½ in cubes
4 oz celeriac, peeled and cut into fine
    julienne strips
6 scallions, finely sliced
8 canned water chestnuts, drained
    and finely sliced
6 oz beansprouts
1 small fresh green chilli, seeded and
    finely chopped
2 tbsp sesame seeds, to serve
1 cup peanuts, to serve

FOR THE DRESSING
1 tbsp dark soy sauce
1 tbsp light soy sauce
1 tbsp honey
1 tbsp rice wine or dry sherry
1 tbsp sesame oil

1 Preheat the oven to 400°F. Cook the egg noodles in boiling water, following the instructions on the side of the package.

2 Drain the noodles, refresh in cold water, then drain again.

3 Mix the noodles with all of the prepared vegetables.

4 Combine the dressing ingredients in a small bowl, then toss into the noodle and vegetable mixture. Divide the salad between 4 plates.

celeriac

beansprouts

green chilli

scallion

sesame seeds

water chestnuts

cucumber

peanuts

carrot

noodles

5 Place the sesame seeds and peanuts on separate cookie sheets and place in the oven. Take the sesame seeds out after 5 minutes and continue to cook the peanuts for a further 5 minutes until evenly browned.

6 Sprinkle the sesame seeds and peanuts evenly over each portion and serve at once.

Pasta is the **perfect** ingredient when it comes to serving food speedily. Fresh tagliatelle and linguine are **ready** as soon as they rise to the surface of the boiling water, and some Asian noodles **cook** even more **quickly.** Dried pasta takes only a little

longer, especially if you choose small shapes or the varieties made for soup. Sauces range from the **simple**—garlic and oil—to the **sophisticated**, with Fettuccine all'Alfredo, Double Tomato Tagliatelle, and Rigatoni with Spicy Sausage and Tomato Sauce among the **favorites**, old and new.

PASTA PRONTO

Penne with Spinach

Serves 4

INGREDIENTS

8 ounces fresh spinach
1 garlic clove, crushed
1 shallot or small onion,
  finely chopped
½ small red bell pepper, seeded and
  finely chopped
1 small red chili, seeded
  and chopped
⅔ cup stock
12 ounces penne
5 ounces smoked turkey bacon
3 tablespoons low-fat sour cream
2 tablespoons grated
  Parmesan cheese
shavings of Parmesan cheese,
  to garnish

red bell pepper

grated
Parmesan cheese

red chilies

shallot

smoked turkey
bacon

penne

stock

low-fat sour
cream

garlic

spinach

2 Put the garlic, shallot or small onion, pepper and chili into a large frying pan. Add the stock, cover and cook for about 5 minutes until tender. Add the prepared spinach and cook quickly for another 2–3 minutes until it has wilted.

1 Wash the spinach and remove the hard central stems. Shred finely.

3 Cook the pasta in a large pan of boiling, salted water until *al dente*. Drain thoroughly.

4 Fry the smoked turkey bacon, cool a little, and chop finely.

5 Stir the sour cream and grated Parmesan into the pasta with the spinach, and toss carefully together.

6 Transfer to serving plates and sprinkle with chopped turkey and shavings of Parmesan cheese.

Green Pasta with Avocado Sauce

This is an unusual sauce with a pale green color, studded with red tomato. It has a luxurious velvety texture. The sauce is rich, so you don't need much for a filling meal.

Serves 6

INGREDIENTS
3 ripe tomatoes
2 large ripe avocados
2 tbsp butter, plus extra for tossing
  the pasta
1 garlic clove, crushed
1½ cups heavy cream
salt and pepper
dash of Tabasco sauce
1 lb green tagliatelle
freshly grated Parmesan cheese
4 tbsp sour cream

tagliatelle

tomatoes

avocado

garlic

1 Halve the tomatoes and remove the cores. Squeeze out the seeds and cut the tomatoes into dice. Set aside.

2 Halve the avocados, take out the pits, and peel. Roughly chop the flesh.

3 Melt the butter in a saucepan and add the garlic. Cook for 1 minute, then add the cream and chopped avocados. Raise the heat, stirring constantly to break up the avocados.

4 Add the diced tomatoes and season to taste with salt, pepper, and a little Tabasco sauce. Keep warm.

5 Cook the pasta in plenty of boiling salted water according to the manufacturer's instructions. Drain well and toss with a knob of butter.

6 Divide the pasta between 4 warmed bowls and spoon over the sauce. Sprinkle with grated Parmesan and top with a spoonful of sour cream.

Mushroom Bolognese

A quick – and exceedingly tasty – vegetarian
version of the classic Italian meat dish.

Serves 4

INGREDIENTS
1 lb mushrooms
1 tbsp olive oil
1 onion, chopped
1 garlic clove, crushed
1 tbsp tomato paste
14 oz can chopped tomatoes
3 tbsp chopped fresh oregano
1 lb fresh pasta
Parmesan cheese, to serve
salt and freshly ground black pepper

mushrooms

chopped tomatoes

oregano

garlic clove

pasta

onion

Parmesan cheese

tomato paste

1 Trim the mushroom stems neatly.
Then cut each mushroom into quarters.

2 Heat the oil in a large pan. Add the
chopped onion and garlic, and cook for
2–3 minutes.

3 Add the mushrooms to the pan, and
cook over a high heat for 3–4 minutes,
stirring occasionally.

4 Stir in the tomato paste, chopped
tomatoes and 1 tbsp of the oregano.
Lower the heat, cover, and cook for
about 5 minutes.

5 Meanwhile, bring a large pan of
salted water to a boil. Cook the pasta for
2–3 minutes until just tender.

COOK'S TIP
If you prefer to use dried pasta, make this the first thing that you cook. It will take 10–12 minutes, during which time you can make the mushroom mixture. Use 12 oz dried pasta.

6 Season the bolognese sauce with salt and pepper. Drain the pasta, turn it into a bowl, and add the mushroom mixture. Toss to mix well. Serve in individual bowls, topped with shavings of fresh Parmesan and the remaining chopped fresh oregano.

Fettuccine all'Alfredo

A classic dish from Rome, Fettuccine all'Alfredo is simply pasta tossed with heavy cream, butter, and freshly grated Parmesan cheese. Popular less classic additions are peas and strips of ham.

Serves 4

INGREDIENTS
2 tbsp butter
⅔ cup heavy cream, plus 4 tbsp extra
1 lb fettuccine
freshly grated nutmeg
½ cup freshly grated Parmesan
  cheese, plus extra to serve
salt and pepper

fettuccine

nutmeg

Parmesan cheese

1 Place the butter and ⅔ cup cream in a heavy saucepan, bring to a boil, and simmer for 1 minute until slightly thickened.

2 Cook the fettuccine in plenty of boiling salted water according to the manufacturer's instructions, but for 2 minutes less time. The pasta should still be a little firm.

3 Drain very well and transfer to the pan with the cream sauce.

4 Place on the heat and toss the pasta in the sauce to coat.

5 Add the extra 4 tbsp cream, the cheese, salt and pepper to taste, and a little grated nutmeg. Toss until well coated and heated through. Serve immediately with extra grated Parmesan cheese.

Spaghetti Olio e Aglio

This is another classic recipe from Rome. A quick and filling dish, originally the food of the poor involving nothing more than pasta, garlic, and olive oil, but now fast becoming fashionable.

Serves 4

INGREDIENTS
2 garlic cloves
2 tbsp fresh parsley
½ cup olive oil
1 lb spaghetti
salt and pepper

spaghetti

olive oil

parsley

garlic

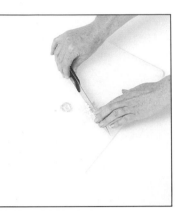

1 Finely chop the garlic.

2 Chop the parsley roughly.

3 Heat the olive oil in a medium saucepan and add the garlic and a pinch of salt. Cook gently, stirring all the time, until golden. If the garlic becomes too brown, it will taste bitter.

4 Meanwhile cook the spaghetti in plenty of boiling salted water according to the manufacturer's instructions. Drain well.

5 Toss with the warm – not sizzling – garlic and oil and add plenty of black pepper and the parsley. Serve immediately.

Double Tomato Tagliatelle

Sun-dried tomatoes add pungency to this dish,
while the broiled fresh tomatoes add bite.

Serves 4

INGREDIENTS
3 tbsp olive oil
1 garlic clove, crushed
1 small onion, chopped
¼ cup dry white wine
6 sun-dried tomatoes, chopped
2 tbsp chopped fresh parsley
½ cup pitted black olives, halved
1 lb fresh tagliatelle
4 tomatoes, halved
Parmesan cheese, to serve
salt and freshly ground black pepper

tomatoes

parsley

garlic clove

sun-dried tomatoes

tagliatelle

dry white wine

onion

black olives

Parmesan cheese

COOK'S TIP

It is essential to buy Parmesan
in a piece for this dish. Find a
good source – fresh Parmesan
should not be unacceptably
hard – and shave or grate it
yourself. The flavor will be
much more intense than that of
the pre-grated product.

1 Heat 2 tbsp of the oil in a pan. Add
the garlic and onion, and cook for
2–3 minutes, stirring occasionally. Add
the wine, sun-dried tomatoes and the
parsley. Cook for 2 minutes. Stir in the
black olives.

2 Bring a large pan of salted water to a
boil. Add the fresh tagliatelle, and cook
for 2–3 minutes until just tender. Preheat
the broiler.

3 Put the tomatoes on a baking sheet,
and brush with the remaining oil. Broil
for 3–4 minutes.

4 Drain the pasta, return it to the pan,
and toss with the sauce. Serve with the
broiled tomatoes, freshly ground black
pepper and shavings of Parmesan.

Spaghetti with Black Olive and Mushroom Sauce

A rich pungent sauce topped with sweet cherry tomatoes.

Serves 4

INGREDIENTS
1 tbsp olive oil
1 garlic clove, chopped
8 oz mushrooms, chopped
 generous ½ cup black olives, pitted
2 tbsp chopped fresh parsley
1 fresh red chili, seeded and chopped
1lb spaghetti
8 oz cherry tomatoes
slivers of Parmesan cheese, to serve
  (optional)

garlic

mushrooms

red chillies

cherry tomatoes

black olives

spaghetti

parsley

1 Heat the oil in a large pan. Add the garlic and cook for 1 minute. Add the mushrooms, cover, and cook over a medium heat for 5 minutes.

2 Place the mushrooms in a blender or food processor with the olives, parsley and red chili. Blend until smooth.

3 Cook the pasta following the instructions on the side of the package until *al dente*. Drain well and return to the pan. Add the olive mixture and toss together until the pasta is well coated. Cover and keep warm.

4 Heat an ungreased frying pan and shake the cherry tomatoes around until they start to split (about 2–3 minutes). Serve the pasta topped with the tomatoes and garnished with slivers of Parmesan, if desired.

Pasta with Pesto Sauce

Don't skimp on the fresh basil – this is the most
wonderful sauce in the world! This pesto can also be
used as a basting sauce for broiled chicken or fish, or
rubbed over a leg of lamb before baking.

Serves 4

INGREDIENTS
2 garlic cloves
salt and pepper
½ cup pine nuts
1 cup fresh basil leaves
⅔ cup olive oil (not extra-virgin as it
   is too strong)
4 tbsp unsalted butter, softened
4 tbsp freshly grated Parmesan cheese
1 lb spaghetti

olive oil

spaghetti

pine nuts

Parmesan cheese

basil

1 Peel the garlic and process in a food
processor with a little salt and the pine
nuts until broken up. Add the basil leaves
and continue mixing to a paste.

2 Gradually add the olive oil, little by
little, until the mixture is creamy and thick.

3 Mix in the butter and season with
pepper. Mix in the cheese. (Alternatively,
you can make the pesto by hand using a
pestle and mortar.)

4 Store the pesto in a jar (with a layer
of olive oil on top to exclude the air) in
the fridge until needed.

5 Cook the pasta in plenty of boiling
salted water according to the
manufacturer's instructions. Drain well.

COOK'S TIP
A good pesto can be made using parsley instead of basil and walnuts instead of pine nuts. To make it go further, add a spoonful or two of fromage frais. 'Red' pesto includes sun-dried tomato paste and pounded roasted red peppers.

6 Toss the pasta with half the pesto and serve in warm bowls with the remaining pesto spooned on top.

Pasta Shells with Tomatoes and Arugula

This pretty-colored pasta dish relies for its success on a salad green called arugula. Available in large supermarkets, it is a leaf easily grown in the garden or a window box and tastes slightly peppery.

Serves 4

INGREDIENTS
1 lb shell pasta
salt and pepper
1 lb very ripe cherry tomatoes
3 tbsp olive oil
3 oz fresh arugula
Parmesan cheese

olive oil

pasta shells

cherry tomatoes

arugula

Parmesan cheese

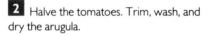

1 Cook the pasta in plenty of boiling salted water according to the manufacturer's instructions. Drain well.

2 Halve the tomatoes. Trim, wash, and dry the arugula.

3 Heat the oil in a large saucepan, add the tomatoes, and cook for barely 1 minute. The tomatoes should only just heat through and not disintegrate.

4 Shave the Parmesan cheese using a rotary vegetable peeler.

5 Add the pasta, then the arugula. Carefully stir to mix and heat through. Season well with salt and freshly ground black pepper. Serve immediately with plenty of shaved Parmesan cheese.

Spaghetti with Fresh Tomato Sauce

The heat from the pasta will release the delicious flavors of this sauce. Only use the really red and soft tomatoes – large ripe beefsteak tomatoes are ideal. Don't be tempted to use small hard tomatoes: they have very little flavor.

Serves 4

INGREDIENTS
4 large ripe tomatoes
2 garlic cloves, finely chopped
4 tbsp chopped fresh herbs such as
  basil, marjoram, oregano, or parsley
⅔ cup olive oil
salt and pepper
1 lb spaghetti

olive oil

garlic

spaghetti

tomato

2 Lift out with a perforated spoon and plunge into a bowl of cold water. Peel off the skins, then dry the tomatoes on paper towels.

3 Halve the tomatoes and squeeze out the seeds. Chop into ¼ in cubes and mix with the garlic, herbs, olive oil, and seasoning in a non-metallic bowl.

I Skin the tomatoes by placing in boiling water for 1 minute – no longer or they will become mushy.

4 Cook the pasta in plenty of boiling salted water.

5 Drain the pasta and mix with the sauce. Cover with a lid and leave for 2–3 minutes, toss again, and serve immediately.

VARIATION
Mix ¾ cup pitted and chopped black Greek-style olives into the sauce just before serving.

Tagliatelle with Gorgonzola Sauce

Gorgonzola is a creamy Italian blue cheese. As an alternative you could use Danish Blue.

Serves 4

INGREDIENTS
2 tbsp butter, plus extra for tossing
    the pasta
½ lb Gorgonzola cheese
⅔ cup heavy or whipping cream
2 tbsp dry vermouth
1 tsp cornstarch
1 tbsp chopped fresh sage
salt and pepper
1 lb tagliatelle

tagliatelle

Gorgonzola cheese

sage

1 Melt 2 tbsp butter in a heavy saucepan (it needs to be thick-based to prevent the cheese from burning). Stir in 6 oz crumbled Gorgonzola cheese and stir over a very gentle heat for 2–3 minutes until the cheese is melted.

2 Pour in the cream, vermouth, and cornstarch, whisking well to amalgamate. Stir in the chopped sage, then taste and season. Cook, whisking all the time, until the sauce boils and thickens. Set aside.

3 Boil the pasta in plenty of salted water according to the manufacturer's instructions. Drain well and toss with a little butter.

4 Reheat the sauce gently, whisking well. Divide the pasta between 4 serving bowls, top with the sauce, and sprinkle over the remaining cheese. Serve immediately.

Pasta with Tomato and Cream Sauce

Here pasta is served with a deliciously rich version of ordinary tomato sauce.

Serves 4–6

INGREDIENTS
2 tbsp olive oil
2 garlic cloves, crushed
14 oz canned chopped tomatoes
⅔ cup heavy or whipping cream
2 tbsp chopped fresh herbs such as
    basil, oregano, or parsley
salt and pepper
4 cups pasta, any variety

olive oil

chopped tomatoes

parsley

pasta

garlic

1 Heat the oil in a medium saucepan, add the garlic, and cook for 2 minutes until golden.

2 Stir in the tomatoes, bring to a boil and simmer uncovered for 20 minutes, stirring occasionally to prevent sticking. The sauce is ready when you can see the oil separating on top.

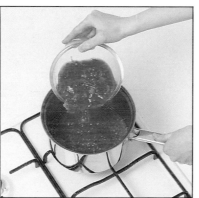

3 Add the cream, bring slowly to a boil again, and simmer until slightly thickened. Stir in the herbs, taste, and season well.

4 Cook the pasta in plenty of boiling salted water according to the manufacturer's instructions. Drain well and toss with the sauce. Serve piping hot, sprinkled with extra herbs if liked.

COOK'S TIP

If you are really in a hurry, buy a good ready-made tomato sauce and simply stir in the cream and simmer until thickened.

Rigatoni with Spicy Sausage and Tomato Sauce

This is really a shortcut to Bolognese sauce, using the wonderful fresh spicy sausages sold at every Italian grocers.

Serves 4

INGREDIENTS

1 lb fresh spicy Italian sausage
2 tbsp olive oil
1 medium onion, chopped
2 cups tomato coulis (strained, crushed tomatoes)
⅔ cup dry red wine
6 sun-dried tomatoes in oil, drained
salt and pepper
1 lb rigatoni or similar pasta
freshly grated Parmesan cheese, to serve

rigatoni

Italian sausage

Parmesan cheese

onion

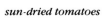

sun-dried tomatoes

1 Squeeze the sausages out of their skins into a bowl and break up the meat.

2 Heat the oil in a medium saucepan and add the onion. Cook for 5 minutes until soft and golden. Stir in the sausage meat, browning it all over and breaking up the lumps with a wooden spoon. Pour in the coulis and the wine. Bring to a boil.

3 Slice the sun-dried tomatoes and add to the sauce. Simmer for 3 minutes until reduced, stirring occasionally. Season to taste.

4 Cook the pasta in plenty of boiling salted water according to the manufacturer's instructions. Drain well and top with the sauce. Serve with grated Parmesan cheese.

Pasta with Fresh Tomato and Smoky Bacon Sauce

A wonderful sauce to prepare in mid-summer when the tomatoes are ripe and sweet.

Serves 4

INGREDIENTS
2 lb ripe tomatoes
6 slices bacon
4 tbsp butter
1 medium onion, chopped
salt and pepper
1 tbsp chopped fresh oregano or 1 tsp dried oregano
1 lb pasta, any variety
freshly grated Parmesan cheese, to serve

pasta

oregano

tomatoes

onion

bacon

Parmesan cheese

1 Plunge the tomatoes into boiling water for 1 minute, then into cold water to stop them from becoming mushy. Slip off the skins. Halve the tomatoes, remove the seeds and cores, and roughly chop the flesh.

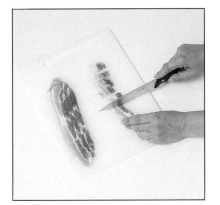

2 Remove the rind and roughly chop the bacon.

3 Melt the butter in a saucepan and add the bacon. Fry until lightly brown, then add the onion and cook gently for 5 minutes until softened. Add the tomatoes, salt, pepper, and oregano. Simmer gently for 10 minutes.

4 Cook the pasta in plenty of boiling salted water according to the manufacturer's instructions. Drain well and toss with the sauce. Serve with grated Parmesan cheese.

Tagliatelle with Prosciutto and Parmesan

A really simple dish, prepared in minutes from the best ingredients.

Serves 4

INGREDIENTS
¼ lb prosciutto
1 lb tagliatelle
salt and pepper
6 tbsp butter
½ cup freshly grated Parmesan
    cheese
few fresh sage leaves, to garnish

tagliatelle

sage

prosciutto

Parmesan cheese

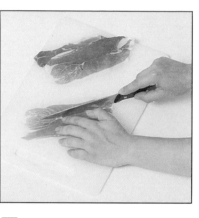

1 Cut the prosciutto into strips the same width as the tagliatelle. Cook the pasta in plenty of boiling salted water according to manufacturer's instructions.

2 Meanwhile, melt the butter gently in a saucepan, stir in the prosciutto strips and heat through, but do not fry.

3 Drain the tagliatelle well and pile into a warm serving dish.

4 Sprinkle over all the Parmesan cheese and pour over the buttery prosciutto. Season well with black pepper and garnish with the sage leaves.

Paglia e Fieno

The title of this dish translates as 'straw and hay', which refers to the yellow and green colors of the pasta when mixed together. Using fresh peas makes all the difference to this dish.

Serves 4

INGREDIENTS
4 tbsp butter
2 cups frozen petits pois (small peas)
    or 2 lb fresh peas, shelled
⅔ cup heavy cream, plus 4 tbsp extra
1 lb tagliatelle (plain and spinach,
    mixed)
½ cup freshly grated Parmesan
    cheese, plus extra to serve
salt and pepper
freshly grated nutmeg

tagliatelle

peas

Parmesan cheese

COOK'S TIP
Sautéed mushrooms and narrow strips of cooked ham also make a good addition.

1 Melt the butter in a heavy saucepan and add the peas. Sauté for 2–3 minutes, then add the cream, bring to a boil, and simmer for 1 minute until slightly thickened.

2 Cook the fettuccine in plenty of boiling salted water according to the manufacturer's instructions, but for 2 minutes' less time. The pasta should still be *al dente*. Drain very well and transfer to the pan with the cream and pea sauce.

3 Place on the heat and toss the pasta in the sauce to coat. Pour in the extra cream, the cheese, salt and pepper to taste, and a little grated nutmeg. Toss until well coated and heated through. Serve immediately with extra Parmesan cheese.

Tagliatelle with Pea Sauce, Asparagus and Broad Beans

A creamy pea sauce makes a wonderful combination with the crunchy young vegetables.

Serves 4

INGREDIENTS
1 tbsp olive oil
1 garlic clove, crushed
6 scallions, sliced
1 cup fresh or frozen baby peas, defrosted
12 oz fresh young asparagus
2 tbsp chopped fresh sage, plus extra leaves, to garnish
finely grated rind of 2 lemons
1¾ cups fresh vegetable stock or water
8 oz fresh or frozen broad beans, defrosted
1 lb tagliatelle
4 tbsp low-fat yogurt

lemon

garlic

asparagus

broad beans

peas

yogurt

tagliatelle

sage

scallions

1 Heat the oil in a pan. Add the garlic and scallions and cook gently for 2–3 minutes until softened.

2 Add the peas and ⅓ of the asparagus, together with the sage, lemon rind and stock or water. Bring to a boil, reduce the heat and simmer for 10 minutes until tender. Purée in a blender until smooth.

3 Meanwhile remove the outer skins from the broad beans and discard.

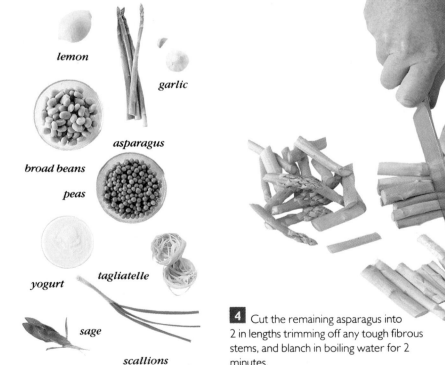

4 Cut the remaining asparagus into 2 in lengths trimming off any tough fibrous stems, and blanch in boiling water for 2 minutes.

5 Cook the tagliatelle following the instructions on the side of the package until *al dente*. Drain well.

COOK'S TIP
Frozen peas and beans have been suggested here to cut down the preparation time, but the dish tastes even better if you use fresh young vegetables when in season.

6 Add the cooked asparagus and shelled beans to the sauce and reheat. Stir in the yogurt and toss into the tagliatelle. Garnish with a few extra sage leaves and serve.

Pasta Bows with Fennel and Walnut Sauce

A scrumptious blend of walnuts and crisp steamed fennel.

Serves 4

INGREDIENTS
½ cup walnuts, shelled and roughly
  chopped
1 garlic clove
1 oz fresh flat-leaf parsley leaves,
  picked from the stems
½ cup ricotta cheese
1 lb pasta bows
1 lb fennel bulbs
chopped walnuts, to garnish

garlic

pasta bows

ricotta

fennel

parsley

walnut halves

chopped walnuts

1 Place the chopped walnuts, garlic and parsley in a food processor. Pulse until roughly chopped. Transfer to a bowl and stir in the ricotta.

2 Cook the pasta following the instructions on the side of the package until *al dente*. Drain well.

3 Slice the fennel thinly and steam for 4–5 minutes until just tender but still crisp.

4 Return the pasta to the pan and add the walnut mixture and the fennel. Toss well and sprinkle with the chopped walnuts. Serve immediately.

Pasta Rapido with Parsley Pesto

Pasta suppers can often be dull. Here's a fresh, lively sauce that will stir the appetite.

Serves 4

INGREDIENTS
1 lb dried pasta
¾ cup whole almonds
½ cup slivered almonds, toasted
¼ cup freshly grated Parmesan
  cheese
pinch of salt

FOR THE SAUCE
1½ oz fresh parsley
2 garlic cloves, crushed
3 tbsp olive oil
3 tbsp lemon juice
1 tsp sugar
1 cup boiling water

1 Bring a large saucepan of salted water to a boil. Toss in the pasta and cook according to the instructions on the package. Toast the whole and slivered almonds separately under a moderate broiler until golden brown. Put the slivered almonds aside until required.

pasta

lemon

parsley

garlic

slivered almonds

Parmesan cheese

almonds

2 For the sauce, chop the parsley finely in a food processor. Add the whole almonds and grind to a fine consistency. Add the garlic, olive oil, lemon juice, sugar and water. Combine to make a sauce.

3 Drain the pasta and combine with half of the sauce. (The remainder of the sauce will keep in a screw-topped jar in the refrigerator for up to ten days.) Top with Parmesan and slivered almonds.

COOK'S TIP

To prevent pasta from sticking together during cooking, use plenty of water and stir well before the water returns to a boil.

Pasta with Shrimp and Feta Cheese

This dish combines the richness of fresh shrimp with the tartness of feta cheese. Goat cheese could be used as an alternative.

Serves 4

INGREDIENTS
1 lb medium raw shrimp
6 scallions
4 tbsp butter
½ lb feta cheese
salt and pepper
small bunch fresh chives
1 lb penne, garganelle, or rigatoni

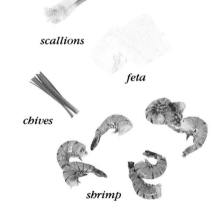

penne

scallions

feta

chives

shrimp

1 Remove the heads from the shrimp by twisting and pulling off. Peel the shrimp and discard the shells. Chop the scallions.

2 Melt the butter in a skillet and stir in the shrimp. When they turn pink, add the scallions and cook gently for 1 minute.

3 Cut the feta into ½ in cubes.

4 Stir the feta cheese into the shrimp mixture, and season with plenty of black pepper.

5 Cut the chives into 1 in lengths and stir half into the shrimp.

6 Cook the pasta in plenty of boiling salted water according to the manufacturer's instructions. Drain well, pile into a warmed serving dish, and top with the sauce. Scatter with the remaining chives and serve.

Spaghetti alla Carbonara

It has been said that this dish was originally cooked by Italian coal miners, or charcoal-burners, hence the name 'carbonara'. The secret of its creamy sauce is not to overcook the egg.

Serves 4

INGREDIENTS
6 oz bacon
1 garlic clove, chopped
3 eggs
1 lb spaghetti
salt and pepper
4 tbsp freshly grated Parmesan cheese

bacon

garlic

eggs

spaghetti

Parmesan cheese

1 Cut the bacon into a dice and place in a medium saucepan. Place over the heat and fry in its own fat with the garlic until brown. Keep warm until needed.

2 Whisk the eggs together in a bowl.

3 Cook the spaghetti in plenty of boiling salted water according to the manufacturer's instructions until *al dente*. Drain well.

4 Quickly transfer the spaghetti to the pan with the bacon and stir in the eggs, a little salt, lots of pepper, and half the cheese. Toss well to mix. The eggs should half-cook with the heat from the spaghetti. Serve in warm bowls with the remaining cheese.

Spaghetti with Tomato and Clam Sauce

Small sweet clams make this a delicately succulent sauce. Mussels would make a good substitute, but don't be tempted to use seafood pickled in vinegar – the result will be inedible!

Serves 4

INGREDIENTS
2 lb live small clams, or 2 × 14 oz
    cans clams in brine, drained
6 tbsp olive oil
2 garlic cloves, crushed
1 lb 5 oz canned chopped tomatoes
3 tbsp chopped fresh parsley
salt and pepper
1 lb spaghetti

spaghetti

olive oil

parsley

garlic

clams

1 If using live clams, place them in a bowl of cold water and rinse several times to remove any grit or sand. Drain.

2 Heat the oil in a saucepan and add the clams. Stir over a high heat until the clams open. Throw away any that do not open. Transfer the clams to a bowl with a perforated spoon.

3 Reduce the clam juice left in the pan to almost nothing by boiling fast; this will also concentrate the flavor. Add the garlic and fry until golden. Pour in the tomatoes, bring to a boil, and cook for 3–4 minutes until reduced. Stir in the clam mixture or canned clams, and half the parsley and heat through. Season.

4 Cook the pasta in plenty of boiling salted water according to the manufacturer's instructions. Drain well and transfer to a warm serving dish. Pour over the sauce and sprinkle with the remaining parsley.

Capellini with Arugula, Snow Peas and Pine Nuts

A light but filling pasta dish with the added pepperiness of fresh arugula.

Serves 4

INGREDIENTS
9 oz capellini or angel-hair pasta
8 oz snow peas
6 oz arugula
¼ cup pine nuts, roasted
2 tbsp Parmesan cheese, finely grated (optional)
2 tbsp olive oil (optional)

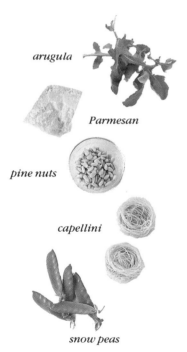

arugula

Parmesan

pine nuts

capellini

snow peas

1 Cook the capellini or angel-hair pasta following the instructions on the side of the package until *al dente*.

2 Meanwhile, carefully top and tail the snow peas.

3 As soon as the pasta is cooked, drop in the arugula and snow peas. Drain immediately.

4 Toss the pasta with the roasted pine nuts, and Parmesan and olive oil if using. Serve at once.

Campanelle with Yellow Pepper Sauce

Roasted yellow peppers make a deliciously sweet and creamy sauce to serve with pasta.

Serves 4

INGREDIENTS
2 yellow peppers
¼ cup soft goat cheese
½ cup low-fat ricotta cheese
salt and freshly ground black pepper
1 lb short pasta such as campanelle or
    fusilli
¼ cup flaked almonds, toasted,
    to serve

1 Place the whole yellow peppers under a preheated grill until charred and blistered. Place in a paper bag to cool. Peel and remove the seeds.

pepper

ricotta cheese

flaked almonds

goat cheese

campanelle

2 Place the pepper flesh in a blender with the goat cheese and ricotta cheese. Blend until smooth. Season with salt and lots of black pepper.

3 Cook the pasta following the instructions on the side of the package until *al dente*. Drain well.

4 Toss with the sauce and serve sprinkled with the toasted flaked almonds.

Spinach and Ricotta Shells with Pine Nuts

Large pasta shells are designed to hold a variety of delicious stuffings. Few are more pleasing than this mixture of chopped spinach and ricotta cheese.

Serves 4

INGREDIENTS
12 oz large pasta shells
scant 2 cups crushed tomatoes or
    tomato purée
10 oz frozen chopped spinach,
    defrosted
2 oz crustless white bread, crumbled
½ cup milk
3 tbsp olive oil
2¼ cups ricotta cheese
pinch of nutmeg
1 garlic clove, crushed
1 tbsp olive oil
½ tsp black olive paste (optional)
¼ cup freshly grated Parmesan
    cheese
2 tbsp pine nuts
salt and freshly ground black pepper

olive paste

ricotta cheese

pine nuts

garlic

spinach

pasta shells

COOK'S TIP

Choose a large saucepan when cooking pasta and give it an occasional stir to prevent shapes from sticking together. You can use either crushed tomatoes or tomato purée.

1 Bring a large saucepan of salted water to a boil. Toss in the pasta and cook according to the directions on the package. Refresh under cold water, drain and reserve until needed.

2 Pour the crushed tomatoes or purée into a nylon sieve over a bowl and strain to thicken. Place the spinach in another sieve and press out any excess liquid with the back of a spoon.

3 Place the bread, milk and oil in a food processor and combine. Add the spinach and ricotta and season with salt, pepper and nutmeg.

4 Combine the crushed tomatoes with the garlic, olive oil and olive paste if using. Spread the sauce evenly over the bottom of an ovenproof dish.

5 Spoon the spinach mixture into a piping bag fitted with a large plain nozzle and fill the pasta shapes (alternatively fill with a spoon). Arrange the pasta shapes over the sauce.

6 Preheat a moderate broiler. Heat the pasta through in a microwave oven at high power (100%) for 4 minutes. Scatter with Parmesan cheese and pine nuts, and finish under the broiler to brown the cheese.

Mushroom Macaroni and Cheese

Macaroni cheese is an all-time classic from the mid-week menu. Here it is served in a light creamy sauce with mushrooms and topped with pine nuts.

Serves 4

INGREDIENTS
1 lb quick-cooking elbow macaroni
3 tbsp olive oil
8 oz field mushrooms, sliced
2 fresh thyme sprigs
4 tbsp plain flour
1 vegetable bouillon cube
2½ cups milk
½ tsp celery salt
1 tsp Dijon mustard
1½ cups grated Cheddar cheese
¼ cup freshly grated Parmesan cheese
2 tbsp pine nuts
salt and freshly ground black pepper

macaroni

thyme

pine nuts

field mushrooms

Parmesan cheese

Dijon mustard

Cheddar cheese

1 Bring a pan of salted water to a boil. Add the macaroni and cook according to the package instructions.

2 Heat the oil in a heavy saucepan. Add the mushrooms and thyme, cover and cook over a gentle heat for 2–3 minutes. Stir in the flour and draw from the heat, add the bouillon cube and stir continuously until evenly blended. Add the milk a little at a time, stirring after each addition. Add the celery salt, mustard and Cheddar cheese and season. Stir and simmer briefly for 1–2 minutes.

3 Preheat a moderate broiler. Drain the macaroni well, toss into the sauce and turn out into four individual dishes or one large flameproof gratin dish. Scatter with grated Parmesan cheese and pine nuts, then broil until brown and bubbly.

COOK'S TIP

Tightly closed mushrooms are best for white cream sauces. Open mushrooms can darken a pale sauce to an unattractive sludgy grey.

Singapore Noodles

A delicious supper dish with a stunning mix of flavors and textures.

Serves 4

INGREDIENTS
8 oz dried egg noodles
3 tbsp peanut oil
1 onion, chopped
1-in piece fresh ginger,
    finely chopped
1 garlic clove,
    finely chopped
1 tbsp Madras curry powder
½ tsp salt
4 oz cooked chicken or pork,
    finely shredded
4 oz cooked peeled shrimp
4 oz Chinese cabbage leaves,
    shredded
4 oz beansprouts
4 tbsp chicken stock
1–2 tbsp dark soy sauce
1–2 fresh red chilies, seeded
    and finely shredded
4 scallions, finely shredded

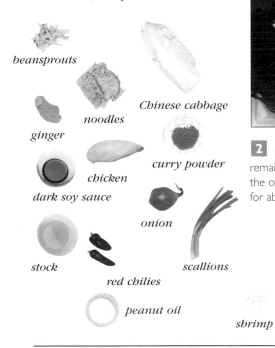

beansprouts

noodles

Chinese cabbage

ginger

curry powder

chicken

dark soy sauce

onion

stock

scallions

red chilies

peanut oil

shrimp

1 Cook the noodles according to the package instructions. Rinse thoroughly under cold water and drain well. Toss in 1 tbsp of the oil and set aside.

2 Heat a wok until hot, add the remaining oil and swirl it around. Add the onion, ginger and garlic and stir-fry for about 2 minutes.

3 Add the curry powder and salt, stir-fry for 30 seconds, then add the egg noodles, chicken or pork and shrimp. Stir-fry for 3–4 minutes.

4 Add the Chinese cabbage and beansprouts and stir-fry for 1–2 minutes. Sprinkle in the stock and soy sauce to taste and toss well until evenly mixed. Serve at once, garnished with the shredded red chilies and scallions.

Oriental Vegetable Noodles

Thin Italian egg pasta is a good alternative to Oriental egg noodles; use it fresh or dried.

Serves 6

INGREDIENTS
1¼ lb thin tagliarini
1 red onion
4 oz shiitake mushrooms
3 tbsp sesame oil
3 tbsp dark soy sauce
1 tbsp balsamic vinegar
2 tsp superfine sugar
1 tsp salt
celery leaves, to garnish

tagliarini

shiitake mushrooms

red onion

balsamic vinegar

soy sauce

1 Boil the tagliarini in a large pan of salted boiling water, following the instructions on the pack.

2 Thinly slice the red onion and the mushrooms, using a sharp knife.

3 Heat the wok, then add 1 tbsp of the sesame oil. When the oil is hot, stir-fry the onion and mushrooms for 2 minutes.

4 Drain the tagliarini, then add to the wok with the soy sauce, balsamic vinegar, sugar and salt. Stir-fry for 1 minute, then add the remaining sesame oil, and serve garnished with celery leaves.

Fried Singapore Noodles

Thai fish cakes vary in their size, and their hotness.
You can buy them from Oriental supermarkets, but,
if you cannot get hold of them, simply omit them
from the recipe.

Serves 4

INGREDIENTS
6 oz rice noodles
4 tbsp vegetable oil
½ tsp salt
3 oz cooked shrimp
6 oz cooked pork, cut into
    matchsticks
1 green pepper, seeded and chopped
    into matchsticks
½ tsp sugar
2 tsp curry powder
3 oz Thai fish cakes
2 tsp dark soy sauce

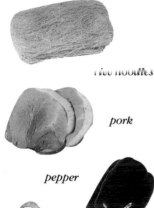

rice noodles

pork

pepper

shrimp

1 Soak the rice noodles in water for
about 10 minutes, drain well, then pat dry
with paper towels.

2 Heat the wok, then add half the oil.
When the oil is hot, add the noodles and
salt and stir-fry for 2 minutes. Transfer to
a heated serving dish to keep warm.

3 Heat the remaining oil and add the
shrimp, pork, pepper, sugar, curry
powder and remaining salt. Stir-fry the
ingredients for 1 minute.

4 Return the noodles to the pan and
stir-fry with the Thai fish cakes for
2 minutes. Stir in the soy sauce and serve.

Mixed Rice Noodles

A delicious noodle dish made extra special by adding avocado and garnishing with shrimp.

Serves 4

INGREDIENTS
1 tbsp sunflower oil
1 in piece ginger root, peeled
    and grated
2 cloves garlic, crushed
3 tbsp dark soy sauce
8 oz peas, thawed if frozen
1 lb rice noodles
1 lb fresh spinach, well washed and
    coarse stalks removed
2 tbsp smooth peanut butter
2 tbsp tahini
⅔ cup milk
1 ripe avocado, peeled and pitted
roasted peanuts and peeled shrimp,
    to garnish

rice noodles

ginger

peas

peanut butter

spinach

1 Heat the wok, then add the oil. When the oil is fairly hot, stir-fry the ginger and garlic for approximately 30 seconds. Add 1 tbsp of the dark soy sauce and ⅔ cup boiling water.

2 Add the peas and noodles, then cook for 3 minutes. Stir in the spinach. Remove the vegetables and noodles, drain and keep warm.

3 Stir the peanut butter, remaining soy sauce, tahini and milk together in the wok, and simmer for 1 minute.

4 Add the vegetables and noodles, slice in the avocado and toss together. Serve piled on individual plates. Spoon some sauce over each portion and garnish with peanuts and shrimp.

Mee Krob

This delicious dish makes a filling meal. Take care when frying vermicelli as it has a tendency to spit when added to hot oil.

Serves 4

INGREDIENTS
½ cup vegetable oil
8 oz rice vermicelli
5 oz green beans, topped, tailed and
  halved lengthwise
1 onion, finely chopped
2 boneless, skinless chicken breasts,
  about 6 oz each, cut into strips
1 tsp chili powder
8 oz cooked shrimp
3 tbsp dark soy sauce
3 tbsp white wine vinegar
2 tsp superfine sugar
fresh coriander sprigs, to garnish

rice vermicelli

chicken breast

onion *green beans*

shrimp

1 Heat the wok, then add 4 tbsp of the oil. Break up the vermicelli into 3 in lengths. When the oil is hot, fry the vermicelli in batches. Remove from the heat and keep warm.

2 Heat the remaining oil in the wok, then add the green beans, onion and chicken and stir-fry for 3 minutes until the chicken is cooked.

3 Sprinkle in the chili powder. Stir in the shrimp, soy sauce, vinegar and sugar, and stir-fry for 2 minutes.

4 Serve the chicken, shrimp and vegetables on the vermicelli, garnished with sprigs of fresh coriander.

PIZZA
PRESTO

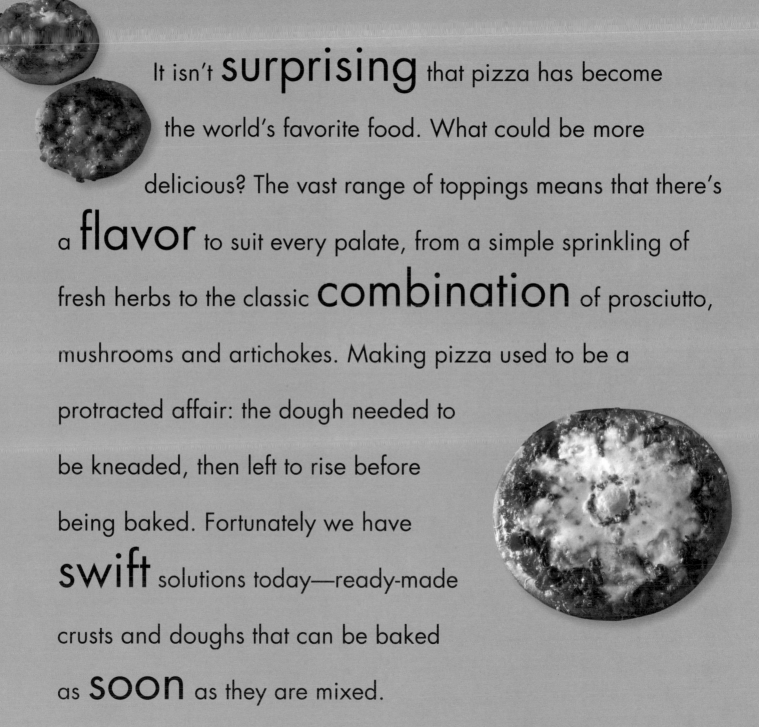

It isn't **surprising** that pizza has become the world's favorite food. What could be more delicious? The vast range of toppings means that there's a **flavor** to suit every palate, from a simple sprinkling of fresh herbs to the classic **combination** of prosciutto, mushrooms and artichokes. Making pizza used to be a protracted affair: the dough needed to be kneaded, then left to rise before being baked. Fortunately we have **swift** solutions today—ready-made crusts and doughs that can be baked as **soon** as they are mixed.

Margherita

(Tomato, Basil and Mozzarella)
This classic pizza is simple to prepare. The sweet flavour of sun-ripened tomatoes works wonderfully with the basil and mozzarella.

Serves 2–3

INGREDIENTS
1 pizza base, about 10–12 in
     diameter
2 tbsp olive oil
1 quantity Tomato Sauce
5 oz mozzarella
2 ripe tomatoes, thinly sliced
6–8 fresh basil leaves
2 tbsp freshly grated Parmesan
black pepper

basil

mozzarella

Parmesan

olive oil

tomatoes

Tomato Sauce

1 Preheat the oven to 425°F. Brush the pizza base with 1 tbsp of the oil and then spread over the Tomato Sauce.

2 Cut the mozzarella into thin slices.

3 Arrange the sliced mozzarella and tomatoes on top of the pizza base.

4 Roughly tear the basil leaves, add and sprinkle with the Parmesan. Drizzle over the remaining oil and season with black pepper. Bake for 15–20 minutes until crisp and golden. Serve immediately.

Marinara

(Tomato and Garlic)

The combination of garlic, good quality olive oil and oregano give this pizza an unmistakably Italian flavor.

Serves 2–3

INGREDIENTS

4 tbsp olive oil
1½ lb plum tomatoes, peeled, seeded and chopped
1 pizza base, about 10–12 in diameter
4 garlic cloves, cut into slivers
1 tbsp chopped fresh oregano
salt and black pepper

olive oil

oregano

plum tomatoes

garlic

1 Preheat the oven to 425°F. Heat 2 tbsp of the oil in a pan. Add the tomatoes and cook, stirring frequently for about 5 minutes until soft.

2 Place the tomatoes in a strainer and leave to drain for about 5 minutes.

3 Transfer the tomatoes to a food processor or blender and purée until smooth.

4 Brush the pizza base with half the remaining oil. Spoon over the tomatoes and sprinkle with garlic and oregano. Drizzle over the remaining oil and season. Bake for 15–20 minutes until crisp and golden. Serve immediately.

Napoletana

(Tomato, Mozzarella and Anchovies)
This pizza is a speciality of Naples. It is both one of the simplest to prepare and the most tasty.

Serves 2–3

INGREDIENTS
1 pizza base, about 10–12 in
 diameter
2 tbsp olive oil
6 plum tomatoes
2 garlic cloves, chopped
4 oz mozzarella, grated
2 oz can anchovy fillets, drained and
 chopped
1 tbsp chopped fresh oregano
2 tbsp freshly grated Parmesan
black pepper

Parmesan

mozzarella

anchovy fillets

olive oil

plum tomatoes

garlic

oregano

1 Preheat the oven to 425°F. Brush the pizza base with 1 tbsp of the oil. Put the tomatoes in a bowl and pour over boiling water. Leave for 30 seconds, then plunge into cold water.

2 Peel, seed and coarsely chop the tomatoes. Spoon the tomatoes over the pizza base and sprinkle over the garlic.

3 Mix the mozzarella with the anchovies and sprinkle over.

4 Sprinkle over the oregano and Parmesan. Drizzle over the remaining oil and season with black pepper. Bake for 15–20 minutes until crisp and golden. Serve immediately.

Quattro Formaggi

(Four Cheeses)

Rich and tasty, these individual pizzas are quick to assemble, and the aroma of melting cheese is irresistible.

Serves 4

INGREDIENTS
1 quantity Superquick Pizza Dough
1 tbsp Garlic Oil
½ small red onion, very thinly sliced
2 oz Saga Blue
2 oz mozzarella
2 oz Gruyère, grated
2 tbsp freshly grated Parmesan
1 tbsp chopped fresh thyme
black pepper

mozzarella

red onion

Parmesan

Garlic Oil

Saga Blue

Gruyère

thyme

1 Preheat the oven to 425°F. Divide the dough into four pieces and roll out each one on a lightly floured surface into a 5 in circle. Place well apart on two greased baking sheets, then pinch up the dough edges to make a thin rim. Brush with Garlic Oil and top with the red onion.

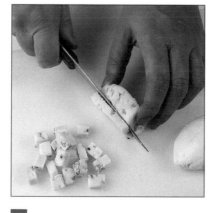

2 Cut the Saga Blue and mozzarella into cubes and scatter over the bases.

3 Mix together the Gruyère, Parmesan and thyme and sprinkle over.

4 Grind over plenty of black pepper. Bake for 15–20 minutes until crisp and golden and the cheese is bubbling. Serve immediately.

Fiorentina

Spinach is the star ingredient of this pizza. A grating of nutmeg to heighten its flavor gives this pizza its unique character.

Serves 2–3

INGREDIENTS
6 oz fresh spinach
3 tbsp olive oil
1 small red onion, thinly sliced
1 pizza base, about 10–12 in diameter
1 quantity Tomato Sauce
freshly grated nutmeg
5 oz mozzarella
1 large egg
1 oz Gruyère, grated

mozzarella

Gruyère

Tomato Sauce

spinach

red onion

nutmeg

egg

1 Preheat the oven to 425°F. Remove the stems from the spinach and wash the leaves in plenty of cold water. Drain well and pat dry with paper towels.

2 Heat I tbsp of the oil and fry the onion until soft. Add the spinach and continue to fry until just wilted. Drain off any excess liquid.

3 Brush the pizza base with half the remaining oil. Spread over the Tomato Sauce, then top with the spinach mixture. Grate some nutmeg over.

4 Thinly slice the mozzarella and arrange over the spinach. Drizzle the remaining oil over. Bake for 10 minutes, then remove from the oven.

5 Make a small well in the center and drop the egg into the hole.

6 Sprinkle over the Gruyère and return to the oven for a further 5–10 minutes until crisp and golden. Serve immediately.

Sun-dried Tomatoes, Basil and Olive Pizza Bites

This quick and easy recipe uses scone pizza dough with the addition of chopped fresh basil.

Makes 24

INGREDIENTS
18–20 fresh basil leaves
1 quantity Scone Pizza Dough
2 tbsp tomato oil (from jar of sun-dried tomatoes)
1 quantity Tomato Sauce
4 oz (drained weight) sun-dried tomatoes in oil, chopped
10 pitted black olives, chopped
2 oz mozzarella, grated
2 tbsp freshly grated Parmesan
shredded basil leaves, to garnish

mozzarella

black olives

Tomato Sauce

Parmesan

tomato oil

basil

sun-dried tomatoes

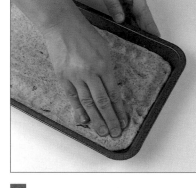

1 Preheat the oven to 425°F. Tear the basil leaves into small pieces. Add half to the scone mix before mixing to a soft dough. Set aside the remainder.

2 Knead the dough gently on a lightly floured surface until smooth. Roll out and use to line a 12 × 7 in jelly roll pan. Pinch up the edges to make a thin rim.

3 Brush the base with 1 tbsp of the tomato oil, then spread the Tomato Sauce over. Scatter the sun-dried tomatoes, olives and remaining basil over.

4 Mix together the mozzarella and Parmesan and sprinkle over. Drizzle the remaining tomato oil over. Bake for about 20 minutes. Cut lengthwise and across into 24 bite-size pieces. Garnish with extra shredded basil leaves and serve immediately.

Mini Pizzas

For a quick supper dish try these delicious little pizzas made with fresh and sun-dried tomatoes.

Makes 4

INGREDIENTS
1 × 5 oz package pizza mix
8 halves sun-dried tomatoes in olive
    oil, drained
½ cup black olives, pitted
8 oz ripe tomatoes, sliced
¼ cup goat cheese
2 tbsp fresh basil leaves

basil

tomatoes

*sun-dried
tomatoes*

black olives

goat cheese

1 Preheat the oven to 400°F. Make up the pizza base following the instructions on the side of the package.

2 Divide the dough into 4 and roll each piece out to a 5 in disc. Place on a lightly oiled cookie sheet.

3 Place the sun-dried tomatoes and olives in a blender or food processor and blend until smooth. Spread the mixture evenly over the pizza bases.

4 Top with the tomato slices and crumble over the goat cheese. Bake for 10–15 minutes. Sprinkle with the fresh basil and serve.

New Potato, Rosemary and Garlic

New potatoes, smoked mozzarella, rosemary and garlic make the flavor of this pizza unique. For a delicious variation, use sage instead of rosemary.

Serves 2–3

INGREDIENTS
12 oz new potatoes
3 tbsp olive oil
2 garlic cloves, crushed
1 pizza base, 10–12 in diameter
1 red onion, thinly sliced
5 oz smoked mozzarella, grated
2 tsp chopped fresh rosemary
salt and black pepper
2 tbsp freshly grated Parmesan, to
  garnish

olive oil

Parmesan

new potatoes

smoked mozzarella

rosemary

red onion

garlic

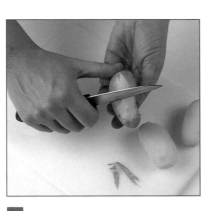

1 Preheat the oven to 425°F. Cook the potatoes in boiling salted water for 5 minutes. Drain well. When cool, peel and slice thinly.

2 Heat 2 tbsp of the oil in a frying pan. Add the sliced potatoes and garlic and fry for 5–8 minutes until tender.

3 Brush the pizza base with the remaining oil. Scatter the onion over, then arrange the potatoes on top.

4 Sprinkle over the mozzarella and rosemary. Grind over plenty of black pepper and bake for 15–20 minutes until crisp and golden. Remove from the oven and sprinkle the Parmesan over to serve.

Fresh Herb

Cut this pizza into thin wedges and serve as part of a mixed antipasti.

Serves 8

INGREDIENTS
4 oz mixed fresh herbs, such as
    parsley, basil and oregano
3 garlic cloves, crushed
½ cup heavy cream
1 pizza base, 10–12 in diameter
1 tbsp Garlic Oil
4 oz Pecorino, grated
salt and black pepper

Garlic Oil

heavy cream

Pecorino

basil

parsley

garlic

1 Preheat the oven to 425°F. Chop the herbs in a food processor if you have one.

2 In a bowl mix together the herbs, garlic, cream and seasoning.

3 Brush the pizza base with the Garlic Oil, then spread the herb mixture over.

4 Sprinkle the Pecorino over. Bake for 15–20 minutes until crisp and golden and the topping is still moist. Cut into thin wedges and serve immediately.

Spinach and Ricotta Panzerotti

These make great party food to serve with drinks or as tasty appetizers for a crowd.

Makes 20–24

INGREDIENTS
4 oz frozen chopped spinach,
  defrosted and squeezed dry
2 oz ricotta
2 oz freshly grated Parmesan
generous pinch freshly grated nutmeg
2 quantities Superquick Pizza Dough
1 egg white, lightly beaten
vegetable oil for deep-frying
salt and black pepper

ricotta

nutmeg

vegetable oil

egg

frozen spinach

Parmesan

1 Place the spinach, ricotta, Parmesan, nutmeg and seasoning in a bowl and beat until smooth.

2 Roll out the dough on a lightly floured surface to about ⅛ in thick. Using a 3 in plain round cutter stamp out 20–24 circles.

3 Spread a teaspoon of spinach mixture over one half of each circle.

4 Brush the edges of the dough with a little egg white.

5 Fold the dough over the filling and press the edges firmly together to seal.

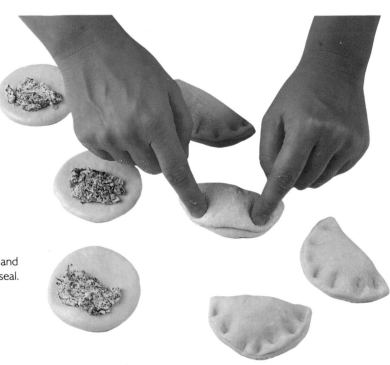

COOK'S TIP
Do serve these as soon as possible after frying, they will become much less appetizing if left to cool.

6 Heat the oil in a large heavy-based pan or deep-fat fryer to 350°F. Deep-fry the panzerotti a few at a time for 2–3 minutes until golden. Drain on paper towels and serve immediately.

Eggplant, Shallot and Sun-dried Tomato Calzone

Eggplant, shallots and sun-dried tomatoes make an unusual filling for calzone. Add more or less red chili flakes, depending on personal taste.

Serves 2

INGREDIENTS
3 tbsp olive oil
3 shallots, chopped
4 baby eggplants
1 garlic clove, chopped
2 oz (drained weight) sun-dried
   tomatoes in oil, chopped
¼ tsp dried red chili flakes
2 tsp chopped fresh thyme
1 quantity Superquick Pizza Dough
3 oz mozzarella, cubed
salt and black pepper
1–2 tbsp freshly grated
   Parmesan, to serve

Parmesan

mozzarella

thyme

olive oil

baby eggplants

shallots

red chili flakes

1 Preheat the oven to 425°F. Heat 2 tbsp of the oil in a frying pan. Add the shallots and cook until soft. Trim the eggplants, then cut into small cubes.

2 Add the eggplants to the shallots with the garlic, sun-dried tomatoes, red chili flakes, thyme and seasoning. Cook for 4–5 minutes, stirring frequently, until the eggplant is beginning to soften. Remove from the heat and let cool.

3 Divide the dough in half and roll out each piece on a lightly floured surface to a 7 in circle.

4 Spread the eggplant mixture over half of each circle, leaving a 1 in border, then scatter the mozzarella over.

5 Dampen the edges with water, then fold over the other half of dough to enclose the filling. Press the edges firmly together to seal. Place on two greased baking sheets.

6 Brush with half the remaining oil and make a small hole in the top of each to allow the steam to escape. Bake for 15–20 minutes until golden. Remove from the oven and brush with the remaining oil. Sprinkle the Parmesan over and serve immediately.

Tomato, Fennel and Parmesan

This pizza relies on the winning combination of tomatoes, fennel and Parmesan. The fennel adds both a crisp texture and a distinctive flavor.

Serves 2–3

INGREDIENTS
1 fennel bulb
3 tbsp Garlic Oil
1 pizza base, 10–12 in diameter
1 quantity Tomato Sauce
2 tbsp chopped fresh Italian parsley
2 oz mozzarella, grated
2 oz Parmesan, grated
salt and black pepper

Italian parsley

mozzarella

Parmesan

Tomato Sauce

fennel bulb

Garlic Oil

1 Preheat the oven to 425°F. Trim and quarter the fennel lengthwise. Remove the core and slice each quarter of fennel thinly.

2 Heat 2 tbsp of the Garlic Oil in a frying pan and sauté the fennel for 4–5 minutes until just tender. Season.

3 Brush the pizza base with the remaining Garlic Oil and spread over the Tomato Sauce. Spoon the fennel on top and scatter the Italian parsley over.

4 Mix together the mozzarella and Parmesan and sprinkle over. Bake for 15–20 minutes until crisp and golden. Serve immediately.

Red Onion, Gorgonzola and Sage

This topping combines the richness of Gorgonzola with the earthy flavors of sage and sweet red onions.

Serves 4

INGREDIENTS
1 quantity Superquick Pizza Dough
2 tbsp Garlic Oil
2 small red onions
5 oz strong Gorgonzola
2 garlic cloves
2 tsp chopped fresh sage
black pepper

sage

Gorgonzola

garlic

Garlic Oil

red onions

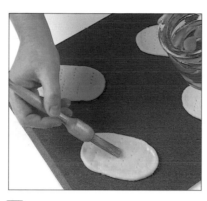

1 Preheat the oven to 425°F. Divide the dough into eight pieces and roll out each one on a lightly floured surface to a small oval about ¼ in thick. Place well apart on two greased baking sheets and prick with a fork. Brush the bases of each oval well with 1 tbsp of the Garlic Oil.

2 Halve, then slice the onions into thin wedges. Scatter over the pizza bases.

3 Remove the rind from the Gorgonzola. Cut the cheese into small cubes, then scatter it over the onions.

4 Cut the garlic lengthwise into thin strips and sprinkle over, along with the sage. Drizzle the remaining oil on top and grind over plenty of black pepper. Bake for 10–15 minutes until crisp and golden. Serve immediately.

Spring Vegetable and Pine Nuts

This colorful pizza is well worth the time it takes to prepare. You can vary the ingredients according to availability.

Serves 2–3

INGREDIENTS
1 pizza base, 10–12 in diameter
3 tbsp Garlic Oil
1 quantity Tomato Sauce
4 scallions
2 zucchini
1 leek
4 oz asparagus tips
1 tbsp chopped fresh oregano
2 tbsp pine nuts
2 oz mozzarella, grated
2 tbsp freshly grated Parmesan
black pepper

Parmesan

mozzarella

Tomato Sauce

scallions

leek

zucchini

asparagus

pine nuts

1 Preheat the oven to 425°F. Brush the pizza base with 1 tbsp of the Garlic Oil, then spread the Tomato Sauce over.

2 Slice the scallions, zucchini, leek and asparagus.

3 Heat half the remaining Garlic Oil in a frying pan and stir-fry the vegetables for 3–5 minutes.

4 Arrange the vegetables over the Tomato Sauce.

5 Sprinkle the oregano and pine nuts over the pizza.

6 Mix together the mozzarella and Parmesan and sprinkle over. Drizzle the remaining Garlic Oil over and season with black pepper. Bake for 15–20 minutes until crisp and golden. Serve immediately.

Quattro Stagioni

(Four Seasons)

This traditional pizza is divided into quarters, each with a different topping to depict the four seasons of the year.

Serves 2–4

INGREDIENTS
3 tbsp olive oil
2 oz mushrooms, sliced
1 pizza base, about 10–12 in diameter
1 quantity Tomato Sauce
2 oz prosciutto
6 pitted black olives, chopped
4 bottled artichoke hearts in oil, drained
3 canned anchovy fillets, drained
2 oz mozzarella, thinly sliced
8 fresh basil leaves, shredded
black pepper

artichoke hearts

mozzarella

olive oil

Tomato Sauce

prosciutto

basil

black olives

mushrooms

anchovy fillets

1 Preheat the oven to 425°F. Heat 1 tbsp of the oil in a frying pan and fry the mushrooms until all the juices have evaporated. Leave to cool.

2 Brush the pizza base with half the remaining oil. Spread over the Tomato Sauce and mark into four equal sections with a knife.

3 Arrange the mushrooms over one section of the pizza.

4 Cut the prosciutto into strips and arrange with the olives on another section.

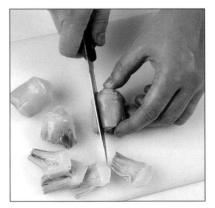

5 Thinly slice the artichoke hearts and arrange over a third section. Halve the anchovies lengthwise and arrange with the mozzarella over the fourth section.

6 Sprinkle the basil over. Drizzle the remaining oil over and season with black pepper. Bake for 15–20 minutes until crisp and golden. Serve immediately.

Pancetta, Leek and Smoked Mozzarella

Smoked mozzarella with its brownish smoky-flavored skin, pancetta and leeks make this an extremely tasty and easy-to-prepare pizza, ideal for a light lunch.

Serves 4

INGREDIENTS
2 tbsp freshly grated Parmesan
1 quantity Superquick Pizza Dough
2 tbsp olive oil
2 medium leeks
8–12 slices pancetta
5 oz smoked mozzarella
black pepper

pancetta

leeks

smoked mozzarella

olive oil

Parmesan

1 Preheat the oven to 425°F. Dust the work surface with the Parmesan, then knead into the dough. Divide the dough into four pieces and roll out each one to a 5 in circle. Place well apart on two greased baking sheets, then pinch up the edges to make a thin rim. Brush with 1 tbsp of the oil.

2 Trim and thinly slice the leeks.

3 Arrange the pancetta and leeks on the pizza bases.

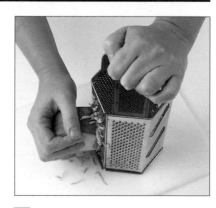

4 Grate the smoked mozzarella and sprinkle over. Drizzle the remaining oil over and season with black pepper. Bake for 15–20 minutes until crisp and golden. Serve immediately.

Ham and Mozzarella Calzone

A calzone is a kind of "inside-out" pizza – the dough is on the outside and the filling on the inside. For a vegetarian version replace the ham with sautéed mushrooms or chopped cooked spinach.

Serves 2

INGREDIENTS
1 quantity Superquick Pizza Dough
4 oz ricotta
2 tbsp freshly grated Parmesan
1 egg yolk
2 tbsp chopped fresh basil
3 oz cooked ham, finely chopped
3 oz mozzarella, cut into small
  cubes
olive oil for brushing
salt and black pepper

basil

ricotta

egg

mozzarella

Parmesan

cooked ham

1 Preheat the oven to 425°F. Divide the dough in to two pieces and roll out each piece on a lightly floured surface to a 7 in circle.

2 In a bowl mix together the ricotta, Parmesan, egg yolk, basil and seasoning.

3 Spread the mixture over half of each circle, leaving a 1 in border, then scatter the ham and mozzarella on top. Dampen the edges with water, then fold over the other half of dough to enclose the filling.

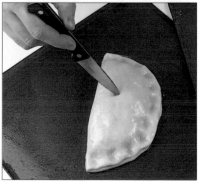

4 Press the edges firmly together to seal. Place on two greased baking sheets. Brush with oil and make a small hole in the top of each to allow the steam to escape. Bake for 15–20 minutes until golden. Serve immediately.

Prosciutto, Mushroom and Artichoke

Here is a pizza full of rich and varied flavors. For a delicious variation use mixed cultivated mushrooms.

Serves 2–3

INGREDIENTS
1 bunch scallions
4 tbsp olive oil
8 oz mushrooms, sliced
2 garlic cloves, chopped
1 pizza base, about 10–12 in
   diameter
8 slices prosciutto
4 bottled artichoke hearts in oil,
   drained and sliced
4 tbsp freshly grated Parmesan
salt and black pepper
thyme sprigs, to garnish

Parmesan

scallions

mushrooms

prosciutto

olive oil

artichoke hearts

1 Preheat the oven to 425°F. Trim the scallions, then chop all the white and some of the green stems.

2 Heat 2 tbsp of the oil in a frying pan. Add the scallions, mushrooms and garlic and fry over a moderate heat until all the juices have evaporated. Season and let cool.

3 Brush the pizza base with half the remaining oil. Arrange the prosciutto, mushrooms and artichoke hearts on top.

4 Sprinkle the Parmesan over, then drizzle the remaining oil over and season. Bake for 15–20 minutes. Garnish with thyme sprigs and serve immediately.

Ham and Pineapple French Bread Pizza

French bread makes a great pizza base. For a really speedy recipe use ready-made pizza topping instead of the Tomato Sauce.

Serves 4

INGREDIENTS
2 small baguettes
1 quantity Tomato Sauce
3 oz sliced cooked ham
4 rings canned pineapple, drained well and chopped
½ small green bell pepper, seeded and cut into thin strips
3 oz sharp Cheddar
salt and black pepper

green bell pepper

sharp Cheddar

pineapple

cooked ham

baguette

Tomato Sauce

1 Preheat the oven to 400°F. Cut the baguettes in half lengthwise and toast the cut sides until crisp and golden.

2 Spread the Tomato Sauce over the toasted baguettes.

3 Cut the ham into strips and arrange on the baguettes with the pineapple and pepper. Season.

4 Grate the Cheddar and sprinkle on top. Bake or broil for 15–20 minutes until crisp and golden.

Prosciutto, Roasted Bell Peppers and Mozzarella Pizzas

Succulent roasted peppers, salty prosciutto and creamy mozzarella – the delicious flavors of these easy pizzas are hard to beat.

Serves 2

INGREDIENTS
½ loaf country bread
1 red bell pepper, roasted and peeled
1 yellow bell pepper, roasted and peeled
4 slices prosciutto, cut into thick strips
3 oz mozzarella
black pepper
tiny basil leaves, to garnish

country bread

basil

mozzarella

prosciutto

red and yellow bell peppers

1 Cut the bread into four thick slices and toast both sides until golden.

2 Cut the roasted peppers into thick strips and arrange on the toasted bread with the prosciutto.

3 Thinly slice the mozzarella and arrange on top. Grind plenty of black pepper over. Place under a hot broiler for 2–3 minutes until the cheese is bubbling.

4 Arrange the basil leaves on top and serve immediately.

Chorizo and Corn

The combination of spicy chorizo and sweet, tender corn works well in this hearty and colorful pizza. For a simple variation you could use chopped fresh basil instead of Italian parsley.

Serves 2–3

INGREDIENTS
1 pizza base, about 10–12 in diameter
1 tbsp Garlic Oil
1 quantity Tomato Sauce
6 oz chorizo sausages
6 oz (drained weight) canned corn kernels
2 tbsp chopped fresh Italian parsley
2 oz mozzarella, grated
2 tbsp freshly grated Parmesan

Tomato Sauce

Italian parsley

mozzarella

Garlic Oil

chorizo sausages

Parmesan

sweetcorn

1 Preheat the oven to 425°F. Brush the pizza base with Garlic Oil and spread over the Tomato Sauce.

2 Skin and cut the chorizo sausages into chunks and scatter over the Tomato Sauce. Bake for 10 minutes then remove from the oven.

3 Sprinkle over the corn and Italian parsley.

4 Mix together the mozzarella and Parmesan and sprinkle over. Bake for a further 5–10 minutes until crisp and golden. Serve immediately.

American Hot

This popular pizza is spiced with green chilies and pepperoni.

Serves 2–3

INGREDIENTS
1 pizza base, about 10–12 in
    diameter
1 tbsp olive oil
4 oz can peeled and chopped green
    chilies in brine, drained
1 quantity Tomato Sauce
3 oz sliced pepperoni
6 pitted black olives
1 tbsp chopped fresh oregano
4 oz mozzarella, grated
oregano leaves, to garnish

mozzarella

oregano

Tomato Sauce

pepperoni

olive oil

green chillies

black olives

1 Preheat the oven to 425°F. Brush the pizza base with the oil.

2 Stir the chilies into the sauce, and spread over the base.

3 Sprinkle the pepperoni over.

4 Halve the olives lengthwise and sprinkle over, with the oregano.

5 Sprinkle the grated mozzarella over and bake for 15–20 minutes until the pizza is crisp and golden.

VARIATION

You can make this pizza as hot as you like. For a really fiery version use fresh red or green chilies, cut into thin slices, in place of the chilies in brine.

6 Garnish with oregano leaves and serve immediately.

Spicy Sausage

This is a tasty and substantial pizza. You may substitute fresh Italian spicy sausages, available from good Italian delicatessens, if you prefer.

Serves 3–4

INGREDIENTS
8 oz good quality pork sausages
1 tsp mild chili powder
½ tsp freshly ground black pepper
2 tbsp olive oil
2–3 garlic cloves
1 pizza base, about 10–12 in
    diameter
1 quantity Tomato Sauce
1 red onion, thinly sliced
1 tbsp chopped fresh oregano
1 tbsp chopped fresh thyme
2 oz mozzarella, grated
2 oz freshly grated Parmesan

thyme and oregano

Tomato Sauce

red onion

Parmesan

mozzarella

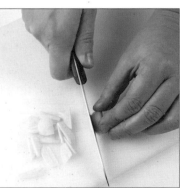
olive oil

pork sausages

1 Preheat the oven to 425°F. Skin the sausages by running a sharp knife down the side of the skins. Place the sausage meat in a bowl and add the chili powder and black pepper; mix well. Break the sausage meat mixture into walnut-sized balls.

2 Heat 1 tbsp of the oil in a frying pan and fry the sausage balls for 2–3 minutes until evenly browned.

3 Using a slotted spoon remove the sausage balls from the pan and drain on paper towels.

4 Thinly slice the garlic cloves.

5 Brush the pizza base with the remaining oil, then spread over the Tomato Sauce. Scatter the sausages, garlic, onion and herbs over.

6 Sprinkle over the mozzarella and Parmesan and bake for 15–20 minutes until crisp and golden. Serve immediately.

mild chili powder

Caramelized Onion, Salami and Black Olive

The flavor of the sweet caramelized onion is offset by the salty black olives and herbes de Provence in the pizza base and the sprinkling of Parmesan to finish.

Serves 4

INGREDIENTS
1½ lb red onions
4 tbsp olive oil
12 pitted black olives
1 quantity Superquick Pizza Dough
1 tsp dried herbes de Provence
6–8 slices Italian salami, quartered
2–3 tbsp freshly grated
  Parmesan
black pepper

Italian salami

olive oil

red onions

Parmesan

black olives

herbes de Provence

1 Preheat the oven to 425°F. Thinly slice the onions.

2 Heat 2 tbsp of the oil in a pan and add the onions. Cover and cook gently for 10 minutes, stirring occasionally until the onions are soft and very lightly colored. Leave to cool.

3 Finely chop the black olives.

4 Knead the dough on a lightly floured surface, adding the black olives and herbes de Provence. Roll out the dough and use to line a 12 × 7 in jelly roll pan. Pinch up the dough edges to make a thin rim and brush with half the remaining oil.

5 Spoon half the onions over the base, top with the salami and the remaining onions.

6 Grind over plenty of black pepper and drizzle over the remaining oil. Bake for 15–20 minutes until crisp and golden. Remove from the oven and sprinkle the Parmesan over to serve.

Pepperoni Pan Pizza

This pizza is made using a scone base which happily does not require proving! The topping can be varied to include whatever you like best – tunafish, shrimp, ham or salami are all good alternatives to the pepperoni.

Serves 2–3

INGREDIENTS
1 tbsp chopped fresh mixed herbs
1 quantity Scone Pizza Dough
2 tbsp tomato paste
14 oz can crushed tomatoes, drained well
2 oz mushrooms, thinly sliced
3 oz sliced pepperoni
6 pitted black olives, chopped
2 oz Edam, grated
2 oz sharp Cheddar, grated
1 tbsp chopped fresh basil, to garnish

1 Add the herbs to the scone mix before mixing to a soft dough.

2 Turn the dough on to a lightly floured surface and knead lightly until smooth. Roll out to fit a well-greased frying pan, about 8½ in diameter.

3 Cook the dough in the pan over a low heat for about 5 minutes until the base is golden. Lift carefully with a spatula to check.

sharp Cheddar

Edam

chopped tomatoes

mushrooms

black olives

basil

fresh mixed herbs

pepperoni

tomato paste

4 Turn the base on to a baking sheet, then slide it back into the pan, with the cooked side uppermost.

5 Mix together the tomato paste and drained tomatoes and spread over the pizza base. Scatter over the mushrooms, pepperoni, olives and cheeses. Continue to cook for about 5 minutes until the underside is golden.

6 When it is ready, transfer the pan to a preheated moderate broiler for 4–5 minutes to melt the cheese. Scatter the basil over and serve immediately.

Beef Chili

Ground beef, red kidney beans and smoky cheese combined with oregano, cumin and chilies give this pizza a Mexican character.

Serves 4

INGREDIENTS
2 tbsp olive oil
1 red onion, finely chopped
1 garlic clove, crushed
½ red pepper, seeded and finely chopped
6 oz lean ground beef
½ tsp ground cumin
2 fresh red chiles, seeded and chopped
4 oz (drained weight) canned red kidney beans
1 quantity Superquick Pizza Dough
1 quantity Tomato Sauce
1 tbsp chopped fresh oregano
2 oz mozzarella, grated
3 oz oak-smoked Cheddar, grated
salt and black pepper

1 Preheat the oven to 425°F. Heat 1 tbsp of the oil in a frying pan, add the onion, garlic and pepper and gently fry until soft. Increase the heat, add the beef and brown well, stirring constantly.

2 Add the cumin and chilies and continue to cook, stirring, for about 5 minutes. Add the beans and seasoning.

3 Roll out the dough on a surface dusted with cornmeal and use to line a 12 × 7 in greased jelly roll pan. Pinch up the dough edges to make a rim.

red onion

Tomato Sauce

ground beef

mozzarella

smoked Cheddar

red chilies

oregano

olive oil

red kidney beans

red bell peppers

4 Spread the Tomato Sauce over.

5 Spoon the beef mixture over then sprinkle the oregano over.

6 Sprinkle the cheeses over and bake for 15–20 minutes until crisp and golden. Serve immediately.

VARIATION

If you prefer a milder version of this spicy pizza, reduce the amount of fresh chilies or leave them out altogether.

Chicken, Shiitake Mushroom and Cilantro

The addition of shiitake mushrooms adds an earthy flavor to this colorful pizza, while fresh red chili provides a hint of spiciness.

Serves 3–4

INGREDIENTS
3 tbsp olive oil
12 oz chicken breast fillets, skinned and cut into thin strips
1 bunch scallions, sliced
1 fresh red chili, seeded and chopped
1 red bell pepper, seeded and cut into thin strips
3 oz fresh shiitake mushrooms, wiped and sliced
3–4 tbsp chopped fresh cilantro
1 pizza base, about 10–12 in diameter
1 tbsp Chili Oil
5 oz mozzarella
salt and black pepper

chicken breast fillets

scallions

red chili

cilantro

red bell pepper

olive oil

Chili Oil

shiitake mushrooms

1 Preheat the oven to 425°F. Heat 2 tbsp of the olive oil in a wok or large frying pan. Add the chicken, scallions, chili, pepper and mushrooms and stir-fry over a high heat for 2–3 minutes until the chicken is firm but still slightly pink within. Season to taste.

2 Pour off any excess oil, then set aside the chicken mixture to cool.

3 Stir the fresh cilantro into the chicken mixture.

4 Brush the pizza base with the chili oil.

5 Spoon the chicken mixture over and drizzle the remaining olive oil over.

6 Grate the mozzarella and sprinkle over. Bake for 15–20 minutes until crisp and golden. Serve immediately.

Smoked Chicken, Yellow Pepper and Sun-dried Tomato Pizzettes

These ingredients complement each other perfectly and make a really delicious topping.

Serves 4

INGREDIENTS
1 quantity Superquick Pizza Dough
3 tbsp olive oil
4 tbsp sun-dried tomato paste
2 yellow bell peppers, seeded and
 cut into thin strips
6 oz sliced smoked chicken or
 turkey, chopped
5 oz mozzarella, cubed
2 tbsp chopped fresh basil
salt and black pepper

basil

mozzarella

yellow bell peppers

olive oil

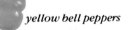

smoked chicken

sun-dried tomato paste

1 Preheat the oven to 425°F. Divide the dough into four pieces and roll out each one on a lightly floured surface to a 5 in circle. Place well apart on two greased baking sheets, then pinch up the dough edges to make a thin rim. Brush with 1 tbsp of the oil.

2 Brush the pizza bases generously with the sun-dried tomato paste.

3 Stir-fry the peppers in half the remaining oil for 3–4 minutes.

4 Arrange the chicken and peppers on top of the sun-dried tomato paste.

5 Scatter the mozzarella and basil over. Season with salt and black pepper.

VARIATION

For a vegetarian pizza with a similar smoky taste, omit the chicken, roast the yellow peppers and remove the skins before using, and replace the mozzarella with Gouda smoked cheese.

6 Drizzle over the remaining oil and bake for 15–20 minutes until crisp and golden. Serve immediately.

Mixed Seafood

Here is a pizza that gives you the full flavor of the Mediterranean, ideal for a summer evening supper!

Serves 3–4

INGREDIENTS
1 pizza base, 10–12 in diameter
2 tbsp olive oil
1 quantity Tomato Sauce
14 oz mixed cooked seafood
 (including mussels, shrimp and
 squid)
3 garlic cloves
2 tbsp chopped fresh parsley
2 tbsp freshly grated Parmesan, to
 garnish

mixed seafood

garlic

olive oil

parsley

Tomato Sauce

Parmesan

1 Preheat the oven to 425°F. Brush the pizza base with 1 tbsp of the oil.

2 Spread the Tomato Sauce over. Bake in the oven for 10 minutes. Remove from the oven.

3 Pat the seafood dry using paper towels, then arrange on top.

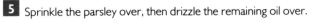

4 Chop the garlic and sprinkle over.

5 Sprinkle the parsley over, then drizzle the remaining oil over.

VARIATION

If you prefer, this pizza can be made with mussels or shrimp on their own, or any combination of your favorite seafood.

6 Bake for a further 5–10 minutes until the seafood is warmed through and the base is crisp and golden. Sprinkle with Parmesan and serve immediately.

Salmon and Avocado

Smoked and fresh salmon make a delicious pizza topping when mixed with avocado. Smoked salmon trimmings are cheaper than smoked salmon slices and could be used instead.

Serves 3–4

INGREDIENTS
5 oz salmon fillet
½ cup dry white wine
1 pizza base, 10–12 in diameter
1 tbsp olive oil
14 oz can chopped tomatoes, drained well
4 oz mozzarella, grated
1 small avocado
2 tsp lemon juice
2 tbsp crème fraîche
3 oz smoked salmon, cut into strips
1 tbsp capers
2 tbsp chopped fresh chives, to garnish
black pepper

lemon

dry white wine

chopped tomatoes

mozzarella

avocado

smoked salmon

salmon fillet

crème fraîche

1 Preheat the oven to 425°F. Place the salmon fillet in a frying pan, pour the wine over and season with black pepper. Bring slowly to a boil, remove from the heat, cover and cool. (The fish will continue to cook in the cooling liquid.) Skin and flake the salmon into small pieces, removing any bones.

2 Brush the pizza base with the oil and spread over the drained tomatoes. Sprinkle 2 oz of the mozzarella over. Bake for 10 minutes, then remove from the oven.

3 Meanwhile, halve, pit and peel the avocado. Cut the flesh into small cubes and toss carefully in the lemon juice.

4 Dot teaspoonsful of the crème fraîche over the pizza base.

5 Arrange the fresh and smoked salmon, avocado, capers and remaining mozzarella on top. Season with black pepper. Bake for a further 5–10 minutes until crisp and golden.

6 Sprinkle the chives over and serve immediately.

Mussel and Leek Pizzettes

Serve these tasty seafood pizzettes with a crisp green salad for a light lunch.

Serves 4

INGREDIENTS
1 lb live mussels
½ cup dry white wine
1 quantity Superquick Pizza Dough
1 tbsp olive oil
2 oz Gruyère
2 oz mozzarella
2 small leeks
salt and black pepper

olive oil

dry white wine

mozzarella

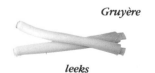

mussels

Gruyère

leeks

1 Preheat the oven to 425°F. Place the mussels in a bowl of cold water to soak, and scrub well. Remove the beards and discard any mussels that are open.

2 Place the mussels in a pan. Pour over the wine, cover and cook over a high heat, shaking the pan occasionally, for 5–10 minutes until the mussels have opened.

3 Drain off the cooking liquid. Remove the mussels from their shells, discarding any that remain closed. Leave to cool.

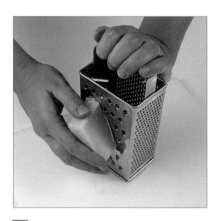

4 Divide the dough into four pieces and roll out each one on a lightly floured surface to a 5 in circle. Place well apart on two greased baking sheets, then pinch up the dough edges to form a thin rim. Brush the pizza bases with the oil. Grate the cheeses and sprinkle half evenly over the bases.

5 Thinly slice the leeks, then scatter over the cheese. Bake for 10 minutes, then remove from the oven.

VARIATION

Frozen or canned mussels can also be used, but will not have the same flavor and texture. Make sure you defrost the mussels properly.

6 Arrange the mussels on top. Season and sprinkle the remaining cheese over. Bake for a further 5–10 minutes until crisp and golden. Serve immediately.

Shrimp, Sun-dried Tomato and Basil Pizzettes

Sun-dried tomatoes with their concentrated caramelized tomato flavor make an excellent topping for pizzas. Serve these pretty pizzettes as an appetizer or snack.

Serves 4

INGREDIENTS
1 quantity Superquick Pizza Dough
2 tbsp Chili Oil
3 oz mozzarella, grated
1 garlic clove, chopped
½ small red onion, thinly sliced
4–6 pieces sun-dried tomatoes, thinly
  sliced
4 oz cooked medium shrimp, peeled
2 tbsp chopped fresh basil
salt and black pepper
shredded basil leaves, to garnish

basil

mozzarella

Chili Oil

red onion

sun-dried tomatoes

garlic

1 Preheat the oven to 425°F. Divide the dough into eight pieces.

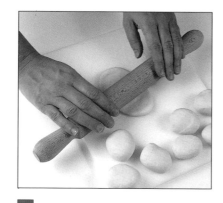

2 Roll out each one on a lightly floured surface to a small oval about ¼ in thick. Place well apart on two greased baking sheets. Prick all over with a fork.

3 Brush the pizza bases with 1 tbsp of the chili oil and top with the mozzarella, leaving a ½ in border.

4 Divide the garlic, onion, sun-dried tomatoes, shrimp and basil between the pizza bases. Season and drizzle the remaining chili oil over. Bake for 8–10 minutes until crisp and golden. Garnish with basil leaves and serve immediately.

Crab and Parmesan Calzonelli

These miniature calzone owe their popularity to their impressive presentation. If preferred, you can use shrimp instead of crab.

Makes 10–12

INGREDIENTS
1 quantity Superquick Pizza Dough
4 oz mixed prepared crab meat, defrosted if frozen
1 tbsp heavy cream
2 tbsp freshly grated Parmesan
2 tbsp chopped fresh parsley
1 garlic clove, crushed
salt and black pepper
parsley sprigs, to garnish

Parmesan

heavy cream

crabmeat

parsley

garlic

1 Preheat the oven to 400°F. Roll out the dough on a lightly floured surface to ⅛ in thick. Using a 3 in plain round cutter stamp out 10–12 circles.

2 In a bowl mix together the crabmeat, cream, Parmesan, parsley, garlic and seasoning.

3 Spoon a little of the filling on to one half of each circle. Dampen the edges with water and fold over to enclose filling.

4 Seal the edges by pressing with a fork. Place well apart on two greased baking sheets. Bake for 10–15 minutes until golden. Garnish with parsley sprigs.

Tuna, Anchovy and Caper

This pizza makes a substantial supper dish which will provide two to three generous portions accompanied by a simple salad.

Serves 2–3

INGREDIENTS
1 quantity Scone Pizza Dough
2 tbsp olive oil
1 quantity Tomato Sauce
1 small red onion
7 oz can tuna, drained
15 ml/1 tbsp capers
12 pitted black olives
3 tbsp freshly grated Parmesan
2 oz can anchovy fillets, drained
    and halved lengthways
black pepper

Tomato Sauce

olive oil

Parmesan

black olives

tuna

red onion

capers

1 Preheat the oven to 425°F. Roll out the dough on a lightly floured surface to a 10 in circle. Place on a greased baking sheet and brush with 1 tbsp of the oil. Spread the Tomato Sauce evenly over the dough.

2 Cut the onion into thin wedges and arrange on top.

3 Coarsely flake the tuna with a fork and scatter the onion over.

4 Sprinkle the capers, black olives and Parmesan over.

5 Lattice the anchovy fillets over the top of the pizza.

6 Drizzle the remaining oil over, then grind over plenty of black pepper. Bake for 15–20 minutes until crisp and golden. Serve immediately.

DAZZLING

Happy endings are only a moment away with this superb

selection of sweet treats. Not surprisingly, fresh fruit features

strongly. Who could resist Pineapple Wedges with Rum Butter Glaze,

Ginger and Banana Brûlée or the warm

promise of Kentucky Fried Peaches?

Nectarines with Marzipan and

Mascarpone can be made in a jiffy, yet are stylish enough to serve after the grandest meal. For children of all ages, from six to sixty-six, Fruit Kebabs with Chocolate and Marshmallow Fondue provide the perfect finale to any meal.

DESSERTS

Caramelized Apples

A sweet, sticky dessert which is very quickly made, and usually very quickly eaten!

Serves 4

INGREDIENTS
1½ lb sweet apples
½ cup unsalted butter
1 oz fresh white bread crumbs
½ cup ground almonds
rind of 2 lemons, finely grated
4 tbsp corn syrup
4 tbsp thick strained yogurt,
   to serve

lemon

corn syrup

ground almonds

apple

1 Peel and core the apples.

2 Carefully cut the apples into ½ in-thick rings.

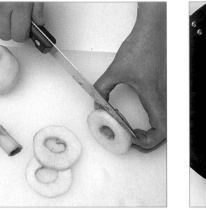

3 Heat the wok, then add the butter. When the butter has melted, add the apple rings and stir-fry for 4 minutes until golden and tender. Remove from the wok, reserving the butter. Add the bread crumbs to the hot butter and stir-fry for 1 minute.

4 Stir in the ground almonds and lemon rind and stir-fry for a further 3 minutes, stirring constantly. Sprinkle the breadcrumb mix over the apples, then drizzle warmed corn syrup over the top. Serve with thick strained yogurt.

Char-grilled Apples on Cinnamon Toasts

This simple, scrumptious dessert is best made with an enriched bread such as brioche, but any light, sweet bread will do.

Serves 4

4 sweet dessert apples
juice of ¹/₂ lemon
4 individual brioches or muffins
4 tbsp melted butter
2 tbsp golden superfine sugar
1 tsp ground cinnamon
cream or plain yogurt, to serve

sweet dessert apples

superfine sugar

lemon

brioches

melted butter

ground cinnamon

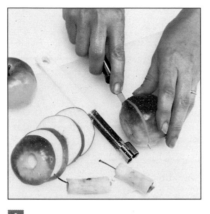

1 Core the apples and then cut them horizontally in 3–4 thick slices. Sprinkle with lemon juice.

2 Cut the brioches or muffins into thick slices. Brush with melted butter on both sides.

3 Mix together the sugar and cinnamon.

4 Place the apple and brioche slices on the hot barbecue and cook them for 3–4 minutes, turning once, until they are beginning to turn golden brown.

5 Sprinkle half the cinnamon sugar over the apple slices and toasts and cook for a further minute, until they are a rich golden brown.

6 To serve, arrange the apple slices over the toasts and sprinkle them with the remaining cinnamon sugar. Serve hot, with cream or yogurt.

Fruit Kebabs with Chocolate and Marshmallow Fondue

Children love these treats – and with supervision they can help to make them.

Serves 4

2 bananas
2 kiwis
12 strawberries
1 tbsp melted butter
1 tbsp lemon juice
1 tsp ground cinnamon

FOR THE FONDUE
8 oz baking chocolate
¹/₂ cup light cream
8 marshmallows
¹/₂ tsp vanilla extract

baking chocolate

bananas

vanilla extract

lemon juice

ground cinnamon

melted butter

light cream

marshmallows

kiwis

strawberries

1 Peel the bananas and cut each into six thick chunks. Peel the kiwis thinly and quarter them. Thread the bananas, kiwis and strawberries onto four wooden or bamboo skewers.

2 Mix together the butter, lemon juice and cinnamon and brush the mixture over the fruits.

3 For the fondue, place the chocolate, cream and marshmallows in a small pan and heat gently on the barbecue, without boiling, stirring until the mixture has melted and is smooth.

4 Cook the kebabs on the barbecue for 2–3 minutes, turning once, or until golden. Stir the vanilla extract into the fondue and serve it with the kebabs.

Barbecued Strawberry Croissants

A deliciously simple, sinful dessert.

Serves 4

4 croissants
½ cup ricotta cheese
½ cup strawberry preserves
  or jam

croissants

ricotta cheese

strawberry preserves

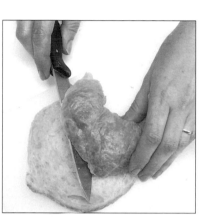

1 Split the croissants in half and open them out on a board.

2 Spread the bottom half of each croissant with ricotta cheese.

3 Top with a generous spoonful of strawberry preserves and replace the top half of the croissant.

4 Place the croissants on a hot barbecue and cook for 2–3 minutes, turning once.

COOK'S TIP

As an alternative to croissants, try fresh scones or muffins, toasted on the barbecue.

Pineapple Wedges with Rum Butter Glaze

Fresh pineapple is even more full of flavor when grilled; this spiced rum glaze makes it into a very special dessert.

Serves 4

1 medium pineapple
2 tbsp dark raw sugar
1 tsp ground ginger
4 tbsp melted butter
2 tbsp dark rum

pineapple

melted butter

dark raw sugar

ground ginger   *dark rum*

 With a large, sharp knife, cut the pineapple lengthwise into four wedges. Cut out and discard the center core.

2 Cut between the flesh and skin, to release the flesh, but leave the skin in place. Slice the flesh across, into chunks.

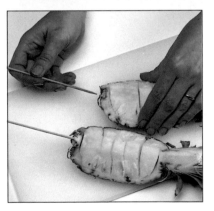

3 Push a bamboo skewer lengthwise through each wedge and into the stalk, to hold the chunks in place.

4 Mix together the sugar, ginger, melted butter and rum and brush over the pineapple. Cook the wedges on a hot barbecue for 3–4 minutes; pour the remaining glaze over the top and serve.

COOK'S TIP

For an easier version, simply cut off the skin and then slice the whole pineapple into thick slices and cook as above.

Nectarines with Marzipan and Mascarpone

A luscious dessert that no one can resist – dieters may like to use low-fat soft cheese or ricotta instead of mascarpone.

Serves 4

4 firm, ripe nectarines or
  peaches
3 oz marzipan
5 tbsp mascarpone cheese
3 macaroons crushed

mascarpone cheese

nectarines

marzipan

macaroons

1 Cut the nectarines or peaches in half, removing the pits.

2 Cut the marzipan into eight pieces and press one piece into the pit cavity of each nectarine half.

COOK'S TIP

Either peaches or nectarines can be used for this recipe. If the pit does not pull out easily when you halve the fruit, use a small, sharp knife to cut around it.

3 Spoon the mascarpone on top. Sprinkle the crushed macaroons over the mascarpone.

4 Place the half-fruits on a hot barbecue for 3–5 minutes, until they are hot and the mascarpone starts to melt.

Mango and Coconut Stir-fry

Choose a ripe mango for this recipe. If you buy one that is a little under-ripe, leave it in a warm place for a day or two before using.

Serves 4

INGREDIENTS
¼ coconut
1 large, ripe mango
juice of 2 limes
rind of 2 limes, finely grated
1 tbsp sunflower oil
1 tbsp butter
1½ tbsp honey
sour cream or yogurt, to serve

coconut

mango

honey

lime

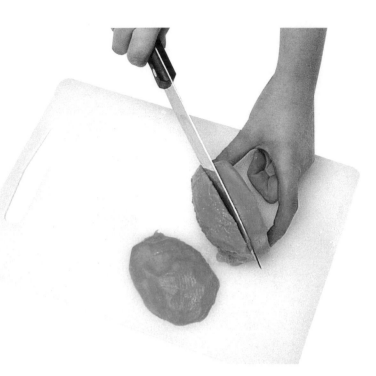

1 Prepare the coconut shreds by draining the milk from the coconut and shredding the flesh with a peeler.

2 Peel the mango. Cut the pit out of the middle of the fruit. Cut each half of the mango into slices.

COOK'S TIP

Because of the delicate taste of desserts, always make sure your wok has been scrupulously cleaned so there is no transference of flavors – a garlicky mango isn't quite the effect you want to achieve!

3 Place the mango slices in a bowl and pour over the lime juice and rind, to marinate them.

4 Meanwhile, heat the wok, then add 2 tsp of the oil. When the oil is hot, add the butter. When the butter has melted, stir in the coconut shreds and stir-fry for 1–2 minutes until the coconut is golden brown. Remove and drain on paper towels. Wipe out the wok. Strain the mango slices, reserving the juice.

5 Heat the wok and add the remaining oil. When the oil is hot, add the mango and stir-fry for 1–2 minutes, then add the juice and allow to bubble and reduce for 1 minute. Then stir in the honey, sprinkle on the coconut and serve with sour cream or yogurt.

Apples and Raspberries in Rose Pouchong Syrup

Inspiration for this dessert stems from the fact that the apple and the raspberry belong to the rose family. The subtle flavors are shared here in an infusion of rose-scented tea.

COOK'S TIP

If fresh raspberries are out of season, use the same weight of frozen fruit or a 14 oz can of well drained fruit.

Serves 4

INGREDIENTS
1 tsp rose pouchong tea
1 tsp rose water (optional)
¼ cup sugar
1 tsp lemon juice
5 dessert apples
1 ½ cups fresh raspberries

tea

apples

sugar

raspberries

1 Warm a large tea pot. Add the rose pouchong tea and 3¾ cups of boiling water together with the rose water, if using. Allow the tea to stand and infuse for 4 minutes.

2 Measure the sugar and lemon juice into a stainless steel saucepan. Strain in the tea and stir to dissolve the sugar.

3 Peel and core the apples, then cut into quarters.

4 Poach the apples in the syrup for about 5 minutes.

5 Transfer the apples and syrup to a large metal tray and leave to cool to room temperature.

6 Pour the cooled apples and syrup into a bowl, add the raspberries and mix to combine. Spoon into individual glass dishes or bowls and serve warm.

Apricot and Almond Bake

This dessert consists of a few apricots, either fresh or canned, strewn over an almond batter. Hot from the oven, this dessert is bound to please with a scoop or two of best vanilla ice cream.

Serves 4

INGREDIENTS
4 tbsp butter, softened, plus extra for
   greasing
¼ cup superfine sugar
¾ ground almonds
1 tbsp self-rising flour
1 egg
½ tsp almond extract
1 cup fresh apricots or 1 × 14 oz can
   apricots in syrup
confectioners' sugar, for dusting
vanilla ice cream, custard or cream,
   to serve

butter

egg

apricots

flour

ground almonds

superfine sugar

1 Preheat the oven to 400°F. Lightly grease a 9 in enamel pie plate with butter and set aside.

2 Soften the butter if necessary in a microwave oven for 20 seconds at 100% high power. Combine the butter and sugar in a mixing bowl.

3 Mix the ground almonds and flour together and add to the butter.

4 Add the egg and almond extract, then combine into a smooth batter.

5 Turn the batter into a pie plate and spread it to the edge. Split the apricots, peel and discard the pits if using fresh fruit, and arrange over the batter. Bake in the preheated oven for 15–20 minutes until springy to the touch.

6 Dust with sugar and serve hot with vanilla ice cream, cream or custard.

Kentucky Fried Peaches

Never mind your diet, when peaches are this good, it's time for a break!

Serves 4

INGREDIENTS
5 large ripe peaches
4 tbsp butter
2 tbsp brown sugar
3 tbsp Kentucky bourbon
2 pints/5 cups vanilla ice
   cream
½ cup pecan nuts, toasted

COOK'S TIP
Peaches that ripen after they are picked will not release their skins when blanched in boiling water.

I Place the peaches in a large bowl and cover with boiling water to loosen their skins. Drain, refresh under cold running water and slice.

2 Heat the butter in a large frying pan until it foams and begins to brown. Add the sugar, peaches and bourbon, turn up the heat and cook until soft and syrupy. Spoon the hot peaches over the ice cream and decorate with pecan nuts.

vanilla ice cream

pecan nuts

bourbon

peaches

butter

brown sugar

Broiled Pineapple with Rum-custard Sauce

Freshly ground black pepper may seem an unusual ingredient to put with pineapple, until you realise that peppercorns are the fruit of a tropical vine. If the idea does not appeal, make the sauce without pepper.

Serves 4

INGREDIENTS
1 ripe pineapple
2 tbsp butter
fresh strawberries, sliced, to serve

FOR THE SAUCE
1 egg
2 egg yolks
2 tbsp superfine sugar
2 tbsp dark rum
½ tsp freshly ground black
  pepper

pineapple

butter

rum

eggs

black pepper

superfine sugar

1 Remove the top and bottom from the pineapple with a serrated knife. Pare away the outer skin from top to bottom, remove the core and cut into slices.

2 Preheat a moderate broiler. Dot the pineapple slices with butter and broil for about 5 minutes.

3 To make the sauce, place all the ingredients in a bowl. Set over a saucepan of simmering water and whisk with a hand-held mixer for about 3–4 minutes or until foamy and cooked. Scatter the strawberries over the pineapple and serve with the sauce.

COOK'S TIP

The sweetest pineapples are picked and exported when ripe. Contrary to popular belief, pineapples do not ripen well after picking. Choose fruit that smells sweet and yields to firm pressure from your thumbs.

Cherry Crêpes

These crêpes are virtually fat-free, and lower in calories and higher in fiber than traditional ones. Serve with plain yogurt or fromage frais.

Serves 4

INGREDIENTS
FOR THE CRÊPES
½ cup all-purpose flour
⅓ cup all-purpose whole wheat flour
pinch of salt
1 egg white
⅔ cup skim milk
⅔ cup water
a little oil for frying

FOR THE FILLING
15 oz can black cherries in juice
1½ tsp arrowroot

1 Sift the flours and salt into a bowl, adding any bran left in the sifter to the bowl at the end.

2 Make a well in the center of the flour and add the egg white. Gradually beat in the milk and water, whisking hard until all the liquid is incorporated and the batter is smooth and bubbly.

skim milk

whole wheat flour

all-purpose flour

arrowroot

black cherries

egg

3 Heat a non-stick pan with a small amount of oil until the pan is very hot. Pour in just enough batter to cover the base of the pan, swirling the pan to cover the base evenly.

4 Cook until the crêpe is set and golden, and then turn to cook the other side. Remove to a sheet of paper towel and then cook the remaining batter to make about eight crêpes.

5 Drain the cherries, reserving the juice. Blend about 2 tbsp of the juice from the can of cherries with the arrowroot in a saucepan. Stir in the rest of the juice. Heat gently, stirring, until boiling. Stir over moderate heat for about 2 minutes, until thickened and clear.

COOK'S TIP

If fresh cherries are in season, cook them gently in enough apple juice just to cover them, and then thicken the juice with arrowroot as in Step 5.

The basic crêpes will freeze very successfully. Layer them with paper towels or wax paper, overwrap them in plastic wrap and seal. Freeze for up to six months. Thaw at room temperature.

6 Add the cherries and stir until thoroughly heated. Spoon the cherries into the crêpes and fold them in quarters.

Crispy Cinnamon Toasts

This recipe is based on a sweet version of French toast. You can use fancy cutters to create a pretty dessert or, if you do not have cutters, simply cut the crusts off the bread and cut it into little fingers.

Serves 4

INGREDIENTS
2 oz raisins
3 tbsp Grand Marnier
4 medium slices white bread
3 medium eggs, beaten
1 tbsp ground cinnamon
2 large oranges
1½ tbsp sunflower oil
2 tbsp unsalted butter
1 tbsp raw sugar
thick strained yogurt, to serve

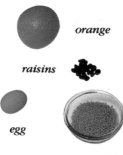

orange

raisins

egg

raw sugar

bread

1 Soak the raisins in the Grand Marnier for 10 minutes.

2 Cut the bread into shapes with a cutter. Place the shapes in a bowl with the eggs and cinnamon to soak.

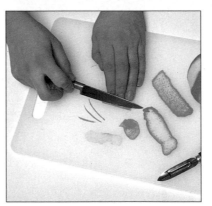

3 Peel the oranges. Remove any excess pith from the peel, then cut it into fine strips and blanch. Refresh it in cold water, then drain.

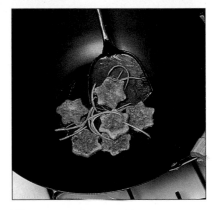

4 Strain the raisins. Heat the wok, then add the oil. When the oil is hot, stir in the butter until melted, then add the bread and fry, turning once, until golden brown. Stir in the raisins and orange rind, and sprinkle with sugar. Serve warm with thick strained yogurt.

Apple Soufflé Omelet

Apples sautéed until they are slightly caramelized make a delicious filling for an omelet dredged with confectioners' sugar and 'branded' with a hot skewer.

Serves 2

INGREDIENTS
4 eggs, separated
2 tbsp light cream
1 tbsp superfine sugar
1 tbsp butter
confectioners' sugar, for dredging

FOR THE FILLING
2 tbsp butter
1 apple, peeled, cored and sliced
2 tbsp brown sugar
3 tbsp light cream

eggs

light cream

superfine sugar

butter

confectioners' sugar

apple

brown sugar

1 Make the filling. Melt the butter in a frying pan. Add the apples and sprinkle them with the brown sugar. Sauté until the apples are just tender and have caramelized a little. Stir in the cream and keep warm while making the omelet.

2 Place the egg yolks in a bowl. Add the cream and sugar and beat well. In a grease-free bowl whisk the egg whites until they hold soft peaks, then fold them into the yolk mixture.

3 Preheat the broiler. Melt the butter in a large, heavy frying pan. Pour in the soufflé mixture and spread evenly. Cook for 1 minute, until golden underneath, then place the pan under the hot broiler to brown the top of the omelet.

4 Heat a metal skewer. Slide the omelet onto a plate, add the apple mixture, then fold it over. Sift the confectioners' sugar over thickly, then mark in a criss-cross pattern with a hot metal skewer. Serve immediately.

Red Berry Sponge Tart

When soft berry fruits are in season, try making this delicious sponge tart. Serve warm from the oven with scoops of vanilla ice cream.

Serves 4

INGREDIENTS
softened butter, for greasing
4 cups soft berry fruits such as
    raspberries, blackberries, black
    currants, red currants, strawberries
    or blueberries
2 eggs, at room temperature
¼ cup superfine sugar, plus extra to
    taste (optional)
1 tbsp flour
¾ cup ground almonds
vanilla ice cream, to serve

1 Preheat the oven to 375°F. Brush a 9 in pic pan with softened butter and line the bottom with a circle of non-stick baking paper. Scatter the fruit in the bottom of the pan with a little sugar if the fruits are tart.

2 Whisk the eggs and sugar together for about 3–4 minutes or until they leave a thick trail across the surface. Combine the flour and almonds, then fold into the egg mixture with a spatula – retaining as much air as possible.

eggs

ground almonds

flour

superfine sugar

red currants

black currants

raspberries   *strawberries*

3 Spread the mixture on top of the fruit base and bake in the preheated oven for 15 minutes. Turn out onto a serving plate and serve with vanilla ice cream.

VARIATION

When berry fruits are out of season, use bottled fruits, but ensure that they are well drained before use.

Orange Yogurt Brûlée

A luxurious treat, but one that is much lower in fat than the classic brûlée, which are made with cream, eggs and large amounts of sugar.

Serves 4

INGREDIENTS
2 medium-size oranges
⅔ cup plain strained yogurt
¼ cup crème fraîche
3 tbsp raw sugar
2 tbsp light brown sugar

light brown sugar

raw sugar

crème fraîche

oranges

yogurt

COOK'S TIP
For a lighter version, simply use ⅞ cup low-fat plain yogurt instead of the strained yogurt and crème fraîche.

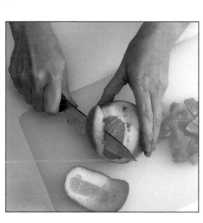

1 With a sharp knife, cut away all the peel and white pith from the oranges and chop the fruit. Or, if there's time, segment the oranges, removing all the membrane.

2 Place the fruit in the bottom of four individual flameproof dishes. Mix together the yogurt and crème fraîche and spoon the mixture over the oranges.

3 Mix together the two sugars and sprinkle them evenly over the tops of the dishes.

4 Place the dishes under a preheated, very hot broiler for 3–4 minutes or until the sugar melts and turns to a rich golden brown. Serve warm or cold.

Raspberry and Passionfruit Puffs

Few desserts are so strikingly easy to make as this one: beaten egg whites and sugar baked in a dish, turned out and served with a handful of soft fruit.

Serves 4

INGREDIENTS
2 tbsp butter, softened
5 egg whites
⅔ cup superfine sugar
2 passionfruit
1 cup ready-made custard from a
    carton or can
milk, as required
6 cups fresh raspberries
confectioners' sugar, for dusting

raspberries

egg whites

passionfruit

confectioners' sugar

VARIATION
If raspberries are out of season, use either fresh, bottled or canned soft berry fruit such as strawberries, blueberries or red currants.

1 Preheat the oven to 350°F. Brush four ½ pint soufflé dishes with a visible layer of soft butter.

2 Whisk the egg whites in a mixing bowl until firm. (You can use an electric mixer.) Add the sugar a little at a time and whisk into a firm meringue.

3 Halve the passionfruit, take out the seeds with a spoon and fold them into the meringue.

4 Turn the meringue out into the prepared dishes, stand in a deep roasting pan which has been half-filled with boiling water and bake for 10 minutes. The meringue will rise above the tops of the soufflé dishes.

5 Turn the puffs out upside-down onto a serving plate.

6 Top with raspberries. Thin the custard with a little milk and pour around the edge. Dredge with confectioners' sugar and serve warm or cold.

Ginger and Banana Brûlée

Desserts don't have to be elaborate to achieve excellent results. The proof of the pudding is this simple ginger and banana brûlée.

Serves 6–8

INGREDIENTS
4 thick slices ginger cake
6 bananas, sliced
2 tbsp lemon juice
1¼ cups whipping cream or fromage frais
4 tbsp fruit juice
3–4 tbsp brown sugar

ginger cake

bananas

lemon

whipping cream

fruit juice

brown sugar

1 Cut the cake into chunks and arrange in an ovenproof dish. Slice the bananas and toss in the lemon juice.

2 Preheat the grill. Whip the cream until firm, then gently whip in the fruit juice. (If using fromage frais, just gently stir in the juice.) Drain the bananas and fold them into the mixture; spoon over the ginger cake.

3 Sprinkle over the sugar in an even layer. Place under the hot grill for 2–3 minutes to caramelize. Serve at once, or allow to cool, then chill for a crisp topping.

VARIATION

For a delicious alternative try chocolate cake and pears instead of ginger cake and bananas. You could also drizzle a little liqueur or sherry over the chocolate cake for a touch of luxury.

Quick Apricot Blender Whip

One of the quickest desserts you could make – and also one of the prettiest.

Serves 4

INGREDIENTS
14 oz can apricot halves in juice
1 tbsp Grand Marnier or brandy
¾ cup plain strained yogurt
2 tbsp slivered almonds

yogurt

Grand Marnier

apricot halves

slivered almonds

1 Drain the juice from the apricots and place the fruit and liqueur in a blender or food processor.

2 Process the apricots until smooth.

3 Spoon the fruit purée and yogurt in alternate spoonfuls into four tall glasses or glass dishes, swirling them together slightly to give a marbled effect.

4 Lightly toast the almonds until they are golden. Let them cool slightly and then sprinkle them on top.

COOK'S TIP

For an even lighter dessert, use low-fat instead of plain yogurt, and, if you prefer to omit the liqueur, add a little of the fruit juice from the can.

Brazilian Coffee Bananas

Rich, lavish and sinful-looking, this dessert
takes only about 2 minutes to make!

Serves 4

INGREDIENTS
4 small ripe bananas
1 tbsp instant coffee granules or
   powder
1 tbsp hot water
2 tbsp dark brown sugar
1⅛ cups strained plain yogurt
1 tbsp toasted slivered almonds

bananas

yogurt

slivered almonds

instant coffee

dark brown sugar

I Peel and slice one banana and mash
the remaining three with a fork.

2 Dissolve the coffee in the hot water
and stir into the mashed bananas.

3 Spoon a little of the mashed banana
mixture into four serving dishes and
sprinkle with sugar. Top with a spoonful
of yogurt, then repeat until all the
ingredients are used up.

4 Swirl the last layer of yogurt for a
marbled effect. Finish with a few banana
slices and slivered almonds. Serve cold.
Best eaten within about an hour of
making.

VARIATION

For a special occasion, add a dash –
just a dash – of dark rum or brandy
to the bananas for extra richness.

Raspberry Granola Layer

As well as being a delicious, low-fat, high-fiber dessert, this can also be served for a quick, healthy breakfast.

Serves 4

INGREDIENTS
2¼ cups fresh or frozen and thawed
    raspberries
1 cup low-fat plain yogurt
½ cup granola

raspberries

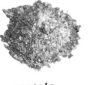

granola

plain yogurt

1 Reserve four raspberries for decoration, and then spoon a few raspberries into four stemmed glasses or glass dishes.

2 Top the raspberries with a spoonful of yogurt in each glass.

3 Sprinkle a layer of granola over the yogurt.

4 Repeat with the raspberries and other ingredients. Top each with a whole raspberry.

COOK'S TIP

This recipe can be made in advance and stored in the fridge for several hours, or overnight if you're serving it for breakfast.

Mixed Melon Salad with Wild Strawberries

Ice-cold melon is a delicious way to end a meal. Here several varieties are combined with strongly flavored wild strawberries. If wild berries are not available, use ordinary strawberries or raspberries.

Serves 4

INGREDIENTS
1 cantaloupe or charentais melon
1 galia or Spanish melon
2 lb watermelon
6 oz wild strawberries
4 sprigs fresh mint

wild strawberries

galia melon

cantaloupe

watermelon

mint

COOK'S TIP
Ripe melons should give slightly when pressed at the base, and should give off a fruity, melony scent. Buy carefully if you plan to use the fruit on the day.

1 Halve the cantaloupe, galia, and watermelons.

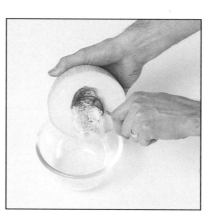

2 Remove the seeds from the cantaloupe and galia with a spoon.

3 With a melon-baller, take out as many balls as you can from all 3 melons. Combine in a large bowl and refrigerate.

4 Add the wild strawberries and transfer to 4 stemmed glass dishes.

5 Decorate with sprigs of mint.

Passionfruit and Apple Mousse

Passionfruit have an exotic, scented flavor that makes this simple apple dessert very special; if passionfruit are not available, use two finely chopped kiwis instead.

Serves 4

INGREDIENTS
1 lb cooking apples
6 tbsp apple juice
3 passionfruit
3 egg whites
1 red-skinned apple, to decorate
lemon juice

apple juice

lemon

cooking apples

red-skinned apple

eggs

passionfruit

1 Peel, core and roughly chop the cooking apples and place them in a pan, with the apple juice.

2 Bring to a boil, and then reduce the heat and cover the pan. Cook gently, stirring occasionally, until the apple is very tender.

3 Remove from the heat and beat the apple mixture with a wooden spoon until it becomes a fairly **smooth** purée (or purée the apple in a **food** processor).

4 Cut the passionfruit in half and scoop out the flesh. Stir the flesh into the apple purée.

5 Place the egg whites in a clean, dry bowl and whisk them until they form soft peaks. Fold the egg whites into the apple mixture. Spoon the apple mousse into four serving dishes.

COOK'S TIP

It's important to use a good cooking apple, such as a Granny Smith, for this recipe, because the fluffy texture of a cooking apple breaks down easily to a purée. You can use eating apples, but you will find it easier to purée them in a food processor.

6 Thinly slice the red-skinned apple and brush the slices with lemon juice, to prevent them from browning. Arrange the slices on top of the apple mousse and serve cold.

Prune and Orange Whip

A simple, storecupboard dessert, made in minutes.
It can be served immediately, but it's best chilled
for about half an hour before serving.

Serves 4

INGREDIENTS
1½ cups ready-to-eat dried prunes
⅔ cup orange juice
1 cup low-fat plain yogurt
shreds of orange rind, to decorate

orange rind

plain yogurt

orange juice

prunes

1 Remove the pits from the prunes and roughly chop them. Place them in a pan with the orange juice.

2 Bring the juice to a boil, stirring. Reduce the heat, cover and leave to simmer for 5 minutes, until the prunes are tender and the liquid is reduced by half.

3 Remove from the heat, allow to cool slightly and then beat well with a wooden spoon, until the fruit breaks down to a rough purée.

4 Transfer the mixture to a bowl. Stir in the yogurt, swirling the yogurt and fruit purée together lightly, to give a marbled effect.

5 Spoon the mixture into stemmed glasses or individual dishes, smoothing the tops.

6 Top each pot with a few shreds of orange rind, to decorate. Chill before serving.

VARIATION

This dessert can also be made with other ready-to-eat dried fruit, such as apricots or peaches. For a special occasion, add a dash of brandy or Cointreau with the yogurt.

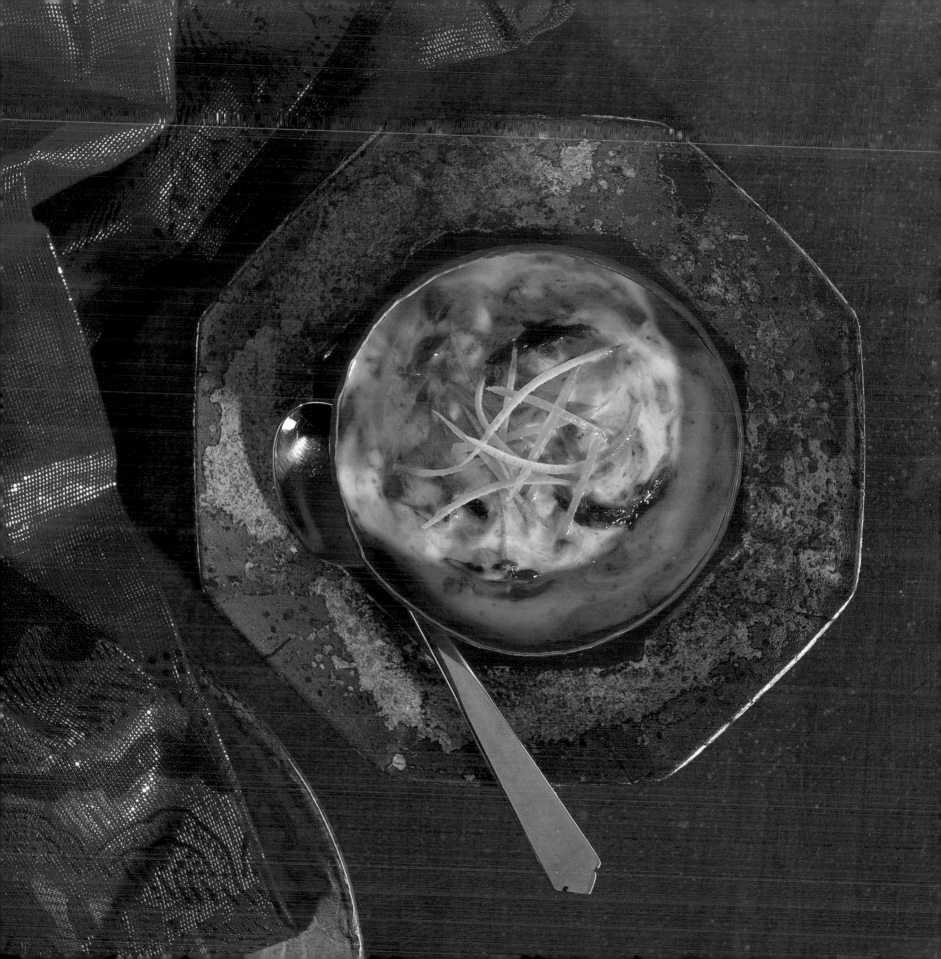

Peach Melba

In the original dish created by Escoffier for the opera singer Dame Nellie Melba, peaches and ice cream were served on an ice swan.

Serves 4

INGREDIENTS
11 oz raspberries
squeeze of lemon juice
confectioners' sugar, to taste
2 large ripe peaches or can (15 oz)
   sliced peaches
8 scoops vanilla ice cream

raspberries

lemon

peaches

*confectioners'
sugar*

*vanilla
ice cream*

1 Press the raspberries through a fine-mesh nylon strainer set over a bowl. Stir in a little lemon juice and sweeten to taste with confectioners' sugar.

2 If using fresh peaches, dip them in boiling water for 4–5 seconds, then slip off the skins. Cut them in half along the indented line, then slice them. If using canned peaches, drain them well.

3 Place two scoops of ice cream in each individual glass dish, top with peach slices, then pour on the raspberry purée. Serve immediately.

COOK'S TIP

If you'd like to prepare this ahead of time, scoop the ice cream onto a cold baking sheet and freeze until ready to serve, then transfer the scoops to the dishes.

Ice Cream Strawberry Shortcake

This American classic couldn't be easier to make. Fresh, juicy strawberries, shop-bought flan cases and rich vanilla ice cream are all you need to create a feast of a dessert.

Serves 4

INGREDIENTS

3 x 6 in sponge flan cases, or shortbread rounds
5 cups vanilla or strawberry ice cream
1½ lb hulled fresh strawberries, halved if large

strawberries

vanilla ice cream

flan case

1 If using flan cases, trim the raised edges with a serrated knife.

2 Set aside a third of the ice cream and strawberries for the topping. Place half the remaining ice cream and strawberries on one flan case or shortcake.

3 Place a second flan case on top and cover with a second layer of ice cream and fruit.

4 Top with the third flan case, the reserved ice cream and strawberries and serve.

COOK'S TIP

Don't worry if the shortcake falls apart when you cut into it. Messy cakes are best. Ice Cream Strawberry Shortcake can be assembled up to 1 hour in advance and kept in the freezer without spoiling the fruit.

Chocolate Mousse on the Loose

Super-light, dark, creamy and delicious; the chocolate mousse is always popular and should maintain a high profile on any dessert menu.

Serves 4

INGREDIENTS
7 oz best quality plain chocolate, plus extra for flaking
3 eggs
2 tbsp dark rum or whisky
¼ cup superfine sugar
½ pint/1¼ cups whipping cream
confectioners' sugar, for dusting

plain chocolate

whipping cream

eggs

superfine sugar

1 Break the chocolate into a bowl, stand over a saucepan of simmering water and melt. Separate the egg whites into a large mixing bowl, remove the chocolate from the heat and stir in the egg yolks and alcohol.

2 Whisk the egg whites until firm, gradually add the sugar and whisk until stiff peaks form.

3 Whip the cream to a dropping consistency and set aside until required.

4 Give the egg whites a final beating with a rubber spatula, add the chocolate and fold all the ingredients together gently, retaining as much air as possible.

5 Fold in the loosely whipped cream, and transfer to four glasses or bowls. If time permits, chill until ready to serve.

COOK'S TIP

It is a false economy to use inexpensive chocolate. Choose the best quality dark chocolate you can find and enjoy it!

6 Decorate with flaked chocolate and dust with confectioners' sugar.

Black Forest Sundae

There's more than one way to enjoy the classic Black Forest Gâteau. Here, the traditional ingredients are layered in a sundae glass to make a superb cold dessert.

Serves 4

INGREDIENTS
can (14 oz) pitted dark, sweet
    cherries in syrup
1 tbsp cornstarch
3 tbsp Kirsch
⅔ cup whipping cream
1 tbsp confectioners' sugar
2½ cups chocolate ice cream
4 oz chocolate cake
8 fresh cherries
vanilla ice cream, to serve

COOK'S TIP
Jarred cherries often have a better flavor than canned ones, especially if the pits are left in. You don't have to remove the pits—just remember to warn your guests.

canned dark, sweet cherries

cornstarch

whipping cream

chocolate ice cream

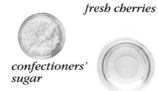
chocolate cake

fresh cherries

confectioners' sugar

Kirsch

1 Strain the cherry syrup from the can into a saucepan. Spoon the cornstarch into a small bowl and stir in 2 tbsp of the strained cherry syrup.

2 Bring the syrup in the saucepan to a boil. Stir in the cornstarch and syrup mixture. Simmer briefly, stirring, until the syrup thickens.

3 Add the drained canned cherries, stir in the Kirsch and spread on a metal tray to cool.

4 Whip the cream with the confectioners' sugar.

5 Place a spoonful of the cherry mixture in the bottom of four sundae glasses. Continue with layers of ice cream, chocolate cake, whipped cream and more cherry mixture until the glasses are full.

6 Finish with a piece of chocolate cake, two scoops of ice cream and more cream. Decorate with the fresh cherries.

INDEX